Quizmaster

D1205335

ENCYCLOPÆDIA
Britannica

International Standard Book Number: 0-85229-793-9

Preface

The quest for knowledge is an ongoing process of searching and learning. When competition and the excitement of success are added to this quest, learning becomes a lot of fun.

One of the most popular methods of acquiring and assimilating knowledge is through quizzing. People of all ages and walks of life enjoy the challenges of quizzing.

The editors of Encyclopædia Britannica bring to quiz fans, and to all who seek knowledge, the *Britannica Quizmaster,* derived from the world's greatest source of knowledge: the *Encyclopædia Britannica.*

The *Britannica Quizmaster* contains questions on art, culture, geography, history, literature, mythology, science, sports, and the Nobel Prize. In this book, the correct answers are not merely showcased. Rather, each correct answer comes with a brief but detailed explanation—verified by our editors—that adds to the reader's understanding and enhances the learning process.

Another unique feature of this quiz book is "Did You Know," a selection of very unusual and fascinating factoids on every page. You'll find these interesting and fun.

As this new Britannica product goes to press, special recognition is due to the editors of the Encyclopædia Britannica (India) team in New Delhi for their efforts in assembling this information and to the editors of Encyclopædia Britannica, Inc., in Chicago for their valuable feedback.

Dale H. Hoiberg, *Vice-President and Editor*
Encyclopædia Britannica, Inc.

Contents

Art, Culture, & Mythology

1. Which one of the following is a Greek vessel made of metal or pottery?
a) Cupola
b) Carafe
c) Urn
d) Krater

2. Which style of painting uses water-based pigments on freshly applied plaster?
a) Sand painting
b) Casein
c) Fresco
d) Acrylic painting

3. What is the name given to the style of play performed near or within a church, that relates stories from the Bible and of the saints?
a) Yiddish drama
b) Fate drama
c) Jesuit drama
d) Liturgical drama

4. In which of the following countries did Su-chou embroidery originate?
a) Korea
b) China
c) Japan
d) Philippines

5. Which of the following techniques is used to produce a "stained-glass" effect through the use of translucent enamels?

a) Plein air painting
b) Plique-a-jour
c) Basse-taille
d) Encrusted enamelling

6. Which one of the following is used to make etched glass?
a) Carving knife
b) Ink
c) Rosin powder
d) Acid

7. What term is used to describe the fixing of pigments with heated wax?
a) Etch
b) Emboss
c) Encaustic
d) Wax

8. Which 19th-century painter is also known for his series on sunflowers?
a) Claude Monet
b) Vincent van Gogh
c) Frederic Bazille
d) Edgar Degas

9. Which one of the following art styles did painter Claude Monet initiate?
a) Cubist
b) Impressionist
c) Baroque
d) Surrealist

Art, Culture, & Mythology

10. Which ritual object was used in the secret rituals by the aborigines of Australia?
a) *Tjurunga*
b) *Eora*
c) *Goonge*
d) *Uluru*

11. What is a masque?
a) A festival
b) A place of worship
c) A poem on masks
d) A French novel

12. What is a Korean priestess called?
a) Mudang
b) Paksu
c) P'ansori
d) Kisaeng

13. What is the popular folk song style of Laos known as?
a) Mohlam
b) Byliny
c) Khon
d) Hat boi

14. Which field of music would you associate Luciano Pavarotti with?
a) Country
b) Jazz
c) Rock
d) Opera

15. Who was the first President of the Academy of Motion Picture Arts and Sciences?
a) Douglas Fairbanks, Sr.
b) William Hanna
c) Louis B. Mayer
d) Ronald Colman

16. Where did Hedwig glass originate?
a) Egypt
b) Germany
c) England
d) Spain

17. What is the statue of Athena Parthenos, housed in the Parthenon, made of?
a) Granite and red stone
b) Silver and gold
c) Marble and sandstone
d) Gold and ivory

18. What is a cameo?
a) A miniature painting
b) A cave painting
c) Small carved gems
d) A tool for engraving

19. In ancient Egypt what were "mastabas"?
a) Granaries
b) Fortifications
c) Funerary structures
d) Sarcophagus

20. Who designed the Sydney Opera House?
a) Jorn Utzon
b) Robert Venturi
c) Ricardo Bofill
d) Hans Hollein

21. Which period in art did Gothic art evolve from?
a) Byzantine art
b) Romanesque art
c) Renaissance art
d) Early Christian art

22. Which printmaking technique is 18th-century artist Francisco de Goya associated with?
a) Engraving
b) Lithography
c) Aquatint
d) Etching

23. What is the spire of the Chrysler Building in New York City made of?
a) Granite
b) Marble
c) Stainless steel
d) Gold-plated metal

24. What is the working drawing in carpet- or tapestry-making called?
a) Template
b) Prototype
c) Blueprint
d) Cartoon

25. Who was responsible for the renovations of old St. Paul's cathedral, London, in the 1630s?
a) Simon Basil
b) Alexander Thomson
c) Inigo Jones
d) Christopher Wren

26. Who was the founder of the British documentary-film movement?
a) Robert Flaherty
b) John Grierson
c) Dziga Vertov
d) Louis de Rochemont

27. Which rock star is featured in D.A. Pennebaker's documentary, *Don't Look Back?*
a) Rod Stewart
b) Jim Morrison
c) Bob Dylan
d) Van Halen

28. Which of these documentaries is a nine-and-a-half-hour examination of Nazi concentration camps?
a) *Shoah*
b) *Hearts and Minds*
c) *Why We Fight*
d) *Fires were Started*

29. Which country produced *Triumph of the Will*, a propaganda documentary?
a) Soviet Union
b) Italy
c) United States of America
d) Germany

30. Which of the following films belong to the genre of musicals?
a) *Fame*
b) *The Towering Inferno*
c) *Ordinary People*
d) *Rancho Notorious*

31. Which society did H.G. Wells, George Bernard Shaw, Augustus John, John Maynard Keynes, and others found in 1925?
a)   Academy of Motion Picture Arts and Sciences
b)   The Lewis Carroll Society
c)   The Film Society of London
d)   The British Federation of Film Societies

32. Where was the first international film festival founded?
a)   Berlin
b)   Tokyo
c)   Venice
d)   Melbourne

33. On what was the traditional art of etching done?
a)   Wood
b)   Copperplate
c)   Sheet glass
d)   Parchment

34. In a Japanese house which architectural feature is called a "tokonoma"?
a)   An alcove to display art
b)   The doorway
c)   The gable
d)   The gatepost

35. What did the early Chinese use for drawing and lettering?
a)   India ink
b)   Natural colour
c)   Coal
d)   Indigo

36. In the field of performing arts in China, what does "hua-chu" denote?
a)   A ritual dance
b)   Western-style drama
c)   A kind of mask
d)   Traditional Chinese theatre

37. Which variety of jade is traditionally used in China?
a)   Jadeite
b)   Olivine
c)   Bowenite
d)   Nephrite

38. In sculpture what is the "cire-perdue" method used for?
a)   Carving
b)   Moulding
c)   Casting
d)   Modelling

39. Which one of the following dances was originally performed to honour the gods or to praise the chiefs?
a)   Rumba
b)   Morris
c)   Hula
d)   Tango

40. To which style of architecture does the Amalienborg, residence of the Danish royal family, belong?
a)   Rococo
b)   Baroque
c)   Gothic
d)   Renaissance

Did You Know?

Cote d'Ivoire is better known as Ivory Coast.

The term fossil comes from a Latin word meaning "to dig".

Pseudofossils, or false fossils, are mineral forms that look like fossils.

41. Where was porcelain first produced?
a) Great Britain
b) France
c) China
d) Japan

42. Who invented bone china?
a) Josiah Spode, the Second
b) William Turner
c) George Ridgway
d) William Copeland

43. Which one of the following dance forms is also known as the "Americanized quadrille"?
a) Twist
b) Square dance
c) Tap dance
d) Waltz

44. To which country did ballerina Anna Pavlova belong?
a) Czechoslovakia
b) Yugoslavia
c) Romania
d) Russia

45. With what were the early Greek and Cretan houses decorated?
a) Colourful stones
b) Tiles
c) Frescos
d) Carvings

46. Which one of the following monuments, in 1899, surpassed the Washington Monument in being the tallest man-made structure of that time?
a) Chrysler Building
b) Empire State Building
c) Eiffel Tower
d) Lincoln Memorial

47. Which one of the following styles of architecture is not British?
a) Regency
b) Prairie
c) Tudor
d) Stuart

48. Where is the Potala Palace situated?
a) Greece
b) Pakistan
c) India
d) China

49. Approximately, how old are the cave murals at Lascaux Grotto, France?
a) 10,000 years
b) 12,000 years
c) 14,000 years
d) 15,000 years

50. What is a griffin?
a) A species of penguin
b) A male goat
c) A kind of bread
d) A mythological animal

The name Accra is derived from the Akan word *nkran* because of the black ants that thrive in the area.

By studying fossils, scientists have proved that the Rocky Mountains, the Alps, and the Himalayas were once below the level of the ocean.

Did You Know?

51. In which ancient civilization would one find pottery having the Marine style?
a) Minoan
b) Greek
c) Harappan
d) Egyptian

52. By what name is shadow theatre known in Indonesia?
a) Wayang kulit
b) Wayang orang
c) Wayang topeng
d) Bedaja

53. Which of these dances is performed by a pair of preadolescent girls?
a) Kathakali
b) Ras Lila
c) Legong
d) Minuet

54. In the classical dance form in India, what are "*hasta-mudras*"?
a) Hand gestures
b) Music
c) Song
d) Rhythm

55. In the *Hayashi* music ensemble of Japan, which instrument is played with percussion instruments?
a) Gong
b) Harp
c) Flute
d) Guitar

56. The *bedaja* dance is performed in which country?
a) Myanmar
b) Japan
c) Indonesia
d) India

57. In which one of these dances are masks worn?
a) Praleng
b) Nupa Jala
c) Ras Lila
d) Bamboo dance

58. Where did the maxixe form of ballroom dancing evolve?
a) Turkey
b) U.S.A.
c) France
d) Brazil

59. Name the trance ritual of Korea, in which singing and dancing are used to invite happiness and repel evil?
a) Kori
b) Mudang
c) Kut
d) Kisaeng

60. Which percussion instrument symbolizes prosperity and social status in China?
a) Drum
b) Xylophone
c) Gong
d) Rattle

61. Which of the following does the no theatre emphasize?
a) Story telling
b) Dances
c) Singing
d) Puppetry

62. Who was the mother of the Greek god Apollo?
a) Leto
b) Venus
c) Diana
d) Medusa

63. Who among the following is the goddess of wild animals, the hunt, vegetation, chastity, and childbirth?
a) Tyndareus
b) Artemis
c) Leto
d) Hera

64. For which Greek god was the epithet *Nomios* used?
a) Zeus
b) Apollo
c) Inachus
d) Hermes

65. Who among the following is considered to be the sky and weather god?
a) Apollo
b) Laertes
c) Odysseus
d) Zeus

66. What was the name of the father of Zeus?
a) Hades
b) Apollo
c) Cronus
d) Poseidon

67. Which Greek god appeared in the *Odyssey* as the messenger of the gods and conductor of the dead to Hades?
a) Hermes
b) Apollo
c) Zeus
d) Aeolus

68. Who among the following was the daughter of the Greek god Inachus?
a) Athena
b) Hera
c) Artemis
d) Io

69. According to Greek legend what does the name of Argus Panoptes mean?
a) All Knowing
b) All Seeing
c) All Hearing
d) Hundred Hands

70. Who among the following was the first to declare that the New Year starts on January 1?
a) King Arthur
b) Henry V
c) Christopher Columbus
d) William the Conqueror

71. Which festival was held in the honour of Poseidon, the sea god, in ancient Greece?
a) Isthmian Games
b) Mardi Gras
c) Saturnalia
d) Lupercalia

72. Whose title translates into "the awakened one"?
a) Jesus Christ
b) Gautama Buddha
c) Zoroaster
d) Confucius

73. During which era did Buddhism become the state religion of Japan?
a) Nara period
b) Heian period
c) Kamakura period
d) Sengoku period

74. Where is the Borobudur Buddhist monument located?
a) India
b) China
c) Indonesia
d) Myanmar

75. In early times, Korean architecture was influenced by what style?
a) Indian
b) Mongolian
c) Japanese
d) Chinese

76. During which period of Korean history did Korean artistic styles begin to influence Japanese art?
a) The Bronze Age
b) The Early Iron Age
c) The Middle Ages
d) The Three Kingdoms Period

77. Which was the first permanent theatre in Paris?
a) Marais Theatre
b) Theatre of the Vieux-Colombier
c) Hotel de Bourgogne
d) Theatre National Populaire

78. Navajo blankets and rugs are examples of the weaving art of which country?
a) India
b) China
c) Mexico
d) United States of America

79. For which one of the following art forms is Roy Lichtenstein best known?
a) Sculpture
b) Portraits
c) Etching
d) Pop art

80. What is the process of preparing stones for hand printing called?
a) Fine-art lithography
b) Block printing
c) Sketching
d) Screen printing

81. Which of the following institutes is the oldest art academy in the U.S.?
a)   Pennsylvania Academy of the Fine Arts
b)   Art Center College of Design (Pasadena)
c)   California Institute of the Arts
d)   Cranbrook Academy of Art

82. Who designed the Lincoln Memorial structure?
a)   Ossip Zadkine
b)   Henry Bacon
c)   Alvar Aalto
d)   Edwin Landseer

83. Which is the oldest theatre still in use in England?
a)   Globe Theatre
b)   Royal Drury Lane Theatre
c)   Royal National Theatre
d)   Blackfriars Theatre

84. Where did no (noh) theatre originate?
a)   Japan
b)   China
c)   Korea
d)   Thailand

85. What name is given to the process of fusing a thin glass layer to a metal object?
a)   Porcelain enamelling
b)   Fresco
c)   Glazing
d)   Lacquering

86. Who among the following sculpted the Oscar Awards statuette?
a)   Cedric Gibbons
b)   Perez Augusto
c)   George Stanley
d)   Frederic Remington

87. Which architectural monument commemorates the Great Fire of London?
a)   London Bridge
b)   Big Ben
c)   Westminster Abbey
d)   The Monument

88. In which of the following types of architecture is the "shoji" (sliding door) used?
a)   Egyptian
b)   Indonesian
c)   Chinese
d)   Japanese

89. Where did the Amarna style of art develop?
a)   India
b)   Egypt
c)   China
d)   Afghanistan

90. Which period is known as the Geometric period in the history of Greek art?
a)   1200–900 BC
b)   900–700 BC
c)   450–400 BC
d)   323–100 BC

91. From where did Black Figure pottery originate?
a) India
b) Japan
c) Greece
d) England

92. What do the metopes, which decorate the roof of Apollo's temple at Thermon, depict?
a) Floral scenes
b) Mythological scenes
c) Geometric designs
d) Animals

93. On the banks of which river were the first communities that can be identified culturally as Chinese settled?
a) Yangtze
b) Han
c) Huang Ho
d) Yalu

94. Who among the following was one of the originators of the form of sculpture called assemblage, in which unlikely objects are joined together in an unorthodox unit?
a) Pazzo Andrea
b) Joseph Cornell
c) Auguste Rodin
d) Constantin Brancusi

95. Who was the first American artist to make welded metal sculpture?
a) David Smith
b) Joseph Cornell
c) Robert Mirek
d) Charles Sheeler

96. Into which kingdom of Korea was Buddhism first introduced?
a) Koguryo
b) Paekche
c) Silla
d) Koryo

97. Who developed a unique style of calligraphy known as the *ch'usa* in Korea?
a) Chao Meng-Fu
b) Kim Chong Hi
c) Eri Takase
d) Huang Shiang

98. Who is best known for his development of Hangul, a phonetic system for writing the Korean language?
a) Sejong
b) Kim Chong Hi
c) Chao Meng-Fu
d) Han Kan

99. Which is Korea's national instrument?
a) *Djunajian*
b) *Komun-go*
c) *Haegum*
d) *Kayagum*

100. Who, other than the Mayo tribe, are the only surviving speakers of the Cahita language group?
a) Aztec
b) Incas
c) Yaqui
d) Zapotec

101. Where did Bonsai originate?
a) China
b) Korea
c) Japan
d) Tibet

102. Who among these developed apartment houses to suit urban conditions?
a) Koreans
b) Romans
c) Greeks
d) French

103. Who invented the first cursive style of Arabic lettering, the nakshi script?
a) Ibn Battutah
b) Ibn Muqlah
c) Ibn al-Bawwab
d) Muzaffar Ali

104. What is the symbolic gateway marking the entrance to the sacred precincts of a Shinto shrine in Japan called?
a) Torana
b) Komainu
c) Kami
d) Torii

105. What is the repertoire of dances of the Japanese Imperial court, derived from traditional dance forms of China, Korea, India, and Southeast Asia, called?
a) Bugaku
b) Togaku
c) Komagaku
d) Gagaku

106. Which Greek building was considered revolutionary because of the presence of an "oculus" in its dome?
a) Parthenon
b) Pantheon
c) Erechtheum
d) Theatre of Dionysus

107. During which Egyptian pharaoh's reign was the sphinx at Giza erected?
a) Khufu
b) Khafre
c) Rameses
d) Akhenaten

108. In architecture what is a "baldachino"?
a) A canopy over the altar
b) A raised platform
c) A niche
d) A railing

109. Which of these was the French sculptor Rodin's first original work?
a) *Les Bourgeois de Calais* ("The Burghers of Calais")
b) *Le Penseur* ("The Thinker")
c) *Le Vaincu* ("The Vanquished")
d) *The Kiss*

110. Which one of the following styles of pottery was developed by the American Indians?
a) Punch'ong pottery
b) Marbled pottery
c) Red Figure pottery
d) Pueblo pottery

Bolivia is named after Simon Bolivar, who drafted the country's first constitution.

Congo was known as Zaire from 1971 to 1997.

Chile leads the world in the production of copper.

Did You Know?

111. What term is used in architecture to describe draped female figurines employed for support, instead of columns?
a) Embedded columns
b) Pillars
c) Atlantes
d) Caryatid

112. With which one of the following materials was the Statue of Liberty constructed?
a) Limestone
b) Copper
c) Marble
d) Gold

113. What is *Pyrrhiche* a form of?
a) Dance
b) Song
c) Painting
d) Drama

114. In Chinese art, what does the dragon symbolize?
a) Teacher
b) Fear
c) Emperor
d) Hatred

115. Which famous Roman god is the son of Mercury and Venus?
a) Saturn
b) Hypnos
c) Cupid
d) Picus

116. Who is the counterpart of Zeus in Roman mythology?
a) Jupiter
b) Cupid
c) Hermes
d) Neptune

117. Which is the most widespread indigenous religious movement among the Native American Indians?
a) Spiritism
b) Naturalism
c) Peyotism
d) Christianity

118. Who is the god of earthquakes in Greek mythology?
a) Vulcan
b) Poseidon
c) Hades
d) Pegasus

119. Who was the mother of the winged horse called Pegasus?
a) Hera
b) Medusa
c) Persephone
d) Leda

120. Which Greek goddess threw an apple and started the Trojan war?
a) Eris
b) Hera
c) Athena
d) Aphrodite

The Congo is named after the Bakongo, one of the major ethnic groups in the country.

The chief river entirely within Costa Rica is the Reventazon.

The Wilderness Road runs through the Cumberland Gap.

121. Who, in Greek mythology, is responsible for the separation of Heaven and Earth?
a) Uranus
b) Cronus
c) Zeus
d) Poseidon

122. Who was the only mortal among the Gorgons?
a) Stheno
b) Euryale
c) Medusa
d) Andromeda

123. What was the name of Cupid's wife?
a) Juno
b) Venus
c) Nyx
d) Psyche

124. What ancient pre-Islamic religion was practised by the Iranians?
a) Zoroastrianism
b) Mithraism
c) Manichaeism
d) Dualism

125. Who is the sculptor of the famous "Pieta" at the St. Peter's Basilica in Rome?
a) Leonardo da Vinci
b) Raphael
c) Michelangelo
d) Rodin

126. Who is known as the "Father of Cubism" in modern painting?
a) Jacob Lawrence
b) Grega Nemec
c) Pablo Picasso
d) Alfonso Michel

127. Which one of these painters, crippled by arthritis, continued to paint by attaching the paintbrush to his hand?
a) Claude Monet
b) Pierre-August Renoir
c) Edgar Degas
d) Alfred Sisley

128. Who among the following French artists died in the Franco-German War?
a) Jean-Frederic Bazille
b) Henri Rousseau
c) Henri Matisse
d) Paul Cezanne

129. Whose work is "Guernica"?
a) Georges Braque
b) Pablo Picasso
c) Juan Gris
d) Gino Severini

130. Of the following Post-Impressionist artists, who is regarded as the "father of modern painting"?
a) Paul Cezanne
b) Paul Gauguin
c) Vincent van Gogh
d) Henri Rousseau

Did You Know?

The Museum of Decorative Arts in Prague houses the world's largest collection of glass.

Dominica derives its name from the Latin *dies dominica,* which means "the Lord's day" or "Sunday".

Guinea has about one-third to one-half of the world's known reserves of bauxite.

131. What kind of art is the Japanese art of Ko?
a) Architectural
b) Floral
c) Ceramic
d) Origami

132. From which of the following did Ch'an painting originate?
a) Chinese colour
b) Buddhist meditation
c) Islamic architecture
d) Korean art

133. What is Henry Moore well known for?
a) Tensile structures
b) Stone sculpture
c) Expressionist painting
d) Lithography

134. What was the Spanish artist El Greco's style of painting?
a) Realistic
b) Impressionistic
c) Expressionistic
d) Romantic

135. Which one of the following public figures does not feature in the Mount Rushmore National Memorial?
a) Theodore Roosevelt
b) George Washington
c) Woodrow Wilson
d) Thomas Jefferson

136. To which one of the following dances does the Charleston belong?
a) Twist
b) Jazz dance
c) Ballet
d) Waltz

137. In which one of the following ceremonies does the Dervish dance take place?
a) *Dhikr*
b) *Kirtan*
c) *Shaadi*
d) *Sagaai*

138. Which of these is a popular peasant theatre of Vietnam?
a) Kabuki
b) Hat boi
c) Hat cheo
d) Wayang kulit

139. Where did the ancient chain dance *syrtos* originate?
a) Spain
b) Cuba
c) Italy
d) Greece

140. What name is given to a carved ornamental motif tied to flowers, foliage, fruit, and cloth with ribbons?
a) Bouquet
b) Pot pourri
c) Lacquer
d) Swag

Geography

1. **Whose book was the first work to have the word "geography" in its title?**
a)   Strabo
b)   Eratosthenes of Cyrene
c)   Ptolemy
d)   Gerardus Mercator

2. **Which is the only extant work covering the whole range of peoples and countries known to both Greeks and Romans during the reign of Augustus?**
a)   *Geography*
b)   *Geographica*
c)   *Historical Sketches*
d)   *Geographia Generalis*

3. **Who wrote *Geographia Generalis*, a 17th-century work that sought scientifically to lay down the general principles of geography?**
a)   Strabo
b)   Leo Africanus
c)   Bernhardus Varenius
d)   Ptolemy

4. **Which is the first modern oceanographic text?**
a)   *The Physical Geography of the Sea*
b)   *Sailing Directions*
c)   *New Voyage Round the World*
d)   *The Depths of the Ocean*

5. **Who was cofounder, with Alexander von Humboldt, of modern geographical science?**
a)   George Perkins Marsh
b)   Carl Ritter
c)   Friedrich Ratzel
d)   Georg Forster

6. **After which volcanic mountain does a wind system, originating at around 15° N-S, derive its name?**
a)   Kilimanjaro
b)   Krakatoa
c)   Fujiyama
d)   Vesuvius

7. **Who, with John Speke, first discovered Lake Tanganyika?**
a)   David Livingstone
b)   James Bruce
c)   Richard Burton
d)   James Grant

8. **Which is the largest drainage system, in terms of volume of flow and area, in the world?**
a)   Amazon River
b)   Congo River
c)   Gambia River
d)   Zambezi River

9. **Which immense canyon cut by the Colorado River into the high-plateau region of northwestern Arizona, is noted for its fantastic shapes and colouration?**
a)   Astoria Canyon
b)   Grand Canyon
c)   Fraser Canyon
d)   Monterey Canyon

It was *Punch* that caused the word cartoon to supplant the overworked designation caricature, by parodying, with great popular success, a series of genuine cartoons, or full-size sketches, to be used as patterns, for the new House of Commons frescoes in 1843.

Did You Know?

10. Who was the first European to reach Lake Victoria in East Africa?
a) Samuel Baker
b) Joseph Thompson
c) John Hanning Speke
d) Henry Morton Stanley

11. Which is the oldest existing freshwater lake in the world?
a) Lake Victoria
b) Lake Baikal
c) Lake Albert
d) Lake Tanganyika

12. Which of these rivers is an outlet of Lake Tanganyika?
a) Malagarasi
b) Ruzizi
c) Lakuga
d) Kalambo

13. Who was the first to reach the South Pole?
a) Robert E. Peary
b) Robert Falcon Scott
c) Lincoln Ellsworth
d) Roald Amundsen

14. What term refers to a flat-bottom depression, also known as a "flat" or a "dry lake", found in interior desert basins?
a) Playa
b) Horst
c) Kopjes
d) Veld

15. Who led the first trans-Arctic air crossings?
a) Roald Amundsen
b) Lincoln Ellsworth
c) Umberto Nobile
d) Herbert Hollick-Kenyon

16. Which is the longest freshwater lake in the world?
a) Lake Victoria
b) Lake Tanganyika
c) Lake Albert
d) Lake Baikal

17. Who was the first European to explore the Amazon?
a) David Livingstone
b) Joseph Thompson
c) Francisco de Orellana
d) John Hanning Speke

18. What term is given to a narrow strip of land connecting two large land areas otherwise separated by the sea?
a) Isthmus
b) Bridge
c) Strait
d) Canal

19. Between which latitudes do the trade winds blow?
a) $0°$ and $30°$ N-S
b) $30°$ and $60°$ N-S
c) $30°$ to $90°$ N-S
d) $60°$ to $90°$ N-S

20. Which of the following terms comes from a Quechua Indian word meaning "flat surface"?
a) Savanna
b) Steppes
c) Pampas
d) Prairies

21. What term is given to the flat land area adjacent to a stream and composed of unconsolidated sedimentary deposits?
a) Beach
b) Bank
c) Floodplain
d) River terrace

22. What term refers to a large submarine volcanic mountain rising at least 3,300 feet (1,000 m) above the surrounding deep-sea floor?
a) Seamount
b) Oceanic ridge
c) Trench
d) Abyssal hill

23. Which are the highest waterfalls in the world?
a) Victoria Falls
b) Niagara Falls
c) Grand Falls
d) Angel Falls

24. Which lake would be considered the headwater of the single drainage system formed by the Great Lakes?
a) Lake Erie
b) Lake Superior
c) Lake Huron
d) Lake Ontario

25. What name is given to all siliciclastic sedimentary rocks composed of silt- and clay-size particles?
a) Dolomites
b) Molasse
c) Mudrocks
d) Sandstone

26. Which mountain system of Central Asia takes its name from the Chinese for "Celestial Mountains"?
a) Pamirs
b) Kopet-Dag
c) Himalaya
d) Tien Shah

27. What name is given to the complex of caves and underground rivers within the Mammoth Cave National Park in Kentucky, U.S.A.?
a) Optimisticheskaya Cave
b) Carlsbad Caverns
c) Flint Ridge Cave System
d) Sistema Huautla

28. By what name is the luminous phenomenon of the upper atmosphere that occurs primarily in high latitudes of both hemispheres known as?
a) Solar flare
b) Aurora
c) Radioluminescence
d) Field aligned currents

The Egyptians used scents lavishly, especially in religious rites; as a result, when they invented glass, it was largely used for perfume vessels. The fashion for perfume spread to Greece, where containers, most often terra-cotta or glass, were made in a variety of shapes and forms such as sandalled feet, birds, animals, and human heads.

Did You Know?

29. What term refers to a bench or step that extends along the side of the valley and represents a former level of the valley floor?
a) Bank
b) River terrace
c) Ridge
d) Horst

30. What term is given to the body of water that, during exceptionally high sea tides, rushes up some rivers?
a) Tsunami
b) Seiche
c) Spring tide
d) Tidal bore

31. Which strong surface oceanic current of the Pacific Ocean flows between Luzon of the Philippines and the east coast of Japan?
a) Kuroshio
b) Anadyr
c) Oya
d) Benguela

32. Which one of these belongs to the low cloud group?
a) Cirrus
b) Cirro-stratus
c) Nimbostratus
d) Cumulonimbus

33. Which of the following have an area larger than China?
a) U.S.A. and Russia
b) U.S.A. and Canada
c) Canada and Russia
d) U.S.A. and Australia

34. What name is given to the anomalous appearance, every few years, of unusually warm ocean conditions along the tropical west coast of South America?
a) Southern oscillation
b) Kelvin waves
c) El Nino
d) La Nina

35. Which country has the greatest contrast in temperature between its northern and southern borders?
a) China
b) India
c) U.S.A.
d) Australia

36. Which of these lakes is entirely within the United States?
a) Lake Erie
b) Lake Huron
c) Lake Michigan
d) Lake Superior

37. In which Australian state is the Cape York Peninsula located?
a) New South Wales
b) Queensland
c) Western Australia
d) Victoria

38. Granite is an example of which rock type?
a) Sedimentary
b) Metamorphic
c) Igneous
d) Basalt

39. Where are the Prince Edward Islands?
a) Indian Ocean
b) Pacific Ocean
c) Atlantic Ocean
d) Arctic Ocean

40. What term refers to the continuous submarine mountain chain extending through all the world's oceans?
a) Reef
b) Oceanic ridge
c) Abyssal hills
d) Seamount

41. Which of these countries is struck most often by tornadoes?
a) United States of America
b) Australia
c) China
d) India

42. In which present-day country was Mesopotamia located?
a) Iran
b) Lebanon
c) Iraq
d) Saudi Arabia

43. Which of the following geographical features links the Persian Gulf and Gulf of Oman?
a) Strait of Hormuz
b) Palk Strait
c) Musandum Peninsula
d) Gulf of Mannar

44. Which of the following islands was discovered by Christopher Columbus?
a) Santa Cruz Island
b) Margarita Island
c) Madeira Islands
d) Falkland Islands

45. The Mercator projection is actually which type of map projection?
a) Conical
b) Cylindrical
c) Conformal
d) Zenithal

46. Which of the following is also known as dry desert gullies?
a) Wadi
b) Buttes
c) Pediments
d) Barchans

47. The Namib desert is adjacent to which body of water?
a) Atlantic Ocean
b) Indian Ocean
c) Pacific Ocean
d) Arctic Ocean

48. Which of these is a deposit of windblown sand and clay weakly cemented by calcite?
a) Loess
b) Mesa
c) Playa
d) Dune

49. Which wind system seasonally reverses its direction?
a) Monsoon
b) Trade wind
c) Doldrums
d) Polar easterlies

50. What is the correct name given to a broad flat-bottomed volcanic crater?
a) Caldera
b) Fumaroles
c) Laccoliths
d) Cinder cones

51. Which is the deepest of the Great Lakes?
a) Lake Superior
b) Lake Erie
c) Lake Huron
d) Lake Ontario

52. Where are the Bonneville salt flats located?
a) Utah
b) Oregon
c) Nevada
d) Ohio

53. Where is the world's highest plateau?
a) Tibet
b) Argentina
c) Ethiopia
d) New Guinea

54. Which of these is the southernmost point of South America?
a) Cape Cod
b) Cape of Good Hope
c) Cape Horn
d) Cape Comorin

55. Between which two pressure belts do the westerlies blow?
a) The equator and the subtropics
b) The subtropics and the temperate
c) The temperate and the poles
d) The equator and the temperate

56. Which sea lies east of Oman, south of Pakistan, and west of India?
a) Baltic Sea
b) Mediterranean Sea
c) Arabian Sea
d) Red Sea

57. In which country is the Karakum Desert located?
a) Uzbekistan
b) Iran
c) Turkmenistan
d) Saudi Arabia

58. Which of the following cities is the capital of Denmark?
a) Prague
b) Copenhagen
c) Amsterdam
d) Brussels

59. What is a meander?
a) Small hill
b) Narrow road that twists from side to side
c) Bend in a river or stream
d) Pile of rock debris left by a glacier

60. Which of the following is a port city on the Strait of Hormuz?
a) Bandar-e-Abbas
b) Bandar-e Bushehr
c) Larak
d) Islands of Qeshm

61. The Pavlof volcano is located in which of the following states in United States?
a) Texas
b) Alaska
c) California
d) Florida

62. The Mayon volcano is located in which of the following countries?
a) U.S.A.
b) Peru
c) Japan
d) Philippines

63. Which of the following is the highest active volcano in Europe?
a) Mount Stromboli
b) Mount Etna
c) Mount Vesuvius
d) Mount Heimaey

64. What is a ria?
a) Narrow mountain valley
b) Wide, shallow river valley
c) Entrance to a cave system, submerged under water
d) Deep, sunken river valley drowned by the sea

65. Madeira Island in the North Atlantic Ocean belongs to which country?
a) Lebanon
b) Portugal
c) Germany
d) Spain

66. Which of the following islands is known as the Isle of Pearls?
a) Canary Islands
b) Margarita Island
c) Madeira Islands
d) Andaman and Nicobar Islands

67. Which geographer wrote the book *Kosmos* and made a significant contribution to the popularization of natural science?
a) Ellsworth Huntington
b) Alexander von Humboldt
c) Carl Ritter
d) Vidal de la Blache

68. Which of the following is the world's highest lake navigable to large vessels?
a) Lake Huron
b) Lake Superior
c) Lake Titicaca
d) Lake Victoria

69. The Gobi desert is located in which of the following geographical regions?
a) South America
b) South Asia
c) West Africa
d) Central Asia

70. In which of these countries is the Atacama Desert located?
a) Tanzania
b) China
c) Chile
d) Brazil

71. What is a pingo?
a) Dome-shaped hill with an ice core
b) Small volcanic vent producing sulphur fumes and steam
c) Type of oasis found in Sahara
d) Large rock outcrop with vertical sides

72. The largest ice sheet in the Northern Hemisphere covers most of which island?
a) Greenland
b) Iceland
c) Sakhalin
d) Novaya Zemlya

73. Which is the smallest ocean in the world?
a) Indian Ocean
b) Arctic Ocean
c) Pacific Ocean
d) Atlantic Ocean

74. Which is the deepest oceanic trench?
a) Java Trench
b) Mariana Trench
c) Puerto Rico Trench
d) South Sandwich Trench

75. Which is the longest river in the world?
a) Mississippi
b) Yangtze
c) Amazon
d) Nile

76. Which of these oceans may be considered an estuary of the Atlantic Ocean?
a) Pacific Ocean
b) Indian Ocean
c) Arctic Ocean
d) Antarctic Ocean

77. Low-salinity waters enter the Arctic Ocean from the Pacific Ocean through which strait?
a) Bering Strait
b) Strait of Magellan
c) Palk Strait
d) Strait of Gibraltar

78. Which continent is known as "Home of the Blizzard" and "White Desert"?
a) Australia
b) Europe
c) Antarctica
d) North America

79. Name the stretch of water that joins the Atlantic Ocean to the Mediterranean Sea?
a) Panama Canal
b) Suez Canal
c) Strait of Gibraltar
d) Strait of Magellan

80. Havana is the capital of which country?
a) Mexico
b) Jamaica
c) Bahamas
d) Cuba

81. Which stretch of water separates Australia and Tasmania?
a) Torres Strait
b) St. George's Channel
c) Cook Strait
d) Baas Strait

82. Which lake in the U.S.A. was formed after the earthquakes of 1811-12?
a) Reelfoot Lake
b) Utah Lake
c) Lake Winnipeg
d) Taal Lake

83. Which country has the largest area in the world?
a) Russia
b) China
c) U.S.A.
d) Canada

84. The source of the Arkansas River is in which mountain range?
a) Cascade
b) Rocky
c) Appalachian
d) Laurentian Highlands

85. The Straits of Mackinac connect Lake Michigan with which other Great Lake?
a) Lake Ontario
b) Lake Superior
c) Lake Erie
d) Lake Huron

86. The San Andreas fault is in which state of the U.S.A.?
a) California
b) Hawaii
c) Missouri
d) Illinois

87. Which canal was opened to traffic on August 15, 1914?
a) Suez Canal
b) Panama Canal
c) Pien Canal
d) Grand Canal

88. Which is the world's largest active volcanic mass?
a) Santa Ana
b) Tajumulco
c) Kilauea
d) Mauna Loa

89. What is an aquifer?
a) A geyser
b) A spring
c) A perched water table
d) A water-bearing stratum

90. Why does the water in artesian wells flow freely without being pumped?
a) The water in them is hard
b) The water in them is soft
c) The water in them is confined and under pressure
d) The water is meant for breweries

91. Which of these means lowering of the land surface by wind erosion?
a) Inflation
b) Deflation
c) Windage
d) Saltation

92. Which is the largest river in North America?
a) Hudson
b) Platte
c) Missouri
d) Mississippi

93. Which plateau lies between the Kunluns in the North and the Himalaya in the South?
a) Plateau of Tibet
b) Pamir Knot
c) Armenian Knot
d) Potwar Plateau

94. What is the savanna region in South Africa also known as?
a) Tundra
b) Prairies
c) Pampas
d) Bushveld

95. Which is the highest point in the Sahara?
a) Mt. Owaynat
b) Mt. Ras Dejen
c) Mt. Koussi
d) Mt. Marrah

96. Where is Krakatoa located?
a) Japan
b) Indonesia
c) Africa
d) Malaysia

97. Where were the aborigines of Tasmania moved to in the 19th century, to save them from extinction?
a) Bruny Island
b) Macquarie Island
c) King Island
d) Flinders Island

98. Which Scottish explorer discovered the Victoria Falls?
a) James Cook
b) David Livingstone
c) John Hanning Speke
d) Francis Drake

99. Which is Europe's longest river?
a) Danube
b) Drieper
c) Volga
d) Elbe

100. Along which country's coast is the world's second largest coral reef situated?
a) Honduras
b) Costa Rica
c) Belize
d) Guatemala

101. What is the Pacific Ring of Fire?
a) Chain of volcanoes
b) Seismic zone
c) Forest fire
d) Atoll

102. Doha is the capital of which country?
a) Indonesia
b) Iran
c) Qatar
d) Saudi Arabia

103. Which mountains separate France and Spain?
a) Alps
b) Andes
c) Ural
d) Pyrenees

104. Which sea separates Indonesia from Australia?
a) Arabian Sea
b) Coral Sea
c) Red Sea
d) Timor Sea

105. What is the term "red tide" associated with?
a) Currents
b) Oceans
c) Algae
d) Lagoons

106. Puerto Rico is a part of which country?
a) Mexico
b) Spain
c) U.S.A.
d) Brazil

107. Christmas Island is a territory of which country?
a) United Kingdom
b) India
c) Australia
d) North America

108. The Serengeti National Park is in which country?
a) Kenya
b) Tanzania
c) Canada
d) India

109. What geographical feature is the Blue Grotto?
a) Island
b) Waterfall
c) Cave
d) River

110. Madagascar is situated in which ocean?
a) Pacific Ocean
b) Indian Ocean
c) Atlantic Ocean
d) Arctic Ocean

111. Where would you find the Qattara Depression?
a) Egypt
b) Israel
c) Saudi Arabia
d) Iran

112. The Sea of Azov is an extension of which sea?
a) Mediterranean Sea
b) Black Sea
c) Caspian Sea
d) Red Sea

Archaeological evidence proves that *Homo sapiens* and *Homo neanderthalensis* inhabited the same general territory in many parts of Europe and the Middle East for thousands of years.

Jim Henson coined the term Muppets as a meld of "marionettes" and "puppets".

Did You Know?

113. Which two countries share the Isthmus of Kra, which connects the Malay penninsula to Southeast Asia?
a) Myanmar and Thailand
b) Indonesia and Malaysia
c) Malaysia and Myanmar
d) Myanmar and Cambodia

114. Which English explorer discovered the South Sandwich Islands and South Georgia Island in the Atlantic?
a) James Cook
b) Richard Grant
c) George Bass
d) Mathew Flinders

115. Which principal river of Australia flows from the Snowy Mountains to the Great Australian Bight of the Indian Ocean?
a) Darling River
b) Murrumbidgee River
c) Mitta Mitta
d) Murray River

116. The two large islands of New Zealand are separated by which strait?
a) Bass Strait
b) Strait of Hormuz
c) Cook Strait
d) Bering Strait

117. The Cape of Good Hope lies at the southern tip of which continent?
a) South America
b) Africa
c) Australia
d) Asia

118. Where is the world's tallest tree located?
a) Texas
b) Missouri
c) California
d) Iowa

119. Rhodesia is the former name of which country?
a) Algeria
b) Somalia
c) Ethiopia
d) Zimbabwe

120. Who among the following classified climate into five major types on the basis of vegetative zones?
a) Karl Wilhelm Humboldt
b) Wladimir Koppen
c) C. Warren Thornthwaite
d) Glen T. Trewartha

121. Which famous U.S. city is situated at the confluence of the Delaware and Schuylkill rivers?
a) Washington D.C.
b) Baltimore
c) Philadelphia
d) Trenton

History

1. The ruling Rana family of which South Asian state entered an agreement with the British after 1860 to ensure the state's autonomy?
a) Bhutan
b) Burma
c) Nepal
d) Tibet

2. Who is the founder of Old Chosun, the first state of Korea?
a) Tan'gun
b) T'aejo
c) Hyokkose
d) Wang Kon

3. Which 8–9th century Buddhist monument was buried under volcanic ash and was rediscovered in 1814 by T.S. Raffles?
a) Angkor Wat
b) Borobudur
c) Sanchi Stupa
d) Angkor Thom

4. The Chinese name of which Southeast Asian port, located to the east of Pearl River, means "fragrant harbour"?
a) Singapore
b) Shanghai
c) Inchon
d) Hong Kong

5. Which dictator of the Philippines was forced to flee the country in 1986 due to charges of corruption and electoral malpractice?
a) Ramon Magsaysay
b) Benigno Aquino
c) Ferdinand Marcos
d) Corazon Aquino

6. Which leader was the president of North Korea from 1972 until his death in 1994?
a) Kim II Sung
b) Kim Jong II
c) Roh Tae Woo
d) Chung Ju Yung

7. Who led the communist government that ruled Cambodia from 1975 to 1979?
a) Norodom Ranariddh
b) Pol Pot
c) Norodom Sihanouk
d) Lon Nol

8. The Potala Palace once served as the seat of government and the residence of which leader?
a) King of Nepal
b) King of Bhutan
c) The Dalai Lama
d) The Japanese Emperor

The name Sahara derives from the Arabic noun *sahra'*, meaning desert, and its plural, *sahara'*.

The founding of Bath in England is attributed in legend to Bladud, son of Lud Hudibras and father of King Lear, who in 863 BC was cured of disease by immersion in the steaming swamps.

Did You Know?

9. Thomas Stamford Raffles established which Asian island port city in 1819?
a) Hong Kong
b) Taiwan
c) Saigon
d) Singapore

10. Which mountain in Sri Lanka is believed by people of different religious faiths to bear the footprint of the Buddha, Adam, and Shiva?
a) Knuckles Peak
b) Pidurutalagala
c) Adam's Peak
d) Kirigalpotta

11. Which king of Afghanistan was deposed in a bloodless coup in 1973?
a) Najibullah
b) Zahir Shah
c) Dost Mohammad Khan
d) Gulbuddin Hekmatyar

12. Which Philippino opposition leader was assassinated in Manila in 1983?
a) Ferdinand Marcos
b) Benigno Aquino
c) Corazon Aquino
d) Fidel Ramos

13. Which Shah was overthrown by Ayatollah Khomeini in 1979?
a) Mohammad Reza Shah Pahlavi
b) Nadir Shah
c) Fath Ali Shah
d) Ahmad Shah

14. Which Arab-Israeli war began on October 6, 1973, the Jewish Day of atonement?
a) Six-day War
b) Yom Kippur War
c) Suez Canal War
d) Golan Heights War

15. Which Asian island was ruled by a dynasty of British rajas for a century?
a) Java
b) Papua New Guinea
c) Sarawak
d) Luzon

16. What were members of the Chinese political elite, convicted for implementing the policies of the Cultural Revolution, called?
a) The Dictators
b) The Last Emperors
c) The Gang of Four
d) The Mandarins

17. From which leader are the Hashimite kings of Jordan believed to have descended?
a) Moses
b) Noah
c) Abraham
d) Prophet Muhammad

18. Which two Asian countries are divided by the 38th parallel?
a) North and South Vietnam
b) North and South Korea
c) Laos and Cambodia
d) Thailand and Malaysia

The traveller's tree of Madagascar (*Ravenala madagascariensis*) gets its name from its leaves which have hollow bases from which, it has been reported, travellers could obtain potable water.

Pieces of money to pay for the passage from this world to the next were placed in the mouth of corpses in ancient Mycenae, Greece, and Rome, and in a pouch in Japan.

19. Which of these Pakistani leaders was imprisoned, sentenced to death, and hanged in 1977?
a) Zia-ul-Haq
b) Yahya Khan
c) Zulfikar Ali Bhutto
d) Nawaz Sharif

20. Who is the chief architect of the British Houses of Parliament?
a) Humphry Repton
b) Richard Boyle Burlington
c) Charles Barry
d) Augustus Welby Northmore Pugin

21. Which Egyptian president was assassinated by extremists while he was reviewing a military parade in 1981?
a) Hafiz al-Assad
b) Muammar Gaddafi
c) Anwar el-Sadat
d) Gamal Abdel Nasser

22. Who was the first woman to become the prime minister of Israel in 1969?
a) Leah Rabin
b) Sholem Aleicheim
c) Golda Meir
d) Sara Netanyahu

23. The parliament of which Asian country is called the Tshogdu?
a) Nepal
b) Bhutan
c) Thailand
d) Korea

24. The parliament of which West Asian country is called the Knesset?
a) Syria
b) Lebanon
c) Israel
d) Jordan

25. Which of the following medieval conquerors' tombs, in Samarkand, is called Gur-e Amir?
a) Genghis Khan
b) Kublai Khan
c) Timur
d) Ogatai Khan

26. Who is the Korean naval officer who built the Korean fleet called *kobukson* ("turtle ship") against the Japanese invasions of Korea in 1592?
a) Ch'oe Ch'ung-hon
b) Yi Sun-shin
c) Yi Song-gye
d) Ch'oe Che-u

27. Who was the first president of Indonesia who was also deposed by the army in 1966?
a) Suharto
b) Lee Kwan Yew
c) U Ne Win
d) Sukarno

28. What were the generals who replaced the kingship in 6th-century Rome called?
a) Consuls
b) Dictators
c) Senate
d) Magistrate

29. Which temple complex in Asia symbolically represents Mount Meru?
a) Shangri La
b) Potala
c) Angkor Wat
d) Amarnath cave

30. Who was Emiliano Zapata?
a) A revolutionary
b) A baseball player
c) A musician
d) A physicist

31. Which was Nazi Germany's largest concentration and extermination camp?
a) Treblinka
b) Auschwitz
c) Belzec
d) Sobibor

32. Who was the only U.S. president to be elected to office four times (1933-45)?
a) John F. Kennedy
b) Harry Truman
c) Ronald Reagan
d) Franklin Roosevelt

33. Where was the final land battle of the Russo-Japanese war in 1905 fought?
a) Mukden
b) Port Arthur
c) Seoul
d) Liaotung Peninsula

34. What was the Democratic Republic of the Congo known as from 1971 to 1997?
a) Zanzibar
b) French Equatorial Africa
c) Zaire
d) Equatorial Guinea

35. Who was the first Queen of England?
a) Elizabeth I
b) Mary I
c) Matilda
d) Victoria

36. Which country did Japan attack in 1904?
a) Korea
b) U.S.A.
c) Britain
d) Russia

37. Who was Benjamin Disraeli?
a) Prime Minister of Israel
b) Founder of Zionism
c) Russian activist
d) Prime Minister of Great Britain

38. Who was called the "Virgin Queen" of England?
a) Elizabeth I
b) Victoria
c) Mary
d) Anne Boleyn

39. Which Queen of England turned power over to her first cousin and husband, Prince Albert?
a) Victoria
b) Duchess of Kent
c) Anne
d) Elizabeth II

40. What was the earliest-known name for the island of Britain?
a) Ierne
b) White Land
c) British Isles
d) Albion

41. Who was the first president of Botswana after it gained independence from Great Britain?
a) Seretse Khama
b) Arthur Bliss
c) William Kirkcaldy
d) William Herschel

42. Who among the following served as prime minister of New Zealand three times?
a) William Bragg
b) Edward William Stafford
c) William Haley
d) William Orpen

43. Which English kingdom was the first to be converted to Christianity in the year 597 in Anglo-Saxon England?
a) Sussex
b) Kent
c) Warwickshire
d) Wessex

44. Who became the prime minister of Britain in the year 1945?
a) Winston Churchill
b) Clement Attlee
c) Stanley Baldwin
d) Neville Chamberlain

45. When was the North Atlantic Treaty signed?
a) April 1949
b) August 1949
c) February 1952
d) May 1955

46. Which of these monarchs had a speech defect?
a) James I
b) Charles I
c) Henry VIII
d) George V

47. Which of these is also known as the Revolution of 1789?
a) Industrial Revolution
b) French Revolution
c) Russian Revolution
d) Cultural Revolution

48. Who among these was guillotined, following a revolution?
a) Maria Theresa
b) Marie Antoinette
c) Astrid
d) Eleanor of Aquitaine

Dragon's blood is a red resin obtained from the fruit of several palms of the genus *Daemonorops*. Once valued as a medicine in Europe because of its astringent properties, dragon's blood now is used as a varnish for violins and in photoengraving for preventing undercutting of the printing surface during etching.

Did You Know?

49. What was the Jacobin Club that was prominent during the French Revolution?
a) A social group
b) A political group
c) An elitist group
d) A peasant group

50. In which country did the Industrial Revolution first take place?
a) France
b) Britain
c) Germany
d) Poland

51. Who coined the term Industrial Revolution?
a) Arnold Toynbee
b) William Cockerill
c) John Cockerill
d) John Stuart Mill

52. What is the first stage of the Russian Revolution of 1917 popularly known as?
a) February Revolution
b) May Revolution
c) July Revolution
d) October Revolution

53. What was name of the test of the plutonium weapon in New Mexico on July 16, 1945?
a) Fat Man
b) Sea-lion
c) Manhattan
d) Trinity

54. Who is credited with having launched the Cultural Revolution in China?
a) Liu Shaoqi
b) Tsar Deng Xiaoping
c) Mao Zedong
d) Jiang Qing

55. Who was the first president of the United States of America?
a) Abraham Lincoln
b) George Washington
c) James Madison
d) John Adams

56. Which American president did not take up residence in the White House?
a) Abraham Lincoln
b) George Washington
c) George Bush
d) John Adams

57. Who adopted "White House" as the official name for the residence of the president of the United States?
a) Thomas Jefferson
b) John Adams
c) Theodore Roosevelt
d) Benjamin Franklin

58. Who among the following is the American president to serve two discontinuous terms?
a) Bill Clinton
b) Grover Cleveland
c) Richard Nixon
d) Ronald Reagan

59. Which American First Lady rescued a Gilbert Stuart portrait of George Washington from the White House when British troops occupied and burned Washington, D.C., in August 1814?
a) Dolley Madison
b) Abigail Smith Adams
c) Martha Washington
d) Martha Jefferson

60. Which American president was referred to as "His Fraudulency"?
a) Grover Cleveland
b) John Adams
c) Bill Clinton
d) Rutherford Hayes

61. The phrase "New Frontier" was associated with the programmes of which U.S. president?
a) John F. Kennedy
b) Ronald Reagan
c) George Bush
d) Bill Clinton

62. Who was the first Roman Catholic ever to be elected U.S. president?
a) Abraham Lincoln
b) Ronald Reagan
c) John F. Kennedy
d) Bill Clinton

63. Who designed the Lincoln Memorial in Washington, D.C.?
a) Piccirilli brothers
b) Henry Bacon
c) Pierre-Charles L'Enfant
d) Daniel Chester French

64. What was the immediate cause of the Peasants' Revolt, the first great popular rebellion in English history, in the year 1381?
a) Imposition of poll tax
b) Economic discontent
c) Statute of labourers
d) Black Death

65. Which political philosopher became the first secretary of state of the United States in 1789?
a) George Washington
b) Thomas Jefferson
c) John Adams
d) Benjamin Franklin

66. Which two former U.S. presidents and friends died within a few hours of each other on the 50th anniversary of the proclamation of the Declaration of Independence?
a) George Washington and John Adams
b) John Adams and Thomas Jefferson
c) Thomas Jefferson and James Madison
d) James Madison and James Monroe

67. Who was the U.S. president during the British-U.S. War of 1812?
a) Thomas Jefferson
b) James Monroe
c) James Madison
d) John Adams

The name hockey—as the organized game came to be known—has been attributed to the French word *hoquet* (shepherd's stick).

Don Bradman, as a youth, perfected his timing by hitting a golf ball against a corrugated metal water tank.

Did You Know?

68. Which of the following U.S. presidents was not a lawyer by profession?
a) Ronald Reagan
b) John Adams
c) Bill Clinton
d) Abraham Lincoln

69. Which German Nazi official was also called "The Hangman"?
a) Herman Goering
b) Reinhard Heydrich
c) Heinrich Himmler
d) Walther Funk

70. Which former U.S. president was given the title of "little magician"?
a) John F. Kennedy
b) James Madison
c) Martin Van Buren
d) John Adams

71. Which former U.S. president was shot at within four months of being sworn into the office?
a) William Harry Harrison
b) Andrew Johnson
c) James Abram Garfield
d) Abraham Lincoln

72. Which U.S. president died within a month of being sworn in as the president?
a) William Henry Harrison
b) Andrew Johnson
c) James Abram Garfield
d) Abraham Lincoln

73. By what name was Richard Saunders more popularly known as?
a) Benjamin Franklin
b) George Washington
c) Max Webber
d) Franklin Roosevelt

74. Whose sonnet is inscribed at the base of the Statue of Liberty?
a) Ralph Waldo Emerson
b) Robert Frost
c) Emma Lazarus
d) Ernest Hemingway

75. Which leader was known by his byname of *Der Fuhrer*?
a) Adolf Hitler
b) Georges Clemenceau
c) Charles De Gaulle
d) Paul Von Hindenburg

76. Who was also known by his byname "The Great Emancipator"?
a) Thomas Paine
b) Charles De Gaulle
c) Abraham Lincoln
d) General Patton

77. Which book was considered to be the bible of National Socialism in Germany's Third Reich?
a) *Das Kapital*
b) *Mein Kampf*
c) *Evangelienbuch*
d) *Hildebrandslied*

78. What was the declaration that outlined proposals for a peace settlement made by Woodrow Wilson during World War I called?
a) Fourteen Points
b) Warsaw Pact
c) Treaty of Versailles
d) Potsdam Conference

79. Which organization was established at the initiative of the victorious Allied Powers at the end of World War I?
a) United Nations
b) League of Nations
c) North Atlantic Treaty Organization
d) World Trade Organization

80. Which German military leader was known by the popular byname of the "Desert Fox"?
a) Adolf Hitler
b) Hermann Goring
c) Erwin Rommel
d) Gustav Stresemann

81. Who is generally considered to be the creator of the League of Nations?
a) Charles De Gaulle
b) Dwight D. Eisenhower
c) Adolf Hitler
d) Woodrow Wilson

82. Who is said to have created the Gestapo, the dreaded police force of the Third Reich?
a) Adolf Hitler
b) Hermann Goering
c) Erwin Rommel
d) Gustav Stresemann

83. Who was also known as Il Duce ("The Leader")?
a) Adolf Hitler
b) Benito Mussolini
c) Hermann Goering
d) Winston Churchill

84. Which German military commander was considered the second most powerful man in the Third Reich?
a) Erwin Rommel
b) Hermann Goering
c) Heinrich Himmler
d) Ludwig Beck

85. Who is considered the chief architect of the July plot, an unsuccessful attempt to assassinate Adolf Hitler?
a) Graf (Count) von Stauffenberg
b) Roland Freisler
c) Erwin Rommel
d) Konrad Henlein

86. Who was the founder of the German Empire in the late 19th century?
a) William I
b) Otto Von Bismarck
c) Frederick I
d) Fredrick III

87. Who is considered to be the father of the U.S. constitution?
a) John Quincy
b) Thomas Jefferson
c) James Madison
d) George Washington

88. Which organization implemented the treaty, signed on April 4, 1949, seeking to establish a military counterweight to the Soviet military presence in eastern Europe?
a) North Atlantic Treaty Organization
b) Non-Aligned Movement
c) United Nations
d) League of Nations

89. Which was the second international organization established in the 20th century that was worldwide in scope and membership?
a) North Atlantic Treaty Organization
b) Non-Aligned Movement
c) United Nations
d) League of Nations

90. Whose speech brought the term "Iron Curtain" into prominence?
a) Joseph Stalin
b) Winston Churchill
c) Franklin Roosevelt
d) Charles De Gaulle

91. Which war was also known as the Great War?
a) World War I
b) World War II
c) Sino-Japanese War
d) Sino-Russian War

92. Which conflict marked the emergence of Japan as a major world power?
a) World War I
b) World War II

c) Sino-Japanese War
d) Sino-Russian War

93. In which year was the Berlin Wall erected?
a) 1961
b) 1962
c) 1969
d) 1989

94. Which of these presidents sent U.S. forces to turn back a communist invasion of South Korea?
a) Harry Truman
b) Dwight Eisenhower
c) Lyndon B. Johnson
d) Gerald Ford

95. What was the coalition headed by Germany, Italy, and Japan in World War II called?
a) Axis Powers
b) Allies
c) Allied Powers
d) Central Powers

96. Which of these countries initiated the Pearl Harbor attack that precipitated the U.S. entry into World War II?
a) Germany
b) Japan
c) Italy
d) Russia

---

97. In which organ of the United Nations are all the members represented?
a) Security Council
b) The General Assembly
c) The Secretariat
d) Trusteeship Council

98. Whose assassination was the immediate cause of World War I?
a) Francis Ferdinand
b) Francis Joseph
c) Joseph Stalin
d) Gavrilo Princip

99. What was the name given to the Normandy invasion, the Allied invasion of Western Europe that began on June 6, 1944?
a) Operation Overlord
b) Operation Sea-Lion
c) Operation Bluestar
d) Operation Desert Storm

100. By what name is the World Court otherwise known?
a) International Labour Organization
b) Permanent Court of International Justice
c) International Court of Justice
d) United Nations International Children's Emergency Fund

101. Who was the German emperor during World War I?
a) Frederick III
b) William II
c) William III
d) Fredrick William III

102. By what name is the Molotov-Ribbentrop Pact better known?
a) German-Soviet Nonaggression Pact
b) Warsaw Pact
c) Anti-Comintern Pact
d) Pact of Steel

103. Which group among the following is also called "Blue Helmets"?
a) The United States Army
b) The United States Air force
c) The United Nations Peacekeeping Force
d) The English Army

104. Who was the founder of the settlement that later became the city of Chicago?
a) King Edward III
b) Christopher Columbus
c) Stephen Austin
d) Jean-Baptist-Point Du Sable

105. Which American historian is best known for the "frontier thesis", the single most influential interpretation of the American past?
a) Louise Phelps Kellogg
b) Mercy Otis Warren
c) Frederick Jackson Turner
d) Herbert Baxter Adams

106. Who among the following circumnavigated the globe in the late 16th century?
a) Martin Frobisher
b) Vasco Da Gama
c) Francis Drake
d) Humphrey Gilbert

The first public clock that struck the hours was made and erected in Milan in 1335.

Peter Henlein, a locksmith in Nurnberg, Germany, was the first to introduce the mainspring in a clock, replacing the cumbersome technique of weights for driving clocks.

Did You Know?

107. What name was given to the surprise attack launched by the North Vietnamese army against American and South Vietnamese forces during the lunar New Year festival of 1968?
a) Summer offensive
b) Equinox offensive
c) June offensive
d) Tet offensive

108. Who led the first European expedition around the Cape of Good Hope opening the sea route to Asia via the Atlantic and Indian oceans?
a) Bartolomeu Dias
b) Duarte Pacheco
c) Amerigo Vespucci
d) Pedro Alvares Cabral

109. Who was the first European to discover the mouth of the Congo River?
a) Pedro Alvares Cabral
b) Diogo Cao
c) Bartolomeu Dias
d) Pero da Covilha

110. Which of these is the oldest federal building in Washington, D.C.?
a) The White House
b) The United States Supreme Court Building
c) The Smithsonian Institution headquarters building
d) The Woolworth Building

111. Which of the following countries has the oldest written national constitution in operation?
a) United States of America
b) India
c) Ireland
d) England

112. Who was the first secretary of war under the U.S. Constitution?
a) Thomas Jefferson
b) Henry Wager Halleck
c) Henry Knox
d) Alexander Hamilton

113. America was named after which of the following?
a) A ship
b) A merchant and navigator
c) A mountain
d) An island

114. The Treaty of Paris was signed by Spain and which of the following countries?
a) Canada
b) United States of America
c) Japan
d) France

115. In the U.S., which political party's traditional symbol is the donkey?
a) Republican Party
b) Democratic Party
c) Whig Party
d) Free-Soil Party

116. Who assassinated the black civil rights movement leader, Martin Luther King, Jr.?
a) James Earl Ray
b) Oswald Lee
c) Jack Ruby
d) John Wilkes Booth

117. Who was the first British Prime Minister in the 20th century to serve three consecutive terms?
a) John Major
b) Winston Churchill
c) Margaret Thatcher
d) Tony Blair

118. Which British political party has the byname "Tories"?
a) Labour Party
b) Conservative Party
c) Liberal Party
d) Whigs

119. Which U.S. president's period of administration has been called the Era of Good Feeling?
a) Thomas Jefferson
b) Abraham Lincoln
c) George Washington
d) James Monroe

120. Who is the founder of the Conservative Party in England?
a) Robert Peel
b) Benjamin Disraeli
c) George Canning
d) Winston Churchill

121. Which country's national flag is also called "Old Glory"?
a) Great Britain
b) Ireland
c) United States of America
d) Canada

122. Which English prime minister is credited with rallying the British people during World War II?
a) Neville Chamberlain
b) Winston Churchill
c) Clement Attlee
d) Harold Wilson

123. Which was the intended second target of the atom bomb to have been dropped on August 11, 1945?
a) Tokyo
b) Nagasaki
c) Yokohama
d) Kokura

124. Who became the king of England after the reign of King Henry II?
a) Henry Fitzhenry
b) William
c) Louis VII
d) Thomas Becket

125. Which famous political figure is known for his words "give me liberty or give me death"?
a) Grover Cleveland
b) Patrick Henry
c) George Washington
d) Thomas Jefferson

126. Which princess played a vital role in secret negotiations with Charles II of England, that led to the Treaty of Dover in 1670?
a) Henrietta Anne
b) Anne-Marie
c) Queen of Sardinia
d) Marie-Louise

127. Which British prime minister is identified with initiating the policy of "appeasement" towards Germany in the period immediately preceding World War II?
a) Joseph Chamberlain
b) Benjamin Disraeli
c) Neville Chamberlain
d) Winston Churchill

128. Which prime minister's term in office coincided with the longest economic recession (1990-93) in Britain since World War II?
a) John Major
b) Margaret Thatcher
c) Clement Attlee
d) Anthony Eden

129. Who was the prime minister of Britain when India gained independence?
a) Clement Attlee
b) Harold Macmillan
c) Anthony Eden
d) Winston Churchill

130. Which British prime minister established the Southeast Asia Treaty Organization (SEATO)?
a) Anthony Eden
b) Margaret Thatcher
c) Clement Attlee
d) Harold Macmillan

131. Which Stuart king of England styled himself as the "king of Great Britain"?
a) Robert Stewart
b) Frederick II of Denmark
c) James I
d) George I

132. Which king of England led the country into a hundred-year war with France?
a) James III
b) Edward III
c) David II
d) Charles IV

133. Which Scottish protestant conspirator murdered the powerful cardinal David Beaton at St. Andrews Castle in May 1546?
a) William Wallace
b) William Kirkcaldy
c) Patrick Hume
d) John Dury

134. Who appoints the secretary-general of the United Nations?
a) General Assembly
b) Security Council
c) Trusteeship Council
d) Secretariat

135. Which permanent specialized agency of the UN was established in October 1945?
a) International Labour Organization
b) United Nations Educational, Scientific and Cultural Organization
c) Food and Agriculture Organization
d) World Health Organization

136. Which famous political figure of America was called "Little Ellick" by his colleagues?
a) John Adams
b) Earl Warren
c) Alexander Hamilton Stephens
d) William Johnson

137. What is the primary function of the United Nations?
a) Conservation of environment
b) Maintenance of international peace and security
c) Economic welfare and cooperation
d) Social welfare and cooperation

138. Where was the first UN conference on environmental issues in 1972 held?
a) Geneva
b) Rio de Janerio
c) Stockholm
d) Paris

139. The International Law Commission was established by which organ of the UN?
a) International Court of Justice
b) Economic and Social Council
c) Secretariat
d) General Assembly

140. The UN efforts for which country represent the most enduring and concerted attempt to promote freedom for a former colony?
a) Brazil
b) Cuba
c) Chile
d) Namibia

141. Which United States army commander was also known as the "Jumping General"?
a) George Washington
b) James Gavin
c) Dwight Eisenhower
d) Abraham Lincoln

142. Which U.S. president issued the Emancipation Proclamation?
a) George Washington
b) Dwight Eisenhower
c) Theodore Roosevelt
d) Abraham Lincoln

143. Which of the following places is famous as Napoleon's place of exile?
a) Elba
b) Waterloo
c) Tuscany
d) Wellington

144. Which famous military leader was also known as "The Little Corporal"?
a) George Washington
b) Benito Mussolini
c) Napoleon Bonaparte
d) Adolf Hitler

Literature

1. In which former English county are the humorous stories of James Herriot based?
a) Buckinghamshire
b) Hampshire
c) Kent
d) Yorkshire

2. Which of the following novels is a work by Jean Webster?
a) *The Little Princess*
b) *Alice in Wonderland*
c) *Daddy-Long-Legs*
d) *The Little Prince*

3. Who wrote the famous *Foundation* trilogy?
a) Michael Crichton
b) Isaac Asimov
c) Jeffrey Archer
d) Arthur Hailey

4. Who compiled fairy tales like "Cinderella" and "Little Red Riding Hood" under the collection titled *Tales of Mother Goose?*
a) Grimm Brothers
b) Charles Perrault
c) Hans Christian Andersen
d) Lewis Carroll

5. Who created animal characters such as "Peter Rabbit" and "Mrs. Tiggy-Winkle"?
a) E.B. White
b) Alan Alexander Milne
c) Hans Christian Andersen
d) Beatrix Potter

6. *Black Boy* is an autobiographical account of which author's boyhood?
a) Thomas Pynchon
b) Richard Wright
c) John Dos Passos
d) Saul Bellow

7. What name is given to the Japanese linked-verse poetry in which two or more poets supplied alternating sections of a poem?
a) Choka
b) Katauta
c) Renga
d) Haiku

8. Who wrote the famous play *She Stoops to Conquer?*
a) Richard Brinsley Sheridan
b) William Shakespeare
c) Oliver Goldsmith
d) Arthur Miller

9. Who among the following is considered to be the greatest master of *renga?*
a) Kobayashi Issa
b) Masaoka Shiki
c) Shohaku
d) Iio Sogi

10. Who among the following was Japan's first great literary figure?
a) Matsuo Basho
b) Iio Sogi
c) Kakinomoto Hitomaro
d) Socho

11. Who produced the first systematic grammar of Western tradition?
a) Apollonius Dyscolus
b) Aelius Donatus
c) Dionysius Thrax
d) Priscian

12. Who wrote the novel *Darkness at Noon?*
a) Kingsley Amis
b) Robert Musil
c) Arthur Koestler
d) Virginia Woolfe

13. Who was the originator of Latin historical plays (*fabulae praetextae*) that were based on Roman historical or legendary figures and events?
a) Quintus Ennius
b) Eusebius Hieronymus
c) Gnaeus Naevius
d) Aelius Donatus

14. Who is known as the founder of Roman literature?
a) Quintus Ennius
b) Lucius Livius Andronicus
c) Virgil
d) Gnaeus Naevius

15. Who was the first of classical Athens' great tragic dramatists?
a) Sophocles
b) Euripides
c) Aeschylus
d) Aristophanes

16. Which is the first anthology of Chinese poetry?
a) *I Ching*
b) *Shu Ching*
c) *Li chi*
d) *Shih Ching*

17. Which is the earliest record of the type of popular entertainment literature circulated by wandering minstrels in the medieval German period?
a) *Koenig Rother*
b) *Salman und Morolf*
c) *Orendel*
d) *Sankt Oswald*

18. Who is credited with the creation of the Gothic alphabet?
a) Ulfilas
b) Notker Labeo
c) Ekkehard IV
d) Otfrid

19. Which famous English author worked with the Indian Imperial Police?
a) Thomas Hardy
b) George Orwell
c) E.M. Forster
d) Allan Sillitoe

Did You Know?

The Book of the Dun Cow, the oldest surviving miscellaneous manuscript in Irish literature, is so called because the original vellum upon which it was written was supposedly taken from the hide of the famous cow of St. Ciaran of Clonmacnoise.

20. Who among the following is one of the most important and celebrated figures in Spanish literature?
a) Bartolome de Las Casas
b) Juan Montalvo
c) Juan de Mariana
d) Miguel de Cervantes Saavedra

21. Who is considered to be the founder of modern Russian literature?
a) Anton Pavlovich Chekov
b) Lev Nikolayevich Tolstoy
c) Aleksandr Pushkin
d) Ivan Turgenev

22. Who wrote *The Wild Swans at Coole?*
a) William Butler Yeats
b) Ezra Loomis Pound
c) Andrew Marvell
d) John Keats

23. Who is best known for his science fiction books, *The Time Machine* and *The War of the Worlds?*
a) Herbert George Wells
b) Isaac Asimov
c) Arthur Charles Clarke
d) Jules Verne

24. Who was largely responsible for the establishment of science fiction as an independent literary form?
a) Hugo Gernsback
b) Arthur Charles Clarke
c) Jules Verne
d) Herbert George Wells

25. In which novel are a group of boys stranded in a beach after a crash?
a) *Lord of the Flies*
b) *Robinson Crusoe*
c) *Treasure Island*
d) *The Adventures of Huckleberry Finn*

26. Who wrote the short story "The Snows of Kilimanjaro"?
a) Thomas Wolfe
b) Robert Penn Warren
c) Mickey Spillane
d) Ernest Hemingway

27. Who wrote the set of stories named *Winnie the Pooh?*
a) Beatrix Potter
b) Robert Lawrence Stine
c) Alan Alexander Milne
d) Enid Blyton

28. Which of the following works features the animal characters Mole, Rat, Badger, and Toad?
a) *The Wind in the Willows*
b) *The Adventures of Tom Sawyer*
c) *Treasure Island*
d) *Harry Potter and the Philosopher's Stone*

29. Who among the following wrote only one novel?
a) Emily Bronte
b) Jane Austen
c) George Eliot
d) Charles Dickens

30. Who compiled the first English dictionary in 1604?
a) Robert Cawdrey
b) Samuel Johnson
c) Thomas Cooper
d) Francis Bacon

31. In which novel by Jerome David Salinger is Holden Caulfield a character?
a) *Franny and Zooey*
b) *Raise High the Roof Beam*
c) *Carpenters*
d) *The Catcher in the Rye*

32. What was the novelist Arthur Conan Doyle's profession?
a) Doctor
b) Lawyer
c) Architect
d) Engineer

33. Which novelist created the lawyer-detective Perry Mason?
a) Josephine Bell
b) Erle Stanley Gardner
c) Ian Fleming
d) Agatha Christie

34. Which novel by George Orwell is based on the story of the Russian Revolution?
a) *Nineteen Eighty-four*
b) *A Clergyman's Daughter*
c) *Keep the Aspidistra Flying*
d) *Animal Farm*

35. Which novel by Thomas Hardy was never published?
a) *A Pair of Blue Eyes*
b) *Far from the Madding Crowd*
c) *The Return of the Native*
d) *The Poor Man and the Lady*

36. Who created the characters Athos, Porthos, and Aramis?
a) Kingsley Amis
b) Arthur Hailey
c) Alexandre Pere Dumas
d) Victor-Marie Hugo

37. Which famous fictional detective lived at 221B, Baker Street, London?
a) Miss Jane Marple
b) Hercule Poirot
c) Sherlock Holmes
d) Perry Mason

38. Which war does Hemingway describe in his novel *For Whom the Bell Tolls*?
a) American Civil War
b) World War I
c) Spanish Civil War
d) Russo-Japanese War

39. Who is the author of the novel *The House of the Seven Gables*?
a) Louisa May Alcott
b) Harold Robbins
c) William Faulkner
d) Nathaniel Hawthorne

40. Who wrote the short story "Rip Van Winkle"?
a) Thomas Wolfe
b) Robert Penn Warren
c) Raymond Chandler
d) Washington Irving

41. Which of the following novelists was a woman?
a) George Eliot
b) O. Henry
c) Joseph Conrad
d) Saki

42. Which of the following poets wrote *The Song of Hiawatha?*
a) Henry Wadsworth Longfellow
b) John Keats
c) Robert Browning
d) Walt Whitman

43. Who wrote *Anne of Green Gables?*
a) Lucy Maud Montgomery
b) Louisa May Alcott
c) Laura Ingalls Wilder
d) Susan Coolidge

44. Who wrote *Little House on the Prairie?*
a) Jean Webster
b) Harriet Beecher Stowe
c) Laura Ingalls Wilder
d) Louisa May Alcott

45. Which poet wrote *The Bell Jar?*
a) Denise Levertov
b) Gwendolyn Brooks
c) Ted Hughes
d) Sylvia Plath

46. Who wrote *Who's Afraid of Virginia Woolf?*
a) Oscar Wilde
b) Noel Coward
c) Edward Albee
d) Arthur Miller

47. Who wrote *A Streetcar Named Desire?*
a) Arthur Miller
b) Eugene O'Neill
c) Lorraine Hansberry
d) Tennessee Williams

48. Which of the following did Saul Bellow write?
a) *The Scarlet Letter*
b) *Leaves of Grass*
c) *Seize the Day*
d) *Death of a Salesman*

49. What is an oxymoron?
a) A comic character in a play
b) A kind of paradox
c) A mythical monster
d) A type of poem

50. Which Shakespearean play has these opening lines, "If music be the food of love, play on..."?
a) *Hamlet*
b) *As You Like It*
c) *King Lear*
d) *Twelfth Night*

51. From which novel by Leo Tolstoy is the statement "All happy families resemble each other; each unhappy family is unhappy in its own way" taken?
a) *Anna Karenina*
b) *War and Peace*
c) *Death of Ivan Ilyich*
d) *Childhood, Boyhood, Youth*

52. Who wrote the book of verse called *Twenty Love Poems and a Song of Despair?*
a) William Blake
b) Pablo Neruda
c) Robert Frost
d) Walt Whitman

53. Paul Morel is the central character of which book by D.H. Lawrence?
a) *The Rainbow*
b) *Sons and Lovers*
c) *Women in Love*
d) *The White Peacock*

54. In which play by George Bernard Shaw is Henry Higgins a character?
a) *Pygmalion*
b) *Mrs. Warren's Profession*
c) *Arms and the Man*
d) *Major Barbara*

55. Who wrote the play *Every Man In His Humour?*
a) William Shakespeare
b) Ben Jonson
c) George Bernard Shaw
d) Oscar Wilde

56. Who wrote the poem *Don Juan?*
a) Robert Browning
b) Lord Byron
c) William Wordsworth
d) William Blake

57. Which was the first book that featured James Bond?
a) *From Russia, with Love*
b) *Dr. No*
c) *Casino Royale*
d) *Goldfinger*

58. Who wrote *Of Human Bondage?*
a) William Somerset Maugham
b) John Steinbeck
c) Jerome David Salinger
d) Pearl S. Buck

59. What is a tercet?
a) A poetic stanza
b) The third act of a play
c) A novella
d) A novel in three parts

60. Who is the author of *The Jungle Books?*
a) Joseph Conrad
b) Rudyard Kipling
c) Ruskin Bond
d) Henry James

61. Who wrote the novel *Madame Bovary?*
a) Lev Nikolayevich Tolstoy
b) Daniel Defoe
c) David Herbert Lawrence
d) Gustave Flaubert

62. Which of the following poems has not been written by William Shakespeare?
a) *The Prelude*
b) *The Phoenix and the Turtle*
c) *The Rape of Lucrece*
d) *Venus and Adonis*

63. Who is the main character of Nathaniel Hawthorne's novel *The Scarlet Letter?*
a) Hester Prynne
b) Roger Chillingworth
c) Arthur Dimmesdale
d) Tess D'Urberville

64. In which novel by Charles Dickens is Pip the hero?
a) *David Copperfield*
b) *A Tale of Two Cities*
c) *Great Expectations*
d) *Oliver Twist*

65. In Herman Melville's novel who or what is Moby Dick?
a) A ship
b) The captain of a ship
c) A whale
d) An imaginary land

66. Which legendary character sells his soul to the devil for the sake of knowledge and power?
a) Merlin
b) Roger Bacon
c) Alberto Magnus
d) Dr. Faustus

67. Who were known collectively as "university wits" in 16th-century England?
a) Singers
b) Actors
c) Poets
d) Playwrights

68. In which of the following Shakespearean plays would one find the character Falstaff?
a) *Henry IV*
b) *Henry VI*
c) *Richard III*
d) *Richard II*

69. Who introduced crucial innovations in satiric comedy in the Elizabethan era?
a) William Shakespeare
b) John Ford
c) Philip Massinger
d) Ben Jonson

70. Who wrote *Songs of Innocence* and *Songs of Experience?*
a) William Wordsworth
b) William Shakespeare
c) William Blake
d) William Ainsworth

71. What is the *masnawi?*
a) An epic
b) A form of drama
c) A form of poetry
d) A monologue

72. Which of the works of T.S. Eliot deals with the legend of the search for the Grail?
a) *The Four Quartets*
b) *Ash Wednesday*
c) *The Waste Land*
d) *The Sacred Wood*

73. Who wrote the story "Baa, Baa Black Sheep"?
a) Hans Christian Andersen
b) Rudyard Kipling
c) Lewis Carroll
d) Grimm Brothers

74. Who wrote *Cry, the Beloved Country* (1948) which turned global attention to apartheid in South Africa?
a) Vidhyadhar Surajprasad Naipaul
b) Chinua Achebe
c) Alan Stewart Paton
d) Jose Craveirinha

75. Which river in North America is the setting for the novel *Huckleberry Finn?*
a) Fraser River
b) Niagara River
c) Mississippi River
d) Snake River

76. Stephen Dedalus is the protagonist of which modern classic?
a) *A Portrait of the Artist as a Young Man*
b) *Ulysses*
c) *A Farewell to Arms*
d) *Gone with the Wind*

77. Who among the following is said to have declared, "God is dead"?
a) Friedrich Nietzsche
b) Jean Paul Sartre
c) Albert Camus
d) Samuel Beckett

78. Who is the author of the play *The Glass Menagerie?*
a) Noel Coward
b) Samuel Beckett
c) Tennessee Williams
d) Arthur Miller

79. Who wrote *The Color Purple?*
a) Alice Walker
b) Arthur Adamov
c) Peter Handke
d) William Saroyan

80. In which of the following plays by Shakespeare does the character called Claudius appear?
a) *Hamlet*
b) *Macbeth*
c) *King Lear*
d) *The Tempest*

81. Which of the following characters has an ass's head in Shakespeare's *A Midsummer Night's Dream?*
a) Nick Bottom
b) Puck
c) Demetrius
d) Oberon

82. Who wrote the *Song of Solomon?*
a) Kenzaburo Oe
b) Kobo Abe
c) Toni Morrison
d) Richard Rive

83. *Elene*, a poem by Cynewulf—the most important of the 9th-century English poets—belongs to which of the following categories?
a) Religious verse
b) Romantic poem
c) War poem
d) Nature poem

84. Who is the author of *Revelations of Divine Love?*
a) Julian of Norwich
b) Margery Kempe
c) John Mandeville
d) Thomas Malory

85. What was the pen name of William Sidney Porter?
a) O. Henry
b) Saki
c) Roald Dahl
d) Graham Greene

86. Who created the characters Clovis and Reginald?
a) Edgar Allan Poe
b) Saki
c) Arthur Conan Doyle
d) Mary Shelley

87. Who wrote *The Fountainhead?*
a) Mario Puzo
b) Ayn Rand
c) Jeffrey Archer
d) Arthur Hailey

88. Which of these dramatists wrote *The Way of the World?*
a) William Congreve
b) Richard Brinsley Sheridan
c) Christopher Marlowe
d) Ben Jonson

89. Which of these poets created the mythological figure of Urizen?
a) William Blake
b) William Wordsworth
c) John Keats
d) Lord Byron

90. Who found and published the diary of Anne Frank after her tragic death?
a) Her sister, Margot
b) Her step-sister, Eva Schloss
c) Her friends
d) Her father, Otto Frank

91. In which of Shakespeare's plays do we find the group of clowns, Feste, Malvolio, Sir Toby Belch, and Sir Andrew Aguecheek?
a) *Comedy of Errors*
b) *Twelfth Night*
c) *As You Like It*
d) *A Midsummer Night's Dream*

92. Which play by Eugene O'Neill is a trilogy based on Aeschylus's *Oresteia?*
a) *Mourning Becomes Electra*
b) *The Iceman Cometh*
c) *Strange Interlude*
d) *Long Day's Journey Into Night*

93. Who among these ancient Greek writers is a poetess?
a) Callimachus
b) Phoenix
c) Hesiod
d) Sappho

94. Who wrote *The Good Earth* that won the Pulitzer Prize for fiction in 1932?
a) Pearl S. Buck
b) Edith Wharton
c) Margaret Mitchell
d) Eudora Welty

95. Which American lyric poet was known as "the New England mystic"?
a) Walt Whitman
b) Robert Frost
c) Emily Dickinson
d) Wallace Stevens

96. Which of these plays by Shakespeare uses the stage-prop of a statue to reveal a most dramatic secret?
a) *Romeo and Juliet*
b) *A Winter's Tale*
c) *King Lear*
d) *Hamlet*

97. Whose novels were known as the Leatherstocking Tales?
a) Mark Twain
b) Herman Melville
c) Henry James
d) James Fenimore Cooper

98. Which of these awards is given by Columbia University for outstanding public service and achievement in American journalism, letters, and music?
a) The Booker Prize
b) The Whitbread Award
c) The Carnegie Medal
d) The Pulitzer Prize

99. Who wrote *One Flew Over the Cuckoo's Nest?*
a) Harper Lee
b) Ken Kesey
c) Toni Morrison
d) Ben Okri

100. Who wrote *Uncle Vanya?*
a) Anton Chekhov
b) Leo Tolstoy
c) Fyodor Dostoyevsky
d) Alexander Pushkin

101. By which name was Mrs. Arthur Bell Nicholls better known as?
a) Jane Austen
b) Emily Bronte
c) Christina Rossetti
d) Charlotte Bronte

There are dialectal differences (regional variations) in birdsongs among populations of a single species living in different areas.

The Chinese and Japanese languages use the same body of characters but pronounce them entirely differently.

Nobel

1. Which one of the following institutions confers the Nobel Prize for Literature?
a) Karolinska Institute
b) Norwegian Nobel Committee
c) Nobel Foundation
d) The Swedish Academy

2. Which one of the following did Alfred Bernhard Nobel invent?
a) Printing press
b) Electricity
c) Telephone
d) Dynamite

3. Which one of the following did Nobel laureate Alexander Fleming discover?
a) Oxygen
b) Gold
c) Penicillin
d) Jupiter

4. In which area of physics was Albert Einstein awarded the Nobel Prize in 1921?
a) Theory of gravitation
b) General theory of relativity
c) Explanation of photoelectric effect
d) Special theory of relativity

5. Who is the Nobel laureate whose daughter and son-in-law were jointly awarded a Nobel Prize?
a) Hendrik Antoon Lorentz
b) Pierre Curie

c) Wilhelm Conrad Rontgen
d) Henri Becquerel

6. Which Nobel laureate's son was also awarded a Nobel Prize?
a) Max Planck
b) Neils Bohr
c) Kai Manne Borje Siegbahn
d) Robert Andrews Millikan

7. Which famous French writer was awarded the Nobel Prize for Literature in 1964 but declined to accept it?
a) Andre Gide
b) Anatole France
c) Jean Paul Sartre
d) Romain Rolland

8. Which Russian writer was forced by his country to decline the Nobel Prize for Literature in 1958?
a) Boris Pasternak
b) Leo Tolstoy
c) Mikhail Aleksandrovich Sholokhov
d) Aleksandr Isayevich Solzhenitsyn

9. Which Asian politician, corecipient with Henry Kissinger, declined the Nobel Peace Prize in 1973?
a) Kim Dae Jung
b) Aung San Suu Kyi
c) Le Duc Tho
d) Dalai Lama

The greatest known reserve of copper ore in one body is the deposit at El Teniente mine in Chile.

Asia is not only the Earth's largest but also its youngest and structurally most complex continent.

Did You Know?

Nobel

10. Who among the following was awarded the Nobel Prize posthumously?
a) Dag Hammarskjold
b) Martin Luther King, Jr.
c) Norman Ernest Borlaug
d) Andrey Dmitriyevich Sakharov

11. Which Swedish writer was posthumously awarded the 1931 Nobel Prize for Literature?
a) Erik Axel Karlfeldt
b) Ola Hansson
c) Sigfrid Siwertz
d) Ludvig Anselm Nordstrom

12. Which institution set up the Nobel Prize for Economic Sciences in 1968?
a) Bank of England
b) Bank of Sweden
c) World Bank
d) Bank of America

13. Besides physics, in which other field was Marie Curie awarded the Nobel Prize?
a) Peace
b) Chemistry
c) Literature
d) Physiology or Medicine

14. For what did Walther Hemann Nernst win the Nobel Prize for Chemistry?
a) Third law of thermodynamics
b) Discoveries in the chemical transmission of nerve impulses
c) Discovery of embryonic induction
d) Developments in harnessing nuclear power

15. Who founded the Swedish Academy, which confers the Nobel Prize for Literature?
a) Alfred Bernhard Nobel
b) Immanuel Nobel
c) King Gustav III
d) John Ericsson

16. Who was the first American to win the Nobel Prize for Literature?
a) Eugene O'Neill
b) William Faulkner
c) Sinclair Lewis
d) Ernest Hemingway

17. For what did Emil von Behring win the Nobel Prize for Physiology or Medicine?
a) Serum therapy
b) Phototherapy
c) Physiology of digestion
d) Tuberculosis research

18. Which Nobel Prize can also be conferred on an institution?
a) Physics
b) Chemistry
c) Peace
d) Economic Sciences

19. Who was the recipient of the first Nobel Prize in Physics?
a) Marie Curie
b) Wilhelm Conrad Rontgen
c) Joseph John Thomson
d) Ernest Rutherford

20. Why was Emil Fischer awarded the Nobel Prize for Chemistry?
a) For work on sugar and purine groups of substances
b) For work on experimental petrology
c) Research on electrolytes
d) Discovery of four noble gases

21. Who won the first Nobel Prize in Literature in 1901?
a) Rabindranath Tagore
b) Sully Prudhomme
c) Rudolf Christoph Eucken
d) Frederic Mistral

22. Who was the first Swedish national to win the Nobel Prize in Chemistry?
a) Svante August Arrhenius
b) Theodor Svedberg
c) Hans von Euler-Chelpin
d) F.W. Kohlrausch

23. For what work in economics did Ragnar Frisch receive the Nobel Prize?
a) Input-output analysis
b) Econometrics
c) Public choice theory
d) Welfare economics

24. Who was the first winner of the Nobel Prize for Chemistry?
a) Jacobus Henricus van't Hoff
b) Emil Hermann Fischer
c) Adolf von Baeyer
d) William Ramsay

25. Which Nobel laureate wrote under the pen-name "Litwos"?
a) Seamus Heany
b) Frederic Mistral
c) Henryk Sienkiewicz
d) Joseph Brodsky

26. Who is considered to be the father of input-output analysis?
a) Eli Hecksher
b) Wassily Leontief
c) John Richard Hicks
d) Ragnar Frisch

27. For research in which area did Ronald Ross win the Nobel Prize for Medicine in 1902?
a) Malaria
b) Tuberculosis
c) Discovery of insulin
d) Discovery of vitamin K

28. Who was awarded the Nobel Prize in 1970 for his fundamental contributions to nearly all branches of economic theory?
a) George Joseph Stigler
b) Edwin Robert Anderson Seligman
c) Paul Anthony Samuelson
d) Eveline Mabel Burns

29. Who among the following won the first Nobel Peace Prize in 1901 along with Henri Dunant?
a) Frederic Passy
b) Randal Cremer
c) Bertha Freifrau von Suttner
d) Theodore Roosevelt

30. For which work did Hendrick Antoon Lorentz win the Nobel Prize for Physics?
a) Theory of electromagnetic radiation
b) Discovery of radioactivity
c) Discovery of electrons
d) Energy levels in atoms

31. How many of the noble gases were discovered by William Ramsay?
a) Three
b) Four
c) Five
d) Six

32. For which work was Adolf von Baeyer awarded the Nobel Prize for Chemistry in 1905?
a) Research on organic dyes
b) Work on sugar and purine syntheses
c) Laws of chemical dynamics
d) Work in thermochemistry

33. Who was the first Englishman to receive the Nobel Prize?
a) William Golding
b) Winston Churchill
c) Patrick White
d) Rudyard Kipling

34. Who discovered the parasite that causes human malaria and was credited with the Nobel Prize for Physiology in 1907?
a) Alphonse Laveran
b) John Michael Bishop
c) Niels Ryberg Finsen
d) Ivan Petrovich Pavlov

35. Where was the Nobel laureate Ronald Ross first employed?
a) Liverpool School of Tropical Medicine
b) King's College Hospital, London
c) University of Liverpool
d) Indian Medical Service

36. Which American president won the Nobel Peace Prize in 1906?
a) Franklin Delano Roosevelt
b) Theodore Roosevelt
c) Grover Cleveland
d) William Howard Taft

37. Who was the first woman Nobel laureate?
a) Bertha Freifrau von Suttner
b) Marie Curie
c) Selma Lagerlof
d) Jane Addams

38. Who shared the Nobel Prize for Economic Sciences in 1972 with Kenneth Joseph Arrow?
a) John Henry Williams
b) Paul Anthony Samuelson
c) John Richard Hicks
d) Wassily Leontief

39. Who was awarded the Nobel Prize for the isolation of the element flourine and the development of the Moissan electric furnace?
a) Theodor Svedberg
b) Hans von Euler-Chelpin
c) Friedrich Wilhelm Georg Kohlrausch
d) Henri Moissan

In Chinese chess the pieces are moved on intersections of lines rather than on squares; the pieces are in the form of flat disks, and have their names written on them in red or blue.

People often yawn when reading or thinking about yawning, when hearing yawning, or when seeing it.

40. For what work was John William Strutt Rayleigh awarded the Nobel Prize for Physics?
a) Research on piezoelectricity
b) Stark effect
c) Isolation of argon gas
d) Study regarding energy levels in atoms

41. For which work was Niels Ryberg Finsen awarded the Nobel Prize for Physiology or Medicine?
a) Discovery of penicillin
b) Research related to mad-cow disease
c) Research related to meningitis
d) Phototheraphy

42. Who was the first woman to receive the Nobel Prize for Literature?
a) Selma Ottilia Lovisa Lagerlof
b) Grazia Deledda
c) Sigrid Undset
d) Pearl Buck

43. For which of his works did Rabindranath Tagore win the Nobel Prize for Literature?
a) *Manasi*
b) *Gitanjali*
c) *Gora*
d) *Ghare-Baire*

44. Who was awarded the Nobel Prize for Physiology or Medicine in 1904 for his work on digestive secretions?
a) Marceli Nencki
b) Louis Pasteur
c) Robert Koch
d) Ivan Petrovich Pavlov

45. Which American president won the Nobel Peace Prize in 1919?
a) Franklin Roosevelt
b) Woodrow Wilson
c) Grover Cleveland
d) William Howard Taft

46. Which Nobel laureate's research is known as the photoelectric effect?
a) Philipp Lenard
b) John William Strutt Rayleigh
c) Joseph John Thomson
d) Wilhelm Rontgen

47. Who shared the Nobel Prize for Economic Sciences with Friedrich von Hayek in 1974?
a) Bertil Ohlin
b) Simon Kuznets
c) John Rogers Commons
d) Gunnar Myrdal

48. For which discovery did Eduard Buchner get the Nobel Prize for Chemistry?
a) Non-cellular fermentation
b) Inert gases
c) Heavy hydrogen
d) Polarography

49. For which of these works did George Bernard Shaw, the 1925 Nobel laureate for Literature, receive the prize?
a) *Saint Joan*
b) *Heartbreak House*
c) *Back to Methuselah*
d) *The Apple Cart*

50. Which physician, who conducted research on tuberculosis and cholera, was awarded the Nobel Prize for Physiology or Medicine in 1905?
a) Robert Koch
b) Paul Greengard
c) Friedrich Gustav Jacob Henle
d) Arvid Carlsson

51. Who shared the 1925 Nobel Peace Prize for his help in bringing about the Locarno Pact?
a) Ludwig Quidde
b) Edouard Daladier
c) Austen Chamberlain
d) Frank Billings Kellogg

52. Who shared the Nobel Prize for Economic Sciences in 1975 with Tjalling Charles Koopmans?
a) Gerard Debreu
b) Gunnar Myrdal
c) Leonid Vitalyevich Kantorovich
d) Milton Friedman

53. Which Nobel laureate in Physics first established the accurate determination of the size of stars?
a) Edmund Halley
b) Guglielmo Marconi
c) Ferdinand Braun
d) Albert Abraham Michelson

54. Who shared the Nobel Prize for Economic Sciences with Arthur Lewis in 1979?
a) Odysseus Elytis
b) Herbert Charles Brown

c) Georg Wittig
d) Theodore William Schultz

55. Allvar Gullstrand received the Nobel Prize for Physiology or Medicine in 1911 for research in which field?
a) Neurology
b) Opthalmology
c) Immunology
d) Pathology

56. Who was awarded the Nobel Prize for Economic Sciences for his pioneering analyses of saving and of financial markets?
a) Franco Modigliani
b) John Maynard Keynes
c) James Mcgill Buchanan
d) Gerard Debreu

57. Who received the Nobel Prize for Economic Sciences for his development of the "public-choice theory"?
a) James Tobin
b) James Mcgill Buchanan
c) James J. Heckman
d) James Alexander Mirrlees

58. Who received a Nobel Prize for Economic Sciences for his contributions to the theory of economic growth?
a) Myron Samuel Scholes
b) Simon Kuznets
c) Herbert Alexander Simon
d) Robert Merton Solow

59. Which Nobel laureate can be called the founder of the field of atomic physics?
a) Joseph John Thomson
b) James Clerk Maxwell
c) Lenard Phillip
d) Ernest Rutherford

60. For which of his works was Gabriel Lippmann awarded the Nobel Prize for Physics in 1908?
a) Studies of piezoelectricity
b) Developing the colour photographic plate
c) Invention of the coleostat
d) Induction in superconductive circuits

61. Which German journalist won the Nobel Prize for Peace in 1935?
a) Carl von Ossietzky
b) Heinrich Boll
c) Rudolf Christoph Eucken
d) Gunter Grass

62. Why was Alexis Carrel awarded the Nobel Prize for Physiology or Medicine?
a) For developing a method of suturing blood vessels
b) For research on the eye as a light-refracting apparatus
c) For research in cellular chemistry
d) For research on tuberculosis

63. For which invention did Nils Dalen receive the Nobel Prize for Physics?
a) Sun valve
b) Cathode ray tube
c) Sphygmomanometer
d) Gas lamps

64. Which Nobel laureate discovered superconductivity?
a) Max Born
b) Niels Bohr
c) Gabriel Lippmann
d) Heike Kamerlingh Onnes

65. With whom was the American Friends Service Committee a corecipient of the Nobel Prize for Peace in 1947?
a) Institute of International Law
b) International Peace Bureau
c) Friends Service Council
d) Nansen International Office for Refugees

66. Which Nobel laureate for Economic Sciences applied the methods of economics to the aspects of human behaviour?
a) Ralph George Hawtrey
b) Robert William Fogel
c) Douglass Cecil North
d) Gary Stanley Becker

67. For which work did Max Planck win the Nobel Prize for Physics in 1918?
a) Special theory of relativity
b) Quantum electrodynamics
c) Quantum theories of electromagnetic phenomena
d) Quantum theory

68. Who was the first writer in Chinese to win the Nobel Prize for Literature?
a) Gao Xingjian
b) Chang Ai-ling
c) Pai Hsien-yung
d) Amy Tan

The glass harmonica, invented by Benjamin Franklin, is a musical instrument consisting of a set of graduated, tuned glass bowls sounded by the friction of wetted fingers on their rims.

Well-formed linen gloves with a drawstring closure at the wrist were found in the tomb of the Egyptian king Tutankhamen (14th century BC).

Did You Know?

69. Who discovered that typhus is transmitted by the body louse and was awarded the Nobel Prize for Physiology or Medicine for his discovery?
a) Charles Brenton Huggins
b) Charles Robert Richet
c) Charles Louis Alphonse Laveran
d) Charles Jules Henri Nicolle

70. Who was the first African to receive the Nobel Prize for Peace?
a) Albert Schweitzer
b) Albert John Luthuli
c) Desmond Tutu
d) Max Theiler

71. For which discovery did Charles Edouard Guillaume win the Nobel Prize for Physics in 1920?
a) A nickel-steel alloy
b) Ultracentrifuge
c) Bubble chamber
d) Contrast microscope

72. Whose demonstration that beriberi is caused by poor diet led to the discovery of vitamins and won him the Nobel Prize for Physiology or Medicine?
a) Henrik Dam
b) Christiaan Eijkman
c) Alphonse Laveran
d) Edward Adelbert Doisy

73. In which two fields was Linus Pauling awarded the Nobel Prize?
a) Chemistry and Physics
b) Chemistry and Peace
c) Physics and Peace
d) Physics and Chemistry

74. For which achievement was Jean Perrin honoured with the Nobel Prize for Physics in 1926?
a) Nuclear magnetic resonance
b) Behaviour of subatomic particles
c) Atomic nature of matter
d) Principle of parity conservation

75. Who received the 1957 Nobel Prize for Physiology or Medicine for his discoveries of certain chemotherapeutic agents?
a) Daniel Bovet
b) Felix Bloch
c) Edward Mills Purcell
d) William Bradford Shockley

76. Who was awarded the Nobel Prize for Peace in 1964?
a) Dag Hammarskjold
b) Albert Schweitzer
c) John Noel-Baker Philip
d) Martin Luther King, Jr.

77. Which of the following teams received the Nobel Prize for Physiology or Medicine for the discovery of insulin?
a) William Parry Murphy and George Hoyt Whipple
b) Edgar Douglas Adrian and Charles Scott Sherrington
c) Archibald Vivian Hill and Otto Meyerhof
d) Frederick Banting and John James Richard Macleod

78. Which organization was awarded the Nobel Prize for Peace in 1965?
a) UNIFEM
b) UNO
c) UNICEF
d) UNESCO

79. Which Indian scientist was the recipient of the Nobel Prize for Physics in 1930?
a) Meghnad Saha
b) Chandrasekhara Venkata Raman
c) Jagadis Chandra Bose
d) Subrahmanyan Chandrasekhar

80. What discovery was made by Charles Thomson Rees Wilson, the 1927 Nobel laureate for physics?
a) Cloud chamber
b) Compton effect
c) X-ray spectroscopy
d) Principle of parity conservation

81. Who shared the Nobel Prize for Economic Sciences in 1997 with Myron S. Scholes?
a) James Alexander Mirrlees
b) Robert C. Merton
c) William Vickrey
d) Robert E. Lucas, Jr.

82. Which Nobel laureate invented the ultramicroscope along with Heinrich Siedentopf?
a) Werner Karl Heisenberg
b) Richard Zsigmondy
c) Marie Curie
d) James Franck

83. Who received the Nobel Prize for Economic Sciences for his contributions to welfare economics?
a) Gary Stanley Becker
b) Amartya Sen
c) Gerad Debreu
d) Tjalling Charles Koopmans

84. Who won the Nobel Prize for Chemistry in 1928 for research on substances, notably vitamin D?
a) Frederick Soddy
b) Adolf Windaus
c) Leon Jouhaux
d) Arthur Harden

85. Which American agricultural scientist was honoured with the Nobel Prize for Peace in 1970?
a) Seaman Asahel Knapp
b) George Washington Carver
c) Franklin Hiram King
d) Norman Ernest Borlaug

86. Which Nobel Prize winner wrote the book *Alcoholic Fermentation?*
a) Frederick Soddy
b) Arthur Harden
c) Leon Jouhaux
d) Hans Von Euler-Chelpin

87. Who shared the 1974 Nobel Prize for Peace with Sean MacBride?
a) Eisaku Sato
b) Rigoberta Menchu
c) Andrei Dmitriyevich Sakharov
d) Willy Brandt

In what is now Mexico, the belief that the Sun needed human nourishment led to sacrifices in which thousands of victims perished annually in the Aztec and Nahua calendrical maize (corn) ritual.

The first contact lens, made of glass, was developed by Adolf Fick in 1887 to correct irregular astigmatism.

Did You Know?

88. For what was Enrico Fermi awarded the Nobel Prize for Physics in 1938?
a) Development of paper partition chromatography
b) Discovery of embryonic induction
c) Developments in harnessing nuclear power
d) Discoveries in the chemical transmission of nerve impulses

89. Who was honoured with the Nobel Prize for Physiology or Medicine for his discovery of cancer-inducing viruses in 1966?
a) Charles Brenton Huggins
b) Haldan Keffer Hartline
c) Francis Peyton Rous
d) George Wald

90. Which of these was the first novel written by Hermann Hesse, the Nobel Prize winner for Literature, in 1946?
a) *Peter Camenzind*
b) *Demian*
c) *Narziss und Goldmund*
d) *Das Glasperlenspiel*

91. For work in which subject was Vincent du Vigneaud awarded a Nobel Prize?
a) Physics
b) Chemistry
c) Medicine
d) Literature

92. For discoveries in which field did Patrick Maynard Stuart Blackett win the Nobel Prize for Physics in 1948?
a) Cosmic radiation

b) Atomic physics
c) Discovery of the ionosphere
d) Thermodynamics

93. For what was Paul Ehrlich awarded the Nobel Prize for Physiology or Medicine?
a) Treatment of eye diseases
b) Methods for dyeing of live tissue
c) Invention of a new staining technique for the TB bacillus
d) Work in immunology and treatment of syphilis

94. For what was Hideki Yukawa awarded the Nobel Prize for Physics in 1949?
a) Research on the theory of elementary particles
b) Invention of the integrated circuit
c) Development of isotopic tracer techniques
d) Discovery of the tau lepton

95. Who among the following Nobel Prize winners discovered the first binary pulsar?
a) Felix Bloch
b) Russell Alan Hulse and Joseph Hooton Taylor, Jr.
c) James Chadwick
d) William Bragg

96. Who was the first surgeon to operate on the thyroid gland and win the Nobel Prize for Physiology or Medicine for his work in 1909?
a) Camillo Golgi
b) Alphonse Laveran
c) Emil Theodor Kocher
d) Elie Mechnikov

97. Which organization won the Nobel Prize for Peace in 1977?
a) Office of the United Nations High Commissioner for Refugees
b) International Labor Organisation
c) Amnesty International
d) United Nations Children's Fund

98. Which 1939 Nobel laureate was forced by the Nazi government to refuse the prize and was able to accept the honour in 1949?
a) Adolf Butenandt
b) Emil Fischer
c) Corneille Heymans
d) Paul Crutzen

99. Which Nobel Prize winner published the best-seller novel *The Townsman* under the name John Sedges?
a) John Galsworthy
b) Nadine Gordimer
c) Pearl Buck
d) William Golding

100. Who shared the 1966 Nobel Prize for Literature with Nelly Sachs?
a) Jean-Paul Sartre
b) Shmuel Yosef Agnon
c) Giorgios Seferis
d) Mikhail Sholokhov

101. With whom did Menachem Begin share the Nobel Prize for Peace in 1978?
a) Mother Teresa
b) Mairead Corrigan-Maguire
c) Betty Williams
d) Anwar el-Sadat

102. Which Nobel laureate was awarded a fellowship at Trinity for his dissertation entitled "An Essay on the Foundations of Geometry"?
a) William Faulkner
b) Leon Jouhaux
c) Bertrand Russell
d) Irene Curie

103. Whose research on the structure and synthesis of nucleotides, nucleosides, and nucleotide coenzymes gained him the 1957 Nobel Prize for Chemistry?
a) Alexander Robertus Todd
b) Cyril Norman Hinshelwood
c) Nikolay Nikolayevich Semyonov
d) Frederick Sanger

104. Which international organization was awarded the Nobel Peace Prize in 1985?
a) International Physicians for the Prevention of Nuclear War
b) United Nations Peace-keeping Forces
c) Pugwash Conferences on Science and World Affairs
d) Office of the United Nations High Commissioner for Refugees

105. Who was the corecipient, with Robert William Holley and Har Gobind Khorana, of the Nobel Prize for Physiology or Medicine in 1968 for deciphering the genetic code?
a) Feodor Lynen
b) Marshall Warren Nirenberg
c) Henry Dale
d) Charles Brenton Huggins

106. Which of these Polish leaders went on to win the Nobel Prize for Peace?
a) Tadeusz Mazowiecki
b) Lech Walesa
c) Aleksander Kwasniewski
d) Mieczyslaw Jagielski

107. Which scientist received, with Ernest T.S. Walton, the Nobel Prize for Physics for pioneering the use of particle accelerators?
a) John Douglas Cockcroft
b) Edwin Mattison McMillan
c) Emilio Gino Segre
d) Chen Ning Yang

108. Which technique, that has wide application in archaeology, was developed by Willard Frank Libby and won him the Nobel Prize?
a) Separation of uranium isotope
b) Development of the vacuum tube
c) Carbon-14 dating
d) Invention of the bubble chamber

109. Which German physicist, corecipient with R.G.W. Norrish and George Porter, was awarded the Nobel Prize for Chemistry in 1967?
a) Hermann Staudinger
b) Otto Paul Hermann Diels
c) Kurt Alder
d) Manfred Eigen

110. Which novelist was awarded the Nobel Peace Prize in 1986?
a) Aung San Suu Kyi
b) Elie Wiesel
c) Alfonso Garcia Robles
d) Alva Reiner Myrdal

111. Whose studies of organic phosphorus compounds made him the corecipient with Herbert C. Brown of the 1979 Nobel Prize for Chemistry?
a) Peter Dennis Mitchell
b) Ernst Otto Fischer
c) Herbert Charles Brown
d) Georg Wittig

112. Who was awarded the Nobel Prize for Chemistry for his development of techniques for high-resolution nuclear magnetic resonance (NMR) spectroscopy?
a) Elias James Corey
b) Rudolph A. Marcus
c) Richard Robert Ernst
d) Michael Smith

113. What law or behaviour did the 1954 Nobel laureates for physics, Walther Bothe and Max Born, discover?
a) Behaviour of subatomic particles
b) Conservation laws and symmetry
c) The law of conservation of parity
d) Conservation law for angular momentum

114. Who received the Nobel Prize for Chemistry in 1998 for his development of the density-functional theory?
a) Walter Kohn
b) Ahmed H. Zewail
c) Paul Delos Boyer
d) John Ernest Walker

Science

1. Who was the first to quantitatively measure blood pressure?
a) Albrecht von Haller
b) Antonio Egas Moniz
c) Antoine-Laurent Lavoisier
d) Stephen Hales

2. Whose work is considered the first textbook of botany?
a) Andreas Caesalpinus
b) Thomas Hunt Morgan
c) Hugo von Mohl
d) Matthias Jakob Schleiden

3. What award in mathematics is considered to be the equivalent of the Nobel Prize?
a) Academy Award
b) Rolf Nevanlinna Prize
c) Fields Medal
d) Emmy Award

4. Who discovered the process of photosynthesis in plants?
a) Theophrastus
b) Dennis Robert Hoagland
c) Nicholas Theodore de Saussure
d) Jan Ingenhousz

5. Who discovered the process of making celluloid?
a) John Wesley Hyatt
b) T.H. Huxley
c) L.H. Baekeland
d) George Eastman

6. Who invented the "dambuster" bombs used in World War II?
a) Barnes Neville Wallis
b) Robert Hooke
c) Alan Cobham
d) Robert Noyce

7. Which German-Dutch chemist is sometimes called the German Boyle?
a) Friedrich Wohler
b) Johann Rudolf Glauber
c) Justus Freiherr von Liebig
d) Andreas Libavius

8. Who among the following was a leading expert in the diagnosis and treatment of intracranial tumours?
a) William Osler
b) William Bragg
c) Harvey William Cushing
d) William Whitney Gull

9. Who is the founder of child psychoanalysis?
a) Josef Breuer
b) Eric Berne
c) Otto Rank
d) Anna Freud

10. Who was the founder of modern psychosurgery?
a) Alfred Adler
b) Antonio Egas Moniz
c) William James
d) Florence Rena Sabin

At its height, the Ottoman Empire created by Turkish tribes in Anatolia included most of southeastern Europe to the gates of Vienna; North Africa up to Algeria; and most of the Arab peninsula.

Chariot races in Rome's Circus Maximus were watched by as many as 250,000 spectators, five times the number that crowded into the Colosseum to enjoy gladiatorial combats.

Did You Know?

11. Who founded the first American journal on psychology and also the first journal in the fields of child and educational psychology?
a) Abraham Harold Maslow
b) Henry Alexander Murray
c) G. Stanley Hall
d) Carl Rogers

12. What is the symbol generally used to represent the atomic number of an element?
a) S
b) Q
c) Z
d) A

13. Into how many sections is the human stomach divided?
a) One
b) Two
c) Three
d) Four

14. Who was the first to make a systematic study of the acquisition of understanding in children?
a) Carl Rogers
b) Ludwig Binswanger
c) Anna Freud
d) Jean Piaget

15. The early windmill transformed the kinetic energy of wind into which of the following forms of energy?
a) Thermal
b) Nuclear
c) Electrical
d) Mechanical

16. Who is believed to be responsible for proposing the concept of molecules in atomic physics?
a) Isaac Newton
b) Joseph John Thomson
c) Amedeo Avogadro
d) Ernest Rutherford

17. What is the smallest structural unit of living matter that is capable of functioning independently?
a) Molecule
b) Nucleus
c) Cell
d) Proton

18. What are the smallest cells in the blood called?
a) Red blood cells
b) White blood cells
c) Blood platelets
d) Plasma

19. Who prepared tables that plot the location of Uranus?
a) Aratus
b) Hipparchus
c) Jean-Baptiste-Joseph Delambre
d) Nicholas Copernicus

20. What determines the blood group in a person?
a) Platelets
b) Red blood cells
c) White blood cells
d) Plasma

21. Rodenticides are used to kill which of the following groups of animals?
a) Grasshoppers and beetles
b) Viruses and bacteria
c) Rats and mice
d) Small birds

22. Which of the following gases was responsible for the death of thousands of people in Bhopal, India?
a) Carbon monoxide
b) Picric acid
c) Ethyl isocynate
d) Methyl isocynate

23. Who wrote the oldest known biography of Hippocrates?
a) Herophilus
b) Erasistratus
c) Meno
d) Soranus

24. Who was the first to lay the mathematical foundation of the science of genetics?
a) Carl Erich Correns
b) Gregor Johann Mendel
c) Ivan Vladimirovich Michurin
d) Erich Tschermak von Seysenegg

25. How many pairs of chromosomes are found in the human body?
a) 21
b) 22
c) 23
d) 24

26. Which of the following countries produced nerve gas as a lethal chemical weapon in World War II?
a) Japan
b) Russia
c) U.S.A.
d) Germany

27. Which of the following gases was used by Germany in the World War I?
a) Methane
b) Ammonia
c) Chlorine
d) Fluorine

28. Which of the following congenital disorders is characterized by the presence of 47 chromosomes?
a) Turner Syndrome
b) Down Syndrome
c) Patau's Syndrome
d) Blue Baby Syndrome

29. Which philosopher is remembered for his theory of water as the essence of all matter?
a) Socrates
b) Anaximander
c) Thales of Miletus
d) Apollodorus

30. Who invented the submarine?
a) John Harrison
b) Karl Benz
c) John E.W. Keely
d) David Bushnell

31. What is a gizzard?
a) A lizard
b) The throat
c) A muscular digestive organ
d) The elbow

32. Who developed the technique known as transactional analysis?
a) Sigmund Freud
b) Abraham Harold Maslow
c) Eric Berne
d) Rollo May

33. Among the following, whose most influential work is considered to be *Anthropology*?
a) Melville J. Herskovits
b) Emile Durkheim
c) Alfred Louis Kroeber
d) E.B. Tylor

34. Who is traditionally credited with the invention of the telescope?
a) Hans Lippershey
b) David Rittenhouse
c) Galileo Galilei
d) Jacques Bovedere

35. What is the radiologic technique for obtaining clear X-ray images of deep internal structures by focusing on a specific plane within the body called?
a) Radiology
b) Topography
c) Tomography
d) Ultrasonography

36. Who coined the word "agnosticism"?
a) Thomas Hobbes
b) Abraham Harold Maslow
c) Thomas Henry Huxley
d) Otto Rank

37. Who discovered the abrasive Carborundum and perfected a method for making graphite?
a) Thomas Edison
b) Edward Acheson
c) Alexander Bell
d) Benjamin Franklin

38. Who is credited with the invention of the cyclotron, the first particle accelerator to achieve high energies?
a) Carl Sontheimer
b) Percy Lavon Julian
c) James Dewar
d) Ernest Orlando Lawerence

39. *Acinonyx jubatus* is the biological name of which famous land animal?
a) Elephant
b) Giraffe
c) Cheetah
d) Deer

40. Who formulated and wrote a paper on the theory of evolution by means of natural selection which predated Charles Darwin's published contributions?
a) Edwin Ray Lankester
b) Thomas Henry Huxley
c) Alfred Russel Wallace
d) Jean-Baptiste Lamarck

Did You Know?

The chair is one of the most ancient forms of furniture, dating back to the 3rd dynasty of ancient Egypt (c. 2650-c. 2575 BC).

Barbadian cricketer Malcolm Marshall's most impressive display was against England in 1984, when he broke his left thumb but went on to bat one-handed and take 7 for 53 to bowl England out.

41. Who is the author of the book *The Principles of Quantum Mechanics?*
a) Paul Adrian Maurice Dirac
b) Julian S. Schwinger
c) Max Born
d) Tomonaga Shin'ichiro

42. Whose work was referred to by Einstein as "the highest form of musicality in the sphere of thought"?
a) Paul Adrian Maurice Dirac
b) Niels Bohr
c) Max Born
d) Carl David Anderson

43. Who is best known for the development of the military rocket?
a) William Congreve
b) Robert Hutchings Goddard
c) Herman Oberth
d) Hyder Ali

44. Who first suggested the idea of putting an artificial satellite into orbit?
a) Plato
b) Galileo Galilei
c) Isaac Newton
d) Albert Einstein

45. Who, besides Francis Crick, James Watson, and Maurice Wilkins, contributed to the discovery of the helical structure of DNA?
a) Alan Lloyd Hodgkin
b) Rosalind Elsie Franklin
c) Andrew Fielding Huxley
d) Peter Brian Medawar

46. Who is the founder of the Red Cross?
a) Petra Kelly
b) Henri Dunant
c) James Lind
d) Philippe Pinel

47. Oilbirds are the inhabitants of which continent?
a) North America
b) South America
c) Africa
d) Asia

48. What is a snail-kite?
a) Mollusc
b) Mammal
c) Reptile
d) Bird

49. What does a ligament connect?
a) Cartilage to bone
b) Bone to muscles
c) Muscles to muscle
d) Bone to bone

50. What is thalassemia?
a) A genetic disorder
b) Heavy metal toxication
c) Nutrient deficiency
d) Disease caused by parasite fungi

51. Who is the author of *Plant Anatomy?*
a) Carl Erich Correns
b) Selman Abraham Waksman
c) Katherine Esau
d) Carolus Linnaeus

52. Which are the only two planets that do not have any satellites?
a) Earth and Jupiter
b) Mercury and Saturn
c) Venus and Mars
d) Mercury and Venus

53. Which planet has the strongest magnetic field ?
a) Earth
b) Mars
c) Saturn
d) Jupiter

54. Which of the following is a device used to capture solar energy and convert it into thermal energy?
a) Flat-plate collector
b) Leyden jar
c) Insulated tanks
d) Solar furnace

55. Jerome Hunsaker, the American aeronautical engineer, is famous for major innovations in the design of which craft?
a) Ships and yachts
b) Rail engines and coaches
c) Passenger buses and trams
d) Aircraft and lighter-than-air ships

56. Who constructed the first ever nuclear reactor?
a) Enrico Fermi
b) John A. Wheeler
c) Niels Bohr
d) Otto Hahn

57. Which is the most reactive metal after uranium?
a) Rubidium
b) Cesium
c) Mercury
d) Bromide

58. Which element is called "the stone that burns"?
a) Bromide
b) Sulphur
c) Lead
d) Gold

59. Which element is known as sal ammoniac in the West, *nao sha* in China, *nao sadar* in India, and *nushadir* in Iran?
a) Mercury
b) Ammonium chloride
c) Sodium
d) Aluminium

60. Which American scientist remade quantum electrodynamics, and thereby changed the way science understands the nature of waves and particles?
a) Thomas Alva Edison
b) Murray Gell-Mann
c) Richard Feynman
d) Charles Goodyear

61. Who published the first manual for physiology?
a) William Harvey
b) Galen of Pergamum
c) Claude Bernard
d) Albrecht von Haller

62. For which of the following inventions is Lawrence Hargrave famous?
a) Anemometer
b) Parachute
c) Elevator
d) Box kite

63. Who invented the semaphore visual telegraph?
a) Nicolaus Copernicus
b) James Alfred Van Allen
c) Claude Chappe
d) Bernard Alfred Charles Lovell

64. Who invented the coronagraph?
a) Isaac Newton
b) Georges Lemaitre
c) Bernard (-Ferdinand) Lyot
d) Jean-Baptiste-Joseph Delambre

65. Who is the American inventor credited to be the originator of frequency modulation systems and communication circuitry?
a) George Washington Carver
b) Jonas Salk
c) Betsy Ancker-Johnson
d) Edwin Armstrong

66. The name of which microorganism is derived from the Latin word meaning "mushroom"?
a) Protozoa
b) Fungi
c) Virus
d) Algae

67. Who discovered parthenogenesis (reproduction without fertilization)?
a) Thomas Hunt Morgan
b) Hermann Joseph Muller
c) Antonie van Leeuwenhoek
d) Charles Bonnet

68. What are epiphytes?
a) Plants dependent on other plants for water
b) Plants dependent on other plants for water and food
c) Plants dependent on other plants for food
d) Plants dependent on other plants for support

69. Which of the following do carnivorous plants obtain from animal bodies?
a) Oxygen
b) Nitrogen
c) Carbon dioxide
d) Sulphur dioxide

70. What is the *Dionaea muscipula* commonly known as?
a) Venus's flytrap
b) Sundew
c) Bladderwort
d) Pitcher-plant

71. Which of the following birds is found only in Australia?
a) Emu
b) Ostrich
c) Penguin
d) Pelican

72. Which bird is also known as the "laughing jackass"?
a) Vulture
b) Dodo
c) Kookaburra
d) Owl

73. What is the young one of a kangaroo called?
a) Calf
b) Lamb
c) Joey
d) Cub

74. The name of which microorganism is derived from the Greek words meaning "first animal"?
a) Virus
b) Bacteria
c) Protozoa
d) Fungi

75. Which of the following is also known as the mastiff, or bulldog, bat?
a) Brown bat
b) Smoky bat
c) Long-eared bat
d) Free-tailed bat

76. Which of the following bats has an odour similar to that of perfumed soap?
a) New Zealand short-tailed bat
b) Philippine bamboo bat
c) Jamaican fruit bat
d) Vampire bat

77. Which is the only animal in the family of "big cats" to live in a group?
a) Tiger
b) Leopard
c) Lion
d) Cheetah

78. Which is the largest frog in the world?
a) Goliath frog
b) Asian tree frog
c) Poison arrow frog
d) Bullfrog

79. Who is the inventor of the threshing machine used for removing the husk from grain?
a) Edmund Lee
b) Andrew Meikle
c) Stephen Hooper
d) William Cubitt

80. In the proposed International Fixed Calendar, each month begins and ends on which day of the week?
a) Begins and ends on a Monday
b) Begins on a Monday and ends on a Sunday
c) Begins on a Sunday and ends on a Saturday
d) Begins and ends on a Sunday

81. Who built the first steam engine?
a) William Murdock
b) John Smeaton
c) Thomas Savery
d) Thomas Newcomen

82. Which Persian scientist, biologist and philosopher's work is among the famous books on the history of medicine?
a) Ibn Battuta
b) Mansur ibn-Nuh
c) Al-Battani
d) Avicenna

83. Who was the chief designer of the first Mercedes automobiles?
a) George Stephenson
b) Gottlieb Daimler
c) Wilhelm Maybach
d) William Murdock

84. Who built the first successful all-metal airplane?
a) Hugo Junkers
b) Wright Brothers
c) George Cayley
d) Glenn Curtiss

85. Where in the human body would you find the humerus?
a) Arm
b) Leg
c) Neck
d) Foot

86. Who discovered the first synthetic dye named "mauve"?
a) August Wilhelm von Hofmann
b) Paul Ehrlich
c) Thomas Alva Edison
d) William H. Perkin

87. What is vertigo?
a) Fear of closed spaces
b) Fear of heights
c) Fear of water
d) Fear of dogs

88. Who performed the first successful human heart transplant?
a) Theodor Kocher
b) Norman Schumway
c) Christiaan Barnard
d) Frederick Treves

89. Who established that both heat and light are electromagnetic radiations?
a) James Clerk Maxwell
b) Guglielmo Marconi
c) Ferdinand Braun
d) Heinrich Rudolf Hertz

90. Which country built the Hubble Space Telescope (HST), the most sophisticated optical observatory ever placed into orbit around the Earth?
a) Russia
b) Canada
c) United Kingdom
d) United States of America

91. Which of the following is William Symington associated with?
a) A steamboat
b) A spacecraft
c) An airplane
d) A bicycle

92. **Who invented portland cement?**
a) Joseph Aspdin
b) John Ambrose Fleming
c) William Crookes
d) Hans Larsen

93. **Which is the weakest force in nature?**
a) Gravitational force
b) Magnetic force
c) Electromagnetic force
d) Nuclear force

94. **What is baking soda?**
a) Sodium carbonate
b) Sodium bicarbonate
c) Sodium sulphate
d) Sodium hydroxide

95. **What is a thermocouple used for?**
a) To make an alloy of two metals
b) To measure temperature
c) To produce mechanical energy
d) To produce thermal energy

96. **What is the history of the evolution of a species or group called?**
a) Phylogeny
b) Phycology
c) Philology
d) Phlebotomy

97. **Who discovered nitroglycerin?**
a) Alfred Bernhard Nobel
b) Robert Boyle
c) Ernest Rutherford
d) Ascanio Sobrero

98. **Binoculars are commonly designated as 6 30, 7 50, or 8 30. What do these numbers indicate?**
a) Size of lens and magnification
b) Depth of vision and magnification
c) Magnification and diameter of lens
d) Diameter of lens and circumference of lens

99. **What name is given to the points on the sun where the gas is cooler than the average photospheric temperature?**
a) Corona
b) Sun spots
c) Neutrinos
d) Black holes

100. **Which of the following is an ancient device for measuring time by the gradual flow of water?**
a) Clepsydra
b) Rikka
c) Seika
d) Nageira

101. **Which of the following are produced in response to substances called antigens?**
a) Lymphocytes
b) Antibodies
c) Toxins
d) Antiglobulin

102. **On what does the pitch of a sound wave depend?**
a) Intensity
b) Wavelength
c) Frequency
d) Vibration

Sports

1. Who was Paavo Nurmi?
a) Cricketer
b) Long-distance runner
c) Footballer
d) Gymnast

2. Where were the first world championships of table tennis held?
a) London
b) Japan
c) Germany
d) Beijing

3. Who won the first prize in the first table tennis World Cup?
a) Victor Barna
b) Richard Bergmann
c) Chuang Tse-tung
d) Guo Yuehua

4. Which game was originally called Criss Cross?
a) Chess
b) Gymnastics
c) Scrabble
d) Lawn Tennis

5. Which stroke is believed to be the oldest of strokes in swimming?
a) Backstroke
b) Butterfly stroke
c) Side stroke
d) Breaststroke

6. Which trophy's official name is the International Lawn Tennis Challenge Trophy?
a) Davis Cup
b) Federation Cup
c) Hyundai Hopman Cup
d) Wimbledon

7. Who is said to have built the first heated swimming pool?
a) Octavian
b) Sextus Pompeius
c) Gaius Maecenas
d) Hadrian

8. Which is the oldest of equestrian sports?
a) Calcio
b) Polo
c) Dressage
d) Horse racing

9. *Chukkers, chukkars,* or *chukkas* is a term associated with which sport?
a) Soccer
b) Horse racing
c) Polo
d) Squash

10. Which sport is also known as water ballet?
a) Synchronized swimming
b) Water polo
c) Underwater diving
d) Skin diving

Sports

11. Which stroke, used in competitive freestyle swimming, has become the fastest of all strokes?
a) Sidestroke
b) Backstroke
c) Crawl
d) Butterfly stroke

12. Which kind of stroke, in swimming, is used predominantly in competition?
a) Butterfly stroke
b) Sidestroke
c) Breaststroke
d) Backstroke

13. Softball and hardball are two different varieties of which sport?
a) Volleyball
b) Water polo
c) Lawn tennis
d) Squash

14. Calisthenics are technical exercises performed in which sports?
a) Pole vaulting
b) Long jumping
c) Gymnastics
d) Skiing

15. Which court or lawn game is named after the country estate of the dukes of Beaufort in Gloucestershire, England, where it was first played, in about 1873?
a) Tennis
b) Volleyball
c) Badminton
d) Lacrosse

16. A pommel horse is related to which sport?
a) Gymnastics
b) Show jumping
c) Sprint
d) Steeplechase

17. Which tennis player was dubbed "Little Mo"?
a) Louise Brough
b) Margaret Osborne DuPont
c) Maureen Connolly
d) Doris Hart

18. What form of motor racing, popular in the US, has two contestants race side by side from a standing start over a flat, straight, measured one-quarter-mile course?
a) Drag racing
b) Formula One
c) Rally driving
d) Grand Prix racing

19. In what kind of automobile racing, over a specified public route, do the driver and navigator attempt to keep to a predetermined schedule between checkpoints?
a) Grand Prix racing
b) Drag race
c) Rally driving
d) Formula One

20. With which game is the Ryder Cup associated?
a) Tennis
b) Archery
c) Golf
d) Shooting

Did You Know?

Chinook is the warm, dry wind descending the eastern slopes of the Rocky Mountains, primarily in winter. Winds of the same kind occur in other parts of the world and are known generally as foehns.

Vesuvius had been dormant for centuries before the great eruption of AD 79 that buried the cities of Pompeii and Stabiae under ashes and the city of Herculaneum under a mud flow.

21. What is the term given to the method of offsetting the varying abilities or characteristics of competitors in order to equalize their chances of winning?
a) Head Start
b) Handicap
c) Breaking even
d) Standardizing

22. Which game, also known as Tenpins, aims at knocking down a group of "pins" with a heavy ball?
a) Croquet
b) Boules
c) Billiards
d) Bowling

23. Which mountaineer first climbed Mont Blanc with his porter, Jacques Belmat?
a) John Hunt
b) George Mallory
c) Edward Whymper
d) Michel-Gabriel Paccard

24. Which form of horse racing is characterized by a "Sulky"?
a) Point-to-point
b) Steeplechase
c) Quarter-horse racing
d) Harness racing

25. With which sport is the term "roving" associated?
a) Rally driving
b) Riding
c) Fox hunting
d) Archery

26. In archery, what is the name given to a target-shooting event consisting of five ends (six arrows each)?
a) York round
b) Clout shooting
c) American round
d) Flight shooting

27. Which sport, related to skating, originated in The Netherlands?
a) Ice jumping
b) Speed skating
c) Ice hockey
d) Figure skating

28. Ville Ritola is associated with which athletics event?
a) 3,000 m steeplechase
b) 5,000 m run
c) 10,000 m run
d) Marathon

29. Which type of canoe, now mostly used for sport, originated with the Eskimos of Greenland?
a) Pirogue
b) Canadian canoe
c) Kayak
d) Flatboat

30. What name is given to the sport of riding breaking waves toward the shore, especially a board?
a) Paddling
b) Surfing
c) Sailing
d) Canoeing

31. With which sport is the name of Lester Piggott associated?
a) Fencing
b) Hog calling
c) Riding
d) Sailing

32. What name is given to the sport of sliding down an ice-covered natural or artificial incline on a four-runner sleigh that carries either two or four persons?
a) Snowshoeing
b) Bobsledding
c) Tobaggoning
d) Slalom

33. Which kind of ski race follows a winding course between pairs of poles topped with flags?
a) Cross-country skiing
b) Ski jumping
c) Freestyle skiing
d) Slalom

34. Who became the first woman of the 20th century to win the Triple Crown at Wimbledon?
a) Helen Hull Jacobs
b) Hazel Hotchkiss Wightman
c) Alice Marble
d) Martina Navratilova

35. Which game, similar to lawn bowls, is played on ice?
a) Slalom
b) Downhill skiing
c) Curling
d) Ice hockey

36. Which winter sport evolved from skateboarding and surfing?
a) Snowboarding
b) Bobsledding
c) Slalom
d) Ski jumping

37. What form of archery has targets of different sizes placed at varying distances on uneven terrain in an attempt to simulate hunting conditions?
a) Target archery
b) Field archery
c) Flight shooting
d) Clout shooting

38. In baseball, what term refers to the pitcher and the catcher together?
a) Team
b) Defense
c) Battery
d) Infielders

39. Which tennis player is known as the "queen mother of American tennis"?
a) Billie Jean King
b) Helen Hull Jacobs
c) Chris Evert
d) Hazel Hotchkiss Wightman

40. Which organized sport uses the epee for attack and defence according to set movements and rules?
a) Shooting
b) Fencing
c) Wrestling
d) Archery

41. Which traditional Japanese style of fencing with a two-handed wooden sword, gets its name from the Japanese for "way of the sword"?
a) Ninjuksu
b) Kung Fu
c) Tae kwon do
d) Kendo

42. What term is used in baseball when the ball is tapped lightly with the bat so as to make it roll slowly along the ground in fair territory?
a) Balk
b) Bunt
c) Swing
d) Strike

43. What name is given to the group of billiard games played with three balls on a table without pockets?
a) Balkline billiards
b) Snooker
c) Pocket billiards
d) Carom

44. Which African-American professional baseball player set a record in the early 1990s for the most stolen bases in major league baseball?
a) Moses Walker
b) Aaron Hank
c) Josh Gibson
d) Rickey Henderson

45. Which variant of baseball, common in the United States, is also known as diamond ball and kitten ball?
a) Stickball
b) Volleyball
c) Softball
d) Rounders

46. What is the maximum number of clubs a player is now permitted to carry in one round in a golf?
a) Ten
b) Twelve
c) Fourteen
d) Sixteen

47. What term is given to the winter sports event that combines cross-country skiing with rifle marksmanship?
a) Classic skiing
b) Nordic skiing
c) Downhill skiing
d) Biathlon

48. What kinds of drugs are often used illegally by sportspersons to maximize their performance in competitions?
a) Amphetamine
b) LSD
c) Barbiturates
d) Tranquillizers

49. Which American professional baseball pitcher (left-handed) popularized the screwball pitch?
a) Carl Hubbell
b) Babe Ruth
c) Dave McNally
d) Curt Flood

Ayers Rock, found in Australia, is perhaps the world's largest monolith. It is composed of arkosic sandstone that changes colour according to the attitude of the sun.

Yalta, in Crimea, was the 1945 meeting place of the three chief Allied leaders, Churchill, Roosevelt, and Stalin, to plan the final defeat and occupation of Nazi Germany.

Did You Know?

50. What term is given to the compound move of the king and the rook in chess?
a) Checkmate
b) Opening
c) Capturing
d) Castling

51. Which British chess master is credited with organizing the first modern international chess tournament in London?
a) Michael Adams
b) Howard Staunton
c) Julian M. Hodgson
d) Mathew Sadler

52. Which Austrian chess master is considered to have been the world champion longer than any other player?
a) Wilhelm Steinitz
b) Alex Wojtkewicz
c) Ivan Sokolov
d) P. Leko

53. What term, in baseball, refers to an infraction the pitcher can commit with a runner or runners on base?
a) Foul
b) Bunt
c) Balk
d) Pitch

54. *Episkuros, calico,* and *melees* are forms of which popular sport?
a) Fencing
b) Boxing
c) Football
d) Gymnastics

55. What term, in baseball, refers to the removal of a player from offensive play until his next turn at bat?
a) Bowled
b) Caught
c) Putout
d) Pitched

56. Which game, similar to billiards, is played with nine balls?
a) Snooker
b) Pool
c) Carom
d) Bagatelle

57. What material was the golf ball originally made of?
a) Rubber
b) Wood
c) Steel
d) Feather

58. Which game, also called French Billiards, is played with three balls in which the object is to drive one of the white balls (cue ball) into both the other balls?
a) Pool
b) Snooker
c) Balkline billiards
d) Carom

59. Which form of billiards, also known as pool, is popular in the United States?
a) Snooker
b) French billiards
c) Pocket billiards
d) Balkline billiards

60. Which competitive game is considered to be the modern version of the North American Indian game of baggataway?
a) Tennis
b) Badminton
c) Lacrosse
d) Squash

61. Which of these is one of the world's oldest continuing rowing races, held annually in England?
a) Henley Royal Regatta
b) The Oxford and Cambridge Boat Race
c) Doggett's Coat and Badge
d) FISA World Rowing Championships

62. Which game is the Indian equivalent of the game Ludo?
a) Chaturanga
b) Shatranj
c) Moksha-Patamu
d) Pachisi

63. What term in basketball refers to throwing, batting, or rolling the ball to another player?
a) Pass
b) Pivot
c) Dribble
d) Dunk

64. Who offered a silver cup, the first known North American horseracing trophy?
a) Henry VIII
b) James I
c) Louis XVI
d) Richard Nicolls

65. Calf roping, bull riding, steer wrestling, saddle bronc-riding, and bareback bronc-riding are the standard types of which horse racing sport?
a) Harness racing
b) Hurdle race
c) Rodeo
d) Match racing

66. Which racing is a kind of preparation for steeplechasing?
a) Barrel race
b) Harness racing
c) Racing on the flat
d) Hurdle race

67. Which is the most famous steeplechase race?
a) The Grand National
b) The Irish Grand National
c) The Grand Steeplechase de Paris
d) The Maryland Hunt Cup

68. For which sport is the Eisenhower Trophy awarded?
a) Soccer
b) Golf
c) Cricket
d) Tennis

69. Who first won the world driving championship according to the modern point system?
a) Ayrton Senna
b) Giuseppe Farina
c) Alberto Ascari
d) Michael Schumacher

70. Which is the oldest continuing harness horseracing series in the United States?
a) Roosevelt International Trot
b) Grand Circuit
c) The International Pace series
d) World Driving Championship

71. From 1930 to 1970 which trophy was awarded to the World Cup Soccer champions?
a) Jules Rimet Trophy
b) Fifa World Cup
c) Heisman Trophy
d) Eisenhower Trophy

72. Which is the oldest of the classic American horse races?
a) Kentucky Derby
b) Belmont Stakes
c) Preakness Stakes
d) Hambletonian Stake

73. The term "pugilism" is synonymous with which sport?
a) Cockfighting
b) Cricket
c) Fencing
d) Boxing

74. Where was the first English cycling race held?
a) Yorkshire
b) Middlesex
c) Surrey
d) Sussex

75. Which cycling game is derived from association football?
a) Cyclo-cross
b) Road race
c) Cycle ball
d) Tandem racing

76. Which is the world's most prestigious and the most difficult bicycle race?
a) Grand Prix des Nations
b) Giro d'Italia
c) Vuelta a Espana
d) Tour de France

77. Supercross relates to which kind of sport?
a) Skiing
b) Football
c) Motorcycle racing
d) Rowing

78. In which type of bicycle racing does each racer compete behind a motorbike or motorcycle?
a) Motor-paced race
b) Pursuit racing
c) Tandem racing
d) Road race

79. Golden Gloves is a competition related to which sport?
a) Cricket
b) Boxing
c) Baseball
d) Shot put

80. Who was called "The Boston Strong Boy" in boxing?
a) John Lawrence Sullivan
b) James J. Corbett
c) Joe Louis
d) Floyd Patterson

81. Who, among the following, became the oldest world heavyweight boxing champion?
a) Cassius Clay
b) Sonny Liston
c) George Foreman
d) Joe Frazier

82. Who was the first important fighter to combine scientific boxing with rapid, rather than hard, punching?
a) Daniel Mendoza
b) Benjamin Brain
c) John ("Gentleman") Jackson
d) James J. Corbett

83. Which boxer was also called "The Brockton Blockbuster"?
a) Jersey Joe Walcott
b) Joe Louis
c) Rocky Marciano
d) Barney Ross

84. Who was the first modern marathon winner?
a) Spyridon Louis
b) Emil Zatopek
c) Ron Clarke
d) Henry Rono

85. Where was the first shooting range or club founded?
a) St. Petersburg
b) Frankfurt
c) Berne
d) Kentucky

86. When was the first World Cup Championship for football held?
a) 1910
b) 1920
c) 1930
d) 1940

87. What are the two forms of play in golf called?
a) Match and stroke
b) Put and stroke
c) Put and match
d) Tee and stroke

88. Who was the first amateur to have won the grand slam in tennis?
a) Don Budge
b) Alice Marble
c) Fred Perry
d) Helen Jacobs

89. With which sport is the term "criterium" associated?
a) Cycling
b) Swimming
c) Wrestling
d) Weightlifting

90. Who invented volleyball?
a) Jimmy George
b) K.C. Elamma
c) William G. Morgan
d) Cyril C. Valloor

91. How many touches is a team allowed in a game of volleyball before the ball must be returned over the net?
a) Two
b) Three
c) Four
d) Five

92. In which major sport is substitution allowed while the game is in play?
a) Ice hockey
b) Football
c) Cricket
d) Volleyball

93. Who is the first American woman to win the world amateur figure-skating championship?
a) Elizabeth Manley
b) Peggy Fleming
c) Sonja Henie
d) Tenley Albright

94. Which of the following sports did Babe Ruth play?
a) Basketball
b) Badminton
c) Baseball
d) Billiards

95. What is a two-beat gait, the fore and hind diagonal pairs of legs following each other almost simultaneously called?
a) Trot
b) Canter
c) Rack
d) Gallop

96. With which of the following sports was Ayrton Senna associated?
a) Formula One car racing
b) Billiards
c) Football
d) Fencing

97. With which sport is Francis Rogallo associated?
a) Parachuting
b) Swimming
c) Cycling
d) Hang gliding

98. Which implement is used in the hammer throw?
a) Discus
b) Javelin
c) A pole
d) A metal ball

99. In which country did tae kwon do originate?
a) Thailand
b) China
c) Korea
d) Japan

100. In which sport is the Sicilian Defence used?
a) Chess
b) Hockey
c) Karate
d) Fencing

101. Which Academy Award-winning film documents Muhammad Ali's eight-round knockout of George Foreman in Zaire?
a) *When We Were Kings*
b) *Gone with the Wind*
c) *Ben Hur*
d) *The English Patient*

102. What does "whist" refer to?
a) A card game
b) A move in chess
c) A type of badminton shot
d) Foul play in tennis

103. How many playing cards are there in a suit?
a) Ten
b) Thirteen
c) Fourteen
d) Fifteen

104. How many active players does a water polo team have?
a) Five
b) Six
c) Seven
d) Eight

105. In which sport are mallets and hoops used?
a) Cricket
b) Croquet
c) Canoeing
d) Carom billiards

106. Which sport features a contest called "Puissance"?
a) Show jumping
b) Surfing
c) Soccer
d) Swimming

107. Which sport features acro, aerials, and moguls?
a) Freestyle skiing
b) Freestyle skating
c) Freestyle swimming
d) Hockey

108. Who won the first Olympic gold medal ever awarded in women's figure skating?
a) Barbara Scott
b) Sonja Henie
c) Madge Cave Syers
d) Tenley Albright

109. Who became the first player to achieve a career Grand Slam in golf?
a) Tiger Woods
b) Jack Nicklaus
c) Ben Hogan
d) Gene Sarazen

110. Which sport is also called draughts?
a) Chess
b) Checkers
c) Darts
d) Dominoes

111. Which of the following does not use a uniform-sized ground?
a) Volleyball
b) Rugby
c) Basketball
d) Australian Rules Football

112. How many members are there in one team of a rugby professional match?
a) Ten
b) Eleven
c) Thirteen
d) Fifteen

113. Which German player is credited with inventing "total football"?
a) Franz Beckenbauer
b) Bobby Charlton
c) Stanley Matthews
d) Joseph Mercer

114. Which famous English cricketer also played football for Arsenal, one of the leading professional Football Association teams?
a) Mike Crawford
b) Peter May
c) Mike Smith
d) Denis Compton

115. Which famous boxer received critical praise as an actor in *The Adventures of Huckleberry Finn*?
a) Rocky Marciano
b) Floyd Patterson
c) Oscar De La Hoya
d) Archie Moore

116. How many basic types of punches are there in boxing?
a) Two
b) Three
c) Four
d) Six

117. How many grams of fine gold are there in the Olympic gold medal?
a) Four
b) Five
c) Six
d) Seven

118. Who is known as the father of figure skating?
a) Brian Boitano
b) Gillis Grafstrom
c) Jackson Haines
d) Scott Hamilton

119. Which figure skater is known as the "Swan of Odessa"?
a) Katarina Witt
b) Oksana Baiul
c) Sonja Henie
d) Tenley Albright

Jupiter has at least 16 satellites, 4 of which were discovered by Italian astronomer Galileo Galilei in 1610. The planet and its moons, in effect, represent a miniature version of the solar system.

In primitive astronomy the term planet was applied to the seven celestial bodies that were observed to move appreciably against the background of the apparently fixed stars.

Art, Culture, & Mythology

1. d) Krater
It is an ancient Greek vessel used for diluting wine with water. It usually stood on a tripod in the dining room, where wine was mixed. Kraters were made of metal or pottery and were often painted or elaborately ornamented.

2. c) Fresco
The method of painting is used usually on wall surfaces. The colours, which are made by grinding dry-powder pigments in pure water, dry and set with the plaster to become a permanent part of the wall. Fresco painting is ideal for making murals because it lends itself to a monumental style, is durable, and has a matte surface.

3. d) Liturgical drama
Although they had their roots in the Christian liturgy, such plays were not performed as essential parts of a standard church service. The language of the liturgical drama was Latin, and the dialogue was frequently chanted to simple monophonic melodies. Music was also used in the form of incidental dance and processional tunes.

4. b) China
In this kind of embroidery, silk, satin, and other textiles are decorated using soft coloured silk threads and were produced at or near the city of Su-chou, in Kiangsu Province, China. The Su-chou school is one of the four most famous schools of embroidery in China (the others being centred in Hunan, Kwangtung, and Szechwan provinces). Embroidered book covers unearthed at Su-chou date the production of embroidery there back to the Five Dynasties period (10th century AD), though the school probably extends back to Han-dynasty times. The Su-chou tradition uses many different types of stitching and variable types of threads to realistically depict the forms and textures of flowers, goldfish, cats, dragons, and other pleasing natural objects.

5. b) Plique-a-jour
The technique is the same as cloisonne enamelling except that the strips of metal forming the cells are only temporarily attached—not soldered—to a metal base to which the enamel will not stick. After the enamel is fused and sufficiently annealed, the metal sheet, usually aluminum-bronze, is removed with a few light taps, leaving a network of metal strips filled with enamel "windows". The enamels can be carefully polished to enhance their appearance.

6. d) Acid
Etched glass is a type of glassware whose decorative design has been cut into the surface by the corrosive action of an acid. An etched-glass surface may be either rough and frosted or satiny smooth and translucent, depending largely on the composition of the glass and the amount of time the glass is exposed to the acid. Design transfer is accomplished by several methods. In one common practice, the glass is coated with a layer of beeswax or paraffin on which patterns or pictures are traced with metal needles. The glass is then dipped in hydrofluoric acid, which etches the design through the grooves made by the needles in the protective coating. Engraving

The colourful onion domes of Saint Basil the Blessed above Red Square are perhaps the most common vision Westerners conjure up in Moscow. The church was commissioned by Ivan the Terrible in honor of the Russian victory over the Tatars in Kazan and Astrakhan.

Did You Know?

and enamelling are often used in conjunction with the etching process to enhance the decorative design.

7. c) Encaustic

Encaustic painting (from the Greek: "burnt in") was probably first practised in Egypt about 3000 BC and is thought to have reached its peak in Classical Greece, although no examples from that period survive. Pigments, mixed with melted beeswax, were brushed onto stone or plaster, smoothed with a metal spatula, and then blended and driven into the wall with a heated iron. The surface was later polished with a cloth. Leonardo and others attempted unsuccessfully to revive the technique. North American Indians used an encaustic method whereby pigments mixed with hot animal fat were pressed into a design engraved on smoothed buffalo hide.

8. b) Vincent van Gogh

Generally considered the greatest Dutch painter after Rembrandt, and one of the greatest of the Post-Impressionists, Van Gogh's work, all of it produced during a period of only 10 years, conveys through its striking colour, emphatic brushwork, and contoured forms his keen observations of nature and the anguish of a mental illness that eventually resulted in suicide. Van Gogh's pictorial style was spontaneous and instinctive for he worked with great speed and intensity, determined to capture an effect or a mood while it possessed him. His subjects during his first great period of painting, beginning February 1888, include blossoming fruit trees, views of the town and surroundings, self-portraits, portraits of Roulin the postman and other friends, interiors and exteriors of the house, a series of sunflowers, and a "starry night".

9. b) Impressionist

The French painter, artist, was the initiator, leader, and unswerving advocate of the Impressionist style. In his mature works, Monet developed his method of producing several studies of the same motif in series, changing canvases with the light or as his interest shifted. These "series" were generally dated and were frequently exhibited in groups, for example, "Haystacks" (1891) and "Rouen Cathedral" (1894). At his home in Giverny, Monet created the water-lily pond that served as inspiration for his "Nympheas" paintings.

10. a) *Tjurunga*

This mythical being and a ritual object traditionally referred to sacred or secret-sacred things set apart, or taboo; for example, certain rites, stone, and wooden slab objects, ritual poles and emblems, headgear, and sacred songs. More popularly, the term is applied to flat, oval, worked stones, normally incised with sacred designs, and to wooden boards ranging in length from about 5 cm (2 inches) to 3 m (10 ft) or so and bearing intricate patterns of mythological significance. At initiation, a youth (not a girl) is introduced to the rituals and *tjurunga* of his local descent group and to those of others. Later he receives his own *tjurunga* object and the knowledge that goes with it (or them). At death, the *tjurunga* might be buried with the corpse, or the dead person's spirit might seek the place where its *tjurunga* "body" (that is, the mythic being itself) rested.

11. a) A festival

A masque is a festival or entertainment in which disguised participants offer gifts to their host and then join in a ceremonial dance. A typical masque consisted of a band of

Tramp art is a type of folk art that fulfills that art form's primary requirements: it is made of found materials by persons who did not necessarily have formal artistic training.

The ancient Egyptians hung a chunk of diorite on a brass ring and raised their walls of stone or clay.

costumed and masked persons of the same sex who, accompanied by torchbearers, arrived at a social gathering to dance and converse with the guests. The masque could be simply a procession of such persons introduced by a presenter, or it could be an elaborately staged show in which a brief lyrical drama heralded the appearance of masquers, who, having descended from their pageant to perform figured dances, reveled with the guests until summoned back into their pageant by farewell speeches and song. The theme of the drama presented during a masque was usually mythological, allegorical, or symbolic and was designed to be complimentary to the noble or royal host of the social gathering.

12. a) Mudang
The priestess employs magic to effect cures, to tell fortunes, to soothe the spirits of the dead, and to repulse evil. Her male counterpart is called a paksu; both, however, are also known by numerous other names in various parts of Korea. Hereditary mudang, especially in former times, formed a separate religious group of low social standing and seldom married into families on a higher social level. The principal occasion for the performance of a mudang is the kut, a trance ritual in which singing and dancing are used to invite happiness and repel evil. As the ritual progresses, the mudang goes into a trance during which the god is said to arrive, to be placated, and then to communicate a message to the client (on behalf of a family, a village, or the state) through the mudang.

13. a) Mohlam
Scores of popular troupes perform plays derived from Thai likay and set to the lively and melodic Lao folk song style known as mohlam. Mohlam balladeers, accompanied by the khen (a complex reed organ), have for centuries travelled the Lao-speaking countryside, which includes Laos and northeast Thailand, singing bawdy songs of physical love and weaving into their performance local gossip and bits from the epics and court plays.

14. d) Opera
The Italian operatic lyric tenor is noted for his mastery of the highest notes of a tenor's range. He is considered one of the finest bel canto opera singers of recent times. Even in the highest register, his voice is noted for its purity of tone.

15. a) Douglas Fairbanks, Sr.
The academy was created in 1927 by 36 film industry leaders after Louis B. Mayer, the head of the powerful Metro-Goldwyn-Mayer studio, actor Conrad Nagel, director Fred Niblo, and producer Fred Beetson had the idea for a new industry organization for handling labour disputes, promoting harmony among the different branches of film production, improving the public image of the film industry, and providing a common ground for the discussion of new production procedures and technologies. Never an effective arbiter, the academy abandoned labour negotiations by 1937, and its focus became cultural and educational.

16. a) Egypt
The Egyptian-made glass of the 11th or 12th century, of which only 12 known examples exist, are among the last cut glass produced in the East. Their designs of stylized lions and griffins among palm leaves are cut in high relief, a technique derived from rock-crystal

cutting. Carried to Europe by returning crusaders, these glasses often became the property of Western churches. Their name derives from St. Hedwig, patron saint of Silesia, who allegedly performed a wine miracle in one of these glasses.

17. d) Gold and ivory
Athena was customarily portrayed wearing body armour and a helmet and carrying a shield and a lance. Two Athenians, the sculptor Phidias and the playwright Aeschylus, contributed significantly to the cultural dissemination of Athena's image. She inspired three of Phidias' sculptural masterpieces, including the massive statue of Athena Parthenos housed in the Parthenon.

18. c) Small carved gems
A cameo is a hard or precious stone carved in relief, or imitations of such stones in glass (called pastes) and mollusc shell. The cameo is usually a gem (commonly agate, onyx, or sardonyx) having two different coloured layers, with the figures carved in one layer so that they are raised on a background of the other.

19. c) Funerary structures
Surrounding the three pyramids are extensive fields of the flat-topped mastabas, arranged in a grid pattern; the mastabas were used for the burials of relatives or officials of the kings. Besides the core mastabas of the 4th dynasty, numerous mastabas have also been found that date from the 5th and 6th dynasties (*c.* 2465-*c.* 2150 BC), as well as from the 3rd dynasty (*c.* 2650-*c.* 2575 BC).

20. a) Jorn Utzon
A serious shortage of theatres and concert halls existed in the city, but this was remedied when the Sydney Opera House—in fact a major arts centre—was opened in 1973. Built on a magnificent site on the harbour, surrounded by water on three sides, it contains a concert hall for the Sydney Symphony Orchestra, a large theatre for opera and ballet, a smaller theatre for plays, a cinema, and rehearsal and recording studios.

21. b) Romanesque art
The painting, sculpture, architecture, and music characteristic of the second of two great international eras that flourished in western and central Europe during the Middle Ages is known as Romanesque art. Gothic art evolved from Romanesque art and lasted from the mid-12th century to as late as the end of the 16th century in some areas. The term Gothic was coined by Italian writers of the Renaissance, who attributed the invention (and what to them was the nonclassical ugliness) of mediaeval architecture to the barbarian Gothic tribes that had destroyed the Roman Empire and its classical culture in the 5th century AD. Although modern scholars have long realized that Gothic art has nothing in truth to do with the Goths, the term Gothic remains a standard one in the study of art history.

22. c) Aquatint
It became the most popular method of producing toned prints in the late 18th century, especially among illustrators. Its textural subtleties, however, remained largely unexplored by well-known artists except for Francisco de Goya. Most of his prints are aquatints, and he is considered the greatest master of the technique.

23. d) Stainless steel
The office building in New York City was designed by William Van Alen and is often cited as the epitome of the Art Deco skyscraper. Its sunburst-patterned stainless steel spire remains one of the most striking features of the Manhattan skyline. Built between 1926 and 1930, the Chrysler Building was briefly the tallest in the world (1,048 ft [319.4 m]) until the Empire State Building opened in 1931.

24. d) Cartoon
The cartoon, or talim, is a full-size paper drawing that is squared, each square representing one knot of a particular colour. The weaver places the talim behind his loom and translates the design directly onto the carpet. The cartoon is used for reproduction of very intricate designs and as a master pattern for the production of more than one carpet. Many of the finest Oriental rugs, which achieve a magnificent effect through wealth of detail, are thought to have been woven from cartoons drawn by manuscript illuminators.

25. c) Inigo Jones
The restoration of Old St. Paul's Cathedral in 1633-42 included not only the repair of the 14th-century choir but the entire recasing, in rusticated masonry, of the Romanesque nave and transepts and the building of a new west front with a portico of 10 columns. This portico, among Jones's most ambitious and subtly calculated works, tragically vanished with the rebuilding of the cathedral after the Great Fire of London in 1666.

26. b) John Grierson
Leader of the British documentary-film movement for almost 40 years, John Grierson was one of the first to see the potential of motion pictures to shape people's attitudes toward life and to urge the use of films for educational purposes. He sponsored his first and only personally directed film, *Drifters* (1929), a study of the lives of North Sea herring fishermen.

27. c) Bob Dylan
The Vietnam War gave rise to a plethora of documentary essays, some of them politically committed, some attempting a balanced exploration of the situation. American cinema verite, sometimes called "direct cinema", matured during the war, though not only in response to it. The first of the rock concert films, D.A. Pennebaker's portrait of Bob Dylan, *Don't Look Back*, first played theatrically in 1967.

28. a) *Shoah*
In the 1980s, many documentaries were increasingly seen on television rather than on movie-theatre screens. Claude Lanzmann's *Shoah* (1985) received limited theatrical distribution in many areas because of its length but still managed to reach wide audiences through the distribution markets provided by the growing cable-television and videocassette industries.

29. d) Germany
In presenting a background, an environment, and characters who behave in a certain way, every motion picture may be said to be propaganda. The term is usually restricted, however, to pictures made deliberately to influence opinion or to argue a point. The most powerful and most consistent use of the cinema for propaganda was seen in the Soviet Union. Nazi Germany produced its own

---

Mice that lack oxytocin cannot remember one another's scent. The finding bolsters the theory that the brain stores "social memory" differently than other types of memory, and it may point to the biological roots of human disorders with a social component, such as autism.

Did You Know?

brand of propaganda in the 1930s, the most striking being Leni Riefenstahl's *Triumph of the Will* (1936), a terrifying spectacle of a huge Nazi rally that had in effect been staged for the film made about it.

30. a) *Fame*
Musicals came into prominence with the introduction of sound. They remained important until the late 1960s, when a number of expensive, overblown productions flooded theatres and met financial failure. The modern musical *Fame* (1980), is more socially conscious and more serious than the colourful, vividly stylized, self-conscious musicals of the 1940s and 1950s.

31. c) The Film Society of London
Film societies and film festivals provide readership for film journals and serious film books, which eventually led to the acceptance of film study in universities. Film societies foster the appreciation of the art of film and emphasize the social dimension of film in culture, sometimes using the film as a prop for the examination and propagation of moral and political ideas.

32. c) Venice
Film festivals provide a forum for promotion and recognition of artistic achievements of national film industries. The first festival was founded in 1932. It remained unique until after World War II, when the Cannes Festival was founded, and festivals began to assume their modern-day importance. Struggling nations, rebuilding their shattered film industries, saw in festivals a chance for world recognition. The growing interest everywhere in film imports made the festivals an international marketplace for distributors. Festivals were initiated at Berlin; Moscow; Karlovy Vary, Czechoslovakia; London; San Francisco; Chicago; and New York City.

33. b) Copperplate
Etching is a method of making prints from a metal plate, usually copper, into which the design has been incised by acid. The copperplate is first coated with an acid-resistant substance, called the etching ground, through which the design is drawn with a sharp tool. The ground is usually a compound of beeswax, bitumen, and resin. The plate is then exposed to nitric acid or dutch mordant, which eats away those areas of the plate unprotected by the ground, forming a pattern of recessed lines. These lines hold the ink, and, when the plate is applied to moist paper, the design transfers to the paper, making a finished print.

34. a) An alcove to display art
In a Japanese room, an alcove is used for the display of paintings, pottery, flower arrangements, and other forms of art. Household accessories are removed when not in use so that the tokonoma found in almost every Japanese house, is the focal point of the interior. A feature of the shoin architectural style, which originated in the Kamakura period (1192-1333), the tokonoma developed from the private altar (butsudan) in Zen Buddhist priests' homes. The butsudan consisted of an alcove containing a narrow wooden table with an incense burner, votive candles, and flower vessels placed before a Buddhist scroll hung on the wall. In its adaptation to the Japanese house, it was used exclusively for the display of art objects.

35. a) India ink
Also called Chinese ink, it is a black pigment in the form of sticks that are moistened before use in drawing and lettering, or the fluid ink consisting of this pigment finely suspended in a liquid medium, such as water, and a glutinous binder. The sticks or cakes consist of specially prepared lampblack, or carbon black, mixed with a gum or glue and sometimes perfume. India ink was used in China and Egypt centuries before the Christian era and is still valued for the opacity and durability that make it one of the finest of inks.

36. b) Western-style drama
A form of Chinese drama featuring realistic spoken dialogue rather than the sung poetic dialogue of the traditional Chinese dramatic forms. Hua-chu was developed in the early 20th century by intellectuals who wanted to replace the traditional Chinese forms with Western-style drama. At first the hua-chu plays consisted exclusively of translations or adaptations of Western works intended for the appreciation of Western-educated intellectuals, but the appeal of hua-chu was later broadened through the efforts of the China Traveling Dramatic Troupe. The form was created during a period of political instability, and it often featured some element of social commentary.

37. d) Nephrite
A crystalline calcium magnesium silicate, nephrite in its pure state is white but may be green, cream, yellow, brown, grey, black, or mottled owing to the presence of impurities, chiefly iron compounds. In historic times, China's chief source of nephrite has been the riverbeds of Yarkand and Ho-t'ien in present-day Xinjiang Central Asian regions in northwestern China, where jade is found in the form of boulders.

38. c) Casting
Also called the lost-wax process, in this method of hollow metal casting a layer of wax corresponding to the desired shape is encased within two heat-proof layers; the process is also used for small solid castings, using a solid wax form. In both variations, the wax is melted and drained off, and molten metal is poured into the resulting cavity. Common on every continent except Australia, the cire-perdue method dates from the 3rd millennium BC and has sustained few changes since then.

39. c) Hula
It is a sensuous, mimetic Hawaiian dance, performed sitting or standing, with undulating gestures to instruments and chant. Originally the hula was a religious dance performed by trained dancers before king or people. Wristlets and anklets of whale teeth or bone and necklaces and fillets of *leis* (interwoven flowers) were common ornaments. The women wore short skirts (*pa'us*) and the men tapa loincloths (*malos*).

40. a) Rococo
The architectural complex in Copenhagen, Denmark, was built during the reign (1746-66) of King Frederick V and comprises the four buildings of the Amalienborg royal palace and the octagonal courtyard surrounded by them. The complex was designed and constructed by the Danish architect Nicolai Eigtved. The Amalienborg complex is said to be one of the finest examples of Rococo-style architecture in Europe. It still serves as the chief residence of the Danish royal family.

The first Barbie doll was unveiled in a toy fair in New York in March 1959.

Mark Twain was the first author to submit a typewritten book manuscript.

The first typewriter had no shift-key mechanism—it wrote capital letters only.

Did You Know?

41. c) China
Porcelain was first made in a primitive form during the T'ang dynasty (618-907) and in the form best known in the West during the Yuan dynasty (1279-1368). Porcelain is vitrified pottery with a white, fine-grained body that is usually translucent, as distinguished from earthenware, which is porous, opaque, and coarser. The word porcelain is derived from porcellana, used by Marco Polo to describe the pottery he saw in China.

42. a) Josiah Spode, the Second
Bone china is hybrid hard-paste porcelain containing bone ash. The initial development of bone china is attributed to Josiah Spode, the Second, who introduced it around 1800. His basic formula of six parts bone ash, four parts china stone, and three and a half parts china clay remains the standard English body. Hard porcelain is strong but chips fairly easily and, unless specially treated, is usually tinged with blue or gray. Somewhat easier to manufacture, bone china is strong, does not chip easily, and has an ivory-white appearance.

43. b) Square dance
The dance begins and progresses rapidly in well-ordered patterns within the framework of a relatively compact square, sets of four couples forming its four sides. To the traditional accompaniment of accordion, banjo, fiddle, and guitar and to prompting, patter, and singing calls made by a "caller", couples perform a variety of movements, all based on a smooth, "shuffling" walk. Formerly danced in five main figures, the contemporary square dance is composed of three.

44. d) Russia
The Russian ballerina was the most celebrated dancer of her time. Pavlova studied at the Imperial School of Ballet at the Mariinsky Theatre from 1891, joined the Imperial Ballet in 1899, and became a prima ballerina in 1906. In 1909 she went to Paris on the historic tour of the Ballets Russes. After 1913 she danced independently with her own company throughout the world.

45. b) Frescos
The palaces and great houses were decorated with complex frescoes whose style was based on Cretan models. Many of the figured scenes are merely decorative and depict landscapes with birds and animals or figures gathering flowers. Others show ceremonies connected with a cult or the court ("The Toreador Fresco") and were probably useful in bolstering the power of the royal or priestly classes.

46. c) Eiffel Tower
The Washington Monument is a memorial to George Washington, the first American president. The structure, based on a design by Robert Mills, is a granite obelisk faced with Maryland marble. It is 16.8 m (55 ft) square at the base, 169.3 m (555 ft 5 inches) high. The monument was the tallest man-made structure in the world from its completion in 1884 until surpassed by the newly built Eiffel Tower in 1889. The Eiffel Tower, a Parisian landmark, is a technological masterpiece in building-construction history. The 300-m (984-ft) tower is, built almost entirely of open-lattice wrought iron. It rests on a base that is 5 m (17 ft) high, and a television antenna atop the tower gives it a total elevation of 322 m (1,056 ft). The Eiffel

Tower was the tallest man-made structure in the world until the completion of the Chrysler Building in New York City in 1930.

47. b) Prairie
The American architectural style is exemplified by the low-lying "prairie houses" such as Robie House (1908) that were for the most part built in the Midwest between 1900 and 1917 by Frank Lloyd Wright. Prairie houses and other buildings were generally two-storey structures with single-storey wings. They utilized horizontal lines, ribbon windows, gently sloping roofs, suppressed, heavy-set chimneys, overhangs, and sequestered gardens.

48. d) China
The immense religious and administrative complex is situated atop Mar-po-ri (Red Mountain), 425 ft (130 m) above the Lhasa River valley in Lhasa, Tibet Autonomous Region, China. In 1645 the fifth Dalai Lama ordered the construction of a new castle that could accommodate his role as both a religious and a government leader. Lhasa was chosen as the location because of its importance as a pilgrimage site and its proximity to the three main Buddhist monasteries of Sera, 'Brasspungs (Drepung), and Dga'-Idan (Ganden). The new Potala was built on Mar-po-ri for the security provided by an elevated position; until its use declined in the mid-18th century, the Potala was a major Tibetan military fortress.

49. d) 15,000 years
Painting has been continuously practised by humans for some 20,000 years. Together with other activities that may have been ritualistic in origin but have come to be designated as artistic painting was one of the earliest ways in which man sought to express his own personality and his emerging understanding of an existence beyond the material world. Unlike music and dance, however, examples of early forms of painting have survived to the present day. The modern eye can derive aesthetic as well as antiquarian satisfaction from the 15,000-year-old cave murals of Lascaux—some examples testify to the considerable powers of draftsmanship of these early artists.

50. d) A mythological animal
The composite mythological creature has a lion's body (winged or wingless) and a bird's head, usually that of an eagle. The griffin was a favourite decorative motif in the ancient Middle Eastern and Mediterranean lands. Probably originating in the Levant in the 2nd millennium BC, the griffin had spread throughout western Asia and into Greece by the 14th century BC. The Asiatic griffin had a crested head, whereas the Minoan and Greek griffin usually had a mane of spiral curls. It was shown either recumbent or seated on its haunches, often paired with the sphinx; its function may have been protective.

51. a) Minoan
Between 1500 and about 1450 BC, however, there flourished the Marine style, possibly the most successful of all Minoan pottery styles. Nearly every form of marine life is accurately reproduced in a riotous allover arrangement: octopuses, argonauts, dolphins, and fish, against a background of rocks and waves. In the 70 or 80 years after 1450 BC, the spontaneity of the early Marine style degenerated into a rigid formality.

---

52. a) Wayang kulit
It is uncertain whether the shadow theatre is indigenous to Java or was brought from India, but the wayang kulit technique of having a single seated puppeteer who manipulates puppets, sings, chants narration, and speaks dialogue seems to be an Indonesian invention. Unlike most court arts, wayang kulit has had centuries of performance in the folk tradition as well, so that today, with several thousand puppeteers active, it is the strongest traditional theatre form in Southeast Asia.

53. c) Legong
The Balinese legong may have only the most tenuous dramatic content. Its interest lies in the girls' unison rapid foot movements and fluttering movements of eyes and hands.

54. a) Hand gestures
In Buddhism and Hinduism, *hasta-mudra*s are symbolic gestures of the hands and fingers, used either in ceremonies and dance or in sculpture and painting. *Mudra*s used in ceremony and dance tend to be numerous, complicated, and often esoteric. The *hasta-mudra*s of Hindu classical dance can express about 500 different meanings, involving not only the hands and fingers but also the wrists, elbows, and shoulders, all in movement.

55. c) Flute
Hayashi, in Japanese music, is any of various combinations of flute and percussion instruments. In no and kabuki drama, the *hayashi* normally consists of a flute plus the hourglass-shaped hand drum (ko-tsuzumi) held on the right shoulder, the larger o-tsuzumi held on the left hip, and the taiko stick-struck barrel drum set on a stand on the floor.

56. c) Indonesia
In the parts of Southeast Asia influenced by Indian forms—everywhere except for Vietnam and the Philippines—nondramatic and dramatic dance are both known. Nondramatic, or "pure", dances that do not express emotional states of characters are numerous in both folk and court traditions. Among court dances, the Javanese bedaja is typical. Nine dancers move in unison, without emotional expression, in precisely fixed choreographic patterns designed to demonstrate sheer grace of movement.

57. a) Praleng
In the Thai praleng, two performers wearing god masks and holding peacock feathers in both hands perform an offertory dance to the god before the main dance-play begins.

58. d) Brazil
The maxixe evolved in Brazil about 1870 and became an international craze in the years before World War I. A fusion of elements from the habanera, the polka, and rural Afro-Brazilian dance, it was danced by couples in ballroom position and often included improvised figures. Related to the tango (and sometimes called tango maxixe), it was the precursor of the ballroom version of the samba.

59. c) Kut
The kut usually comprises 12 *kori* (procedures), each of which is addressed to such specific gods or spirits as the god of childbirth, good harvest, and property, the goddesses in control of specific diseases, the patron spirit of shamans, or the protector god of households.

60. c) Gong

Gongs function as accompaniment to dance, theatre, and song and are used to transmit messages. Frequently, they are considered to have magical or protective qualities. In China they symbolize prosperity and mark social status. They are the leading instruments of the gamelan orchestras of Indonesia, where they are used both singly and as gong chimes (Javanese bonang)-sets of tuned, deep-rimmed, bossed gongs suspended on ropes in a wooden frame and producing bell-like tones.

61. a) Story telling

No, meaning "talent" or "skill", is unlike Western narrative drama. Rather than being actors or "representers" in the Western sense, no performers are simply storytellers who use their visual appearances and their movements to suggest the essence of their tale rather than to enact it.

62. a) Leto

In classical mythology, Leto is believed to have been a Titan, the daughter of Coeus and Phoebe, and mother of the god Apollo and the goddess Artemis. The chief places of her legend were Delos and Delphi. Leto, pregnant by Zeus, sought a place of refuge to be delivered. She finally reached the barren isle of Delos, which, according to some, was a wandering rock borne about by the waves until it was fixed to the bottom of the sea for the birth of Apollo and Artemis.

63. b) Artemis

She was identified by the Romans with Diana. Artemis was the daughter of Zeus and Leto and the twin sister of Apollo. Among the rural populace, Artemis was the favourite goddess. Her character and function varied greatly from place to place, but, apparently, behind all forms lay the goddess of wild nature, who danced, usually accompanied by nymphs, in mountains, forests, and marshes.

64. b) Apollo

Among Apollo's other epithets was *Nomios* (herdsman), and he is said to have served King Admetus of Pherae in the lowly capacities of groom and herdsman as penance for slaying Zeus's armourers, the Cyclopes. He was also called Lyceius, presumably because he protected the flocks from wolves (*lykoi*); because herdsmen and shepherds beguiled the hours with music, scholars have argued that this was Apollo's original role.

65. d) Zeus

In ancient Greek religion, Zeus was considered the chief deity of the pantheon, a sky and weather god who was identical with the Roman god Jupiter. Zeus was regarded as the sender of thunder and lightning, rain, and winds, and his traditional weapon was the thunderbolt. He was called the father (the ruler and protector) of both gods and men.

66. c) Cronus

According to a Cretan myth that was later adopted by the Greeks, Cronus, king of the Titans, upon learning that one of his children was fated to dethrone him, swallowed his children as they were born. But Rhea, his wife, saved the infant Zeus by substituting a stone wrapped in swaddling clothes for Cronus to swallow and hiding Zeus in a cave on Crete. After Zeus grew to manhood he led a revolt against the Titans and succeeded in dethroning Cronus, perhaps with the help of his brothers, Hades and Poseidon, with whom he then divided dominion over the world.

The first watches appeared shortly after 1500, when Peter Henlein, a locksmith in Nurnberg, Germany, introduced the mainspring as a replacement for weights in driving clocks.

A warm-blooded insect eater has an enormous advantage in being able to capture insects when they are cold and slow to react.

Did You Know?

67. a) Hermes
Both in literature and cult Hermes was constantly associated with the protection of cattle and sheep, and he was often closely connected with deities of vegetation, especially Pan and the nymphs.

68. d) Io
Inachus was the river god of Argos. Under the name of Callithyia, Io was regarded as the first priestess of Hera, the wife of Zeus. Zeus fell in love with her and, to protect her from the wrath of Hera, changed her into a white heifer.

69. b) All Seeing
The figure in Greek legend is described variously as the son of Inachus, Agenor, or Arestor or as an aboriginal hero (autochthon). His surname derives from the hundred eyes in his head or all over his body. Argus was appointed by the goddess Hera to watch the cow into which Io (Hera's priestess) had been transformed, but he was slain by Hermes. His eyes were transferred by Hera to the tail of the peacock. This Argus was often confused with the son of Niobe who gave his name to the city of Argos.

70. d) William the Conqueror
He decreed that the year start on January 1, but, later, England began its year with the rest of Christendom on March 25. January 1 was restored as New Year's Day by the Gregorian calendar (1582), immediately adopted by Roman Catholic countries.

71. a) Isthmian Games
The festival of athletic and musical competitions in honour of the sea god Poseidon was held in the spring of the second and fourth years of each Olympiad at his sanctuary on the Isthmus of Corinth. Legend attributed their origin either to Sisyphus, king of Corinth, or to Theseus. Open to all Greeks, the Isthmian Games were especially popular with Athenians. The victors' prize, originally a crown of dry wild celery, was changed to a pine wreath in Roman times, the pine being sacred to Poseidon. Celebration of the festival died out when Christianity became dominant in the 4th century AD.

72. b) Gautama Buddha
Also called Siddhartha, he was the founder of Buddhism, the predominant religious and philosophical system of much of Asia. The term buddha, literally means "awakened one" or "enlightened one".

73. a) Nara Period
During this period (710-784), Buddhism became the state religion of Japan. Emperor Shomu actively propagated the faith, making the imperial capital, Nara—with its "Great Buddha" statue (Daibutsu)—the national cult centre.

74. c) Indonesia
A massive Buddhist monument in central Java, Indonesia, the Borobudur monument combines the symbolic forms of the stupa (a Buddhist commemorative mound usually containing holy relics), the temple mountain (based on Mount Meru of Hindu mythology), and the mandala (a mystic Buddhist symbol of the universe, combining the square as Earth and the circle as heaven).

75. d) Chinese
Korean architecture shows Chinese influence, but it is adapted to local conditions, utilizing

wood and granite, the most abundant building materials. Beautiful examples are found in old palaces, Buddhist temples, stone tombs, and Buddhist pagodas. Western-style architecture became common from the 1970s, fundamentally changing the urban landscape.

76. d) The Three Kingdoms Period

During the Three Kingdoms period there were three political and cultural centres: P'yongyang, the capital of Koguryo, in the northwest; the Kongju-Puyo region, the Paekche heartland, in the southwest; and Kyongju, the capital of Silla, in the southeast. Silla and Paekche, along with the minor state of Kaya (also known as Kara or Karak; Japanese: Mimana) in the south, maintained close cultural contacts with Japan, and it was at this time that the significant Korean influence on Japanese art began.

77. c) Hotel de Bourgogne

It was built in 1548 on the ruins of the palace of the dukes of Burgundy. The theatre was built by the Confrerie de la Passion ("Confraternity of the Passion"), a group of artisans and tradesmen who held a monopoly on the presentation of plays in the city. The long and narrow theatre had a small playing area that was further restricted by the use of multiple settings on the stage. Most of the audience stood in the pit, and galleries lined the side and back walls. The theatre's total capacity was 1,600. The same year their theatre was finished, the Confrerie was forbidden to perform religious plays and was reduced to acting farces and plays of medieval romance, without much success. Toward the end of the 16th century, it gave up acting and rented the theatre to travelling players, including Italian and English companies.

78. d) United States of America

Navajo blankets and rugs are thought to be some of the most colourful and best-made textiles produced by North American Indians. The Navajo, formerly a seminomadic tribe, settled in the southwestern United States in the 10th and 11th centuries and were well established by 1500.

79. d) Pop art

The American painter was a founder and foremost practitioner of Pop art, a movement that countered the techniques and concepts of Abstract Expressionism with images and techniques taken from popular culture. At the start of his artistic career, Lichtenstein painted themes from the American West in a variety of modern art styles; he dabbled in 1957 even in Abstract Expressionism, a style he later reacted against. His interest in the comic-strip cartoon as an art theme probably began with a painting of Mickey Mouse and Donald Duck he made in 1960 for his children.

80. a) Fine-art lithography

The method of preparing stones for hand printing, which is still the lithographic method preferred by artists, has remained substantially unchanged since Senefelder's time. The materials and procedures of the 19th-century lithographer are duplicated in almost every respect by the contemporary hand printer. Although stone is the preferred printing surface in fine art, zinc and aluminium plates are also used, and, like stone, the metal plates can be reground.

81. a) Pennsylvania Academy of the Fine Arts

It was founded in 1805. Specializing in American painting and sculpture of the 18th to the 20th century, the Academy's Art

Although the first Olympic champion listed in the records was one Coroebus of Elis, a cook, who won the sprint race in 776 BC, it is generally accepted that the Games were probably at least 500 years old at that time.

Did You Know?

Museum was built between 1872 and 1876 according to designs by architect Frank Furness (1839-1912). The building's architectural style is high Victorian.

82. b) Henry Bacon
The stately monument in Washington, D.C., honours Abraham Lincoln and "the virtues of tolerance, honesty, and constancy in the human spirit". Designed by Henry Bacon on a plan similar to that of the Parthenon in Athens, the structure includes 36 columns (each 44 ft [13.4 m] high) of Colorado marble surrounding the building, one for each state that comprised the Union in Lincoln's time. The colossal (19-ft) seated statue of Lincoln, composed of Georgia white marble and resting on a pedestal of Tennessee marble, was designed by Daniel Chester French and carved by the Piccirilli brothers of New York; it dominates the interior and looks eastward across a reflecting pool at the Washington Monument and Capitol. On the South Wall is inscribed Lincoln's Gettysburg Address and on the North Wall his Second Inaugural Address. The cornerstone was laid in 1915 and the completed Memorial was dedicated on Memorial Day, May 30, 1922.

83. b) Royal Drury Lane Theatre
It stands in the eastern part of the City of Westminster, London. The theatre was built by the dramatist Thomas Killigrew for his company of actors as the Theatre Royal under a charter from Charles II. It opened May 7, 1663, in the propitious era of Restoration drama, and produced plays by John Dryden, among others. It was closed in 1665-66 but then prospered until being destroyed by fire (1672). Rebuilt on its present site in Drury Lane in 1674 with Christopher Wren as its probable architect, the second Theatre Royal soon featured the works of William Congreve.

84. a) Japan
The traditional Japanese theatrical form is one of the oldest extant theatrical forms in the world. No developed from ancient forms of dance drama and from various types of festival drama at shrines and temples that had emerged by the 12th or 13th century. No became a distinctive form in the 14th century and was continually refined up to the years of the Tokugawa period (1603-1867). It became a ceremonial drama performed on auspicious occasions by professional actors for the warrior class—as, in a sense, a prayer for peace, longevity, and the prosperity of the social elite.

85. a) Porcelain enamelling
The process of fusing a thin layer of glass to a metal object prevents corrosion and enhances its beauty. Porcelain-enamelled iron is used extensively for such articles as kitchen pots and pans, bathtubs, refrigerators, chemical and food tanks, and equipment for meat markets. In architecture it serves as facing for buildings. Being a glass, porcelain enamelling has the properties of glass: a hard surface, resistance to solution, corrosion, and scratching. Enamelware is usually quite resistant to acid and impact, but may crack if the base metal is deformed.

86. c) George Stanley
The design for the award statuette—a knight standing on a reel of film and holding a sword—is credited to Metro-Goldwyn-Mayer (MGM) art director Cedric Gibbons. Sculptor George Stanley was commissioned to create the original statuette based on Gibbons' design. For many years the statuettes were cast

in bronze, with 24-karat gold plating. During World War II the statuettes were made of plaster because of metal shortages. They are now made of gold-plated britannium. The design, however, has remained unchanged, with the exception of the pedestal base, whose height was increased in 1945. The statuette stands 34.3 cm (13.5 inches) tall and weighs 8.5 pounds (3.8 kg).

87. d) The Monument
The column is located in the City of London, just north of London Bridge. It was most likely designed by the physicist and architect Robert Hooke, although some sources credit Christopher Wren. Erected in the 1670s near the site of the fire's origin (on Pudding Lane), it stands 61.5 m (202 ft) above the pavement. Its viewing platform is accessible via an internal spiral staircase.

88. d) Japanese
The sliding outer partition doors and windows made of a latticework wooden frame and covered with a tough, translucent white paper. When closed, they softly diffuse light throughout the house. In summer they are often removed completely, opening the house to the outside—a desirable arrangement in Japan because of the extreme humidity. The shoji is a feature of the shoin style, which first appeared in the Kamakura period (1192-1333).

89. b) Egypt
The revolutionary style of Egyptian art, created by Amenhotep IV, took the name Akhenaton during his reign (1353-36 BC) in the 18th dynasty. Often referred to as the Amarna heresy, Akhenaton's alteration of the artistic and religious life of Egypt was drastic.

After the banishment of all Egyptian gods except Aton, Akhenaton limited aristic subject matter mainly to depictions of himself and his family. It was in the method of portraying the Pharaoh and his family that the most remarkable aspect of Amarna art lies, for the old stiff canon was abandoned in favour of a "naturalistic" depiction, which showed them more as actual human beings.

90. b) 900-700 BC
The Geometric style arose in Athens about 900 BC. It built upon the foundations of the previous period, though the area covered by painted patterns expanded and new motifs were incorporated into the painters' repertoire. The meander, swastika, and crenellation (battlement) patterns were prominent and, together with the older concentric circles, were used by the painters to push back the large areas of solid black characteristic of Protogeometric vases and to create a pleasing halftone decorative effect. A few human and animal figures were introduced into this otherwise severely geometric scheme, but it was not until about 760 BC that a renewed interest in figures became paramount.

91. c) Greece
Black figure pottery originated in Corinth *c.* 700 BC and continued to be popular until the advent of red-figure pottery *c.* 530 BC. In black-figure painting, figures and ornamentation were drawn on the natural clay surface of a vase in glossy black pigment; the finishing details were incised into the black.

92. b) Mythological scenes
The earliest reasonably well-preserved temple decoration comes from the temple of Apollo at Thermon, in central Greece, and dates from

the later 7th century BC. The temple roof was decorated with a series of square terra-cotta frieze plaques, called metopes, bearing mythological scenes.

93. c) Huang Ho
They settled chiefly in the basin of the Huang Ho (Yellow River). Gradually they spread out, influencing other tribal cultures, until, by the Han dynasty (206 BC-AD 220), most of China proper was dominated by the culture that had been formed in the "cradle" of northern Chinese civilization. Over this area there spread slowly a common written language, as well as a common belief in the power of heaven and the ancestral spirits to influence the living and in the importance of ceremony and sacrifice to achieve harmony among heaven, nature, and humankind. These beliefs were to have a great influence on the character of Chinese art.

94. b) Joseph Cornell
He was self-taught, and in the 1930s and 1940s Cornell associated with Surrealist artists and writers, concerned with expressing the subconscious, his works being presented in the first U.S. exhibition of Surrealists (New York City, 1932). Many of Cornell's works take the form of glass-fronted boxes containing objects and collage elements arranged in enigmatic, often poetic juxtaposition. Recurrent themes and motifs include astronomy, music, commedia dell'arte, birds, seashells, broken crystal, and souvenirs of travel. "Chocolat Menier" (1950), for example, is a spare yet fanciful boxed collage of tattered labels and worn surfaces.

95. a) David Smith
The American sculptor's pioneering welded metal sculpture and massive painted geometric forms made him the most original American sculptor in the decades after World War II. His work greatly influenced the brightly coloured "primary structures" of Minimal art during the 1960s. Smith was never trained as a sculptor, but he learned to work with metal in 1925, when he was briefly employed as a riveter at the Studebaker automobile plant in South Bend, Indiana.

96. a) Koguryo
The first major period of Korean art during recorded history is that of the Three Kingdoms (c. 57 BC-AD 668). Northernmost of the Three Kingdoms was the Koguryo kingdom (37 BC-AD 668), into which the Buddhist religion was introduced from China in AD 372. This development (together with the subsequent conversion to Buddhism of the Paekche [18 BC-AD 660] and Silla [57 BC-AD 668] kingdoms) brought about a flowering of the arts on the Korean Peninsula, and, until the 15th century, Buddhism remained the major source of inspiration in Korean visual art.

97. b) Kim Chong Hi
The best-known Korean calligrapher of the 19th century, Kim Chong Hi developed a unique style from the famous li shu calligraphy of Han China known as the ch'usa; it has continued to be one of the major calligraphic styles in Korea.

98. a) Sejong
A monarch of the Yi dynasty during whose reign (1419-50) cultural achievements in Korea reached their highest point. Sejong is best known for his development of Hangul (ha'gul), a phonetic system for writing the Korean language, considered one of the most scientific alphabets in use in any country.

99. d) *Kayagum*

The kayagum, Korea's national instrument, is heard in both folk and classical Korean music and dance. It consists of a Korean board zither with 12 silk strings, movable bridges, and a convex upper surface. It is a rectangle about 5 ft (1.5 m) in length. Although related to similar Chinese and Japanese instruments, such as the cheng, ch'in, koto, and wagon, it is played in a distinctive Korean manner.

100. c) Yaqui

They are an Indian people centred in southern Sonora state, on the west coast of Mexico. They speak the Yaqui dialect of the language called Cahita, which belongs to the Uto-Aztecan language family. (The only other surviving speakers of the Cahita language group are the related Mayo people.) The Yaqui are Roman Catholic, but the form of their worship is clearly influenced by aboriginal practices. The Yaqui numbered about 25,000 in the late 20th century, with several thousand also living in Arizona in the United States.

101. a) China

Bonsai (Japanese: "tray-planted") is a living dwarf tree or trees or the art of training and growing them in containers. Bonsai specimens are ordinary trees and shrubs, not hereditary dwarfs; they are dwarfed by a system of pruning roots and branches and training branches by tying with wire. The art originated in China, where, perhaps over 1,000 years ago, trees were cultivated in trays, wooden containers, and earthenware pots and trained in naturalistic shapes. Bonsai, however, has been pursued and developed primarily by the Japanese. The first Japanese record of dwarfed potted trees is in the Kasuga-gongen-genki, a picture scroll by Takashina Takakane (1309).

102. b) Romans

The apartment house was developed independently by the imperial Romans of antiquity to suit urban conditions and by the American Indians to suit agricultural conditions. Group architecture may be power architecture as well, particularly when land values are too high to permit even the wealthy to build privately, as in the 17th-century Place des Vosges in Paris, where aristocratic mansions were designed uniformly around a square, or in the 18th-century flats in English towns and spas.

103. b) Ibn Muqlah

One of the foremost calligraphers of the 'Abbasid Age (750-1258), Ibn Muqlah's nakshi script replaced the angular Kufic as the standard of Islamic calligraphy. In the nakshi script Ibn Muqlah introduced the rounded forms and curved lines that in later styles were refined to give Arabic writing the flowing beauty for which it is renowned. Although nakshi was originally intended for use in copying the Qur'an, by the 11th century it was used widely for royal and common correspondence and as architectural decoration.

104. d) Torii

The torii, which has many variations, characteristically consists of two cylindrical vertical posts topped by a cross-wise rectangular beam extending beyond the posts on either side and a second crosswise beam a short distance below. Some authorities relate it to the Indian gateway arch, the torana, which reached Japan with the spread of Buddhism. Others connect the torii with traditional gates in Manchuria and elsewhere in China. The torii, often painted bright red, demarcates the

Although comets can be present in any region of the sky, they are often discovered near the western horizon after sunset or near the eastern horizon before sunrise, since they are brightest when closest to the Sun.

Because of the Earth's rotation and direction of motion in its orbit, discoveries of comets before sunrise are more likely, as confirmed by discovery statistics.

Did You Know?

boundary between the sacred space of the shrine and ordinary space. Torii also identify other sacred spots, such as a mountain or rock.

105. a) Bugaku
The dances comprise two basic forms: *saho no mai* ("dances of the left"), accompanied by togaku (music derived mainly from Chinese forms); and *uho samai no mai* ("dances of the right"), accompanied primarily by komagaku (music introduced from Korea). Bugaku are of four genres: civil dances (also called even, or level, dances), warrior dances, running dances, and dances for children. All bugaku consist of highly conventionalized movements cued by the beat of a drum. Positions of arms, hands, and ft are highly stylized, and overall choreography consists of simple geometric patterns.

106. b) Pantheon
The porch is conventional in design, but the body of the building, an immense circular space lit solely by the light that floods through the 8-m (27-ft) "eye", or oculus, opening at the centre of the dome, was revolutionary; possibly this was the first of several great buildings of antiquity that were designed to favour the interior rather than the exterior.

107. b) Khafre
The earliest and most famous example in art is the colossal recumbent Sphinx at Giza, Egypt, dating from the reign of King Khafre (4th king of 4th dynasty, *c.* 2575-*c.* 2465 BC). This is known to be a portrait statue of the king, and the sphinx continued as a royal portrait type through most of Egyptian history. (Arabs, however, know the Sphinx of Giza by the name of Abu al-Hawl, or "Father of Terror".)

108. a) A canopy over the altar
Also called ciborium, the canopy over an altar or tomb is supported on columns, especially when freestanding and disconnected from any enclosing wall. The term originates from the Spanish *baldaquin*, an elaborately brocaded material imported from Baghdad that was hung as a canopy over an altar or doorway. Later it came to stand for a freestanding canopy over an altar.

109. c) *Le Vaincu* ("The Vanquished")
The French sculptor of sumptuous bronze and marble figures is considered by some critics to be the greatest portraitist in the history of sculpture. In 1875, at the age of 35, Rodin had yet to develop a personally expressive style because of the pressures of the decorative work. The inspiration of Michelangelo and Donatello rescued him from the academicism of his working experience. Under those influences, he moulded the bronze *Le Vaincu* ("The Vanquished"), his first original work, the painful expression of a vanquished energy aspiring to rebirth. The realism of the work contrasted so greatly with the statues of Rodin's contemporaries that he was accused of having formed its mould upon a living person.

110. d) Pueblo pottery
It is still produced in a manner almost identical to the method developed during the Classic Pueblo period about AD 1050-1300. Pueblo pots, made only by the women of the tribe, are constructed not on a potter's wheel but by hand. Long "sausages" of clay are coiled upward around a flat base of clay until the pot reaches the desired height; when the coiling is completed, the interior and exterior of the pot are smoothed, and the round coils are pressed together to form a smooth wall of

the pot. The pots are then coated with slip, a watery clay substance, polished, decorated, and fired.

111. d) Caryatid
In marble architecture they first appeared in pairs in three small buildings (treasuries) at Delphi (550-530 BC), and their origin can be traced back to mirror handles of nude figures carved from ivory in Phoenicia and draped figures cast from bronze in archaic Greece. According to a story related by the 1st-century-BC Roman architectural writer Vitruvius, caryatids represented the women of Caryae, who were doomed to hard labour because the town sided with the Persians in 480 BC during their second invasion of Greece.

112. b) Copper
Standing 305 ft (93 m) high including its pedestal, it represents a woman holding a torch in her raised right hand and a tablet bearing the adoption date of the Declaration of Independence (July 4, 1776) in her left. The statue was constructed of copper sheets, hammered into shape by hand and assembled over a framework of four gigantic steel supports, designed by Eugene-Emmanuel Viollet-le-Duc and Alexandre-Gustave Eiffel. In 1885 the completed statue, 151 ft 1 inch (46 m) high and weighing 225 tons, was disassembled and shipped to New York City.

113. a) Dance
A dance form that originated in Crete and flourished in Greece, the pyrrhiche was a weapon dance. Practised in Sparta as part of military training, it was a basis for the claim of the philosopher Socrates that the best dancer is also the best warrior.

114. c) Emperor
In the broadest sense, all Chinese art is symbolic, for everything that is painted reflects some aspect of a totality of which the painter is intuitively aware. At the same time Chinese art is full of symbols of a more specific kind, some with various possible meanings. Bamboo suggests the spirit of the scholar, which can be bent by circumstance but never broken, and jade symbolizes purity and indestructibility. The dragon, in remote antiquity perhaps an alligator or rain deity, is the wholly benevolent symbol of the emperor; the crane, of long life; paired mandarin ducks, of wedded fidelity.

115. c) Cupid
According to myth, Cupid was the son of Mercury, the winged messenger of the gods, and Venus, the goddess of love; he usually appeared as a winged infant carrying a bow and a quiver of arrows, whose wounds inspired love or passion in his every victim.

116. a) Jupiter
Also called Jove, he is the chief ancient Roman and Italian god. Like Zeus, the Greek god with whom he is etymologically identical (root diu, "bright"), Jupiter was a sky god. One of his most ancient epithets is Lucetius ("Light-Bringer").

117. c) Peyotism
The religious movement is also one of the most influential forms of Pan-Indianism. The term peyote derives from the Nahuatl name peyotl for a cactus. The tops of the plants contain mescaline, an alkaloid drug that has hallucinogenic effects. It was used in Mexico in pre-Columbian times to induce supernatural visions and as a medicine.

The first grammar of a South American Indian language (Quechua) appeared in 1560.

In America north of Mexico, more than 50 percent of the surviving languages have fewer than 1,000 speakers each.

Did You Know?

118. b) Poseidon
The name Poseidon means either "husband of earth" or "lord of the earth". Traditionally he was a son of Cronus, an ancient chief god, and Rhea, a fertility goddess, and was brother of Zeus, the chief god, and Hades, god of the underworld. When the three brothers deposed their father, the kingdom of the sea fell by lot to Poseidon. His weapon was the trident, but it may originally have been a long-handled fish spear. Poseidon was also the god of earthquakes, and many of his oldest places of worship in Greece were inland.

119. b) Medusa
In Greek mythology, Pegasus was a winged horse that sprang from the blood of the Gorgon Medusa as she was beheaded by the hero Perseus. The winged horse became a constellation and the servant of Zeus. Pegasus' story was a favourite theme in Greek art and literature, and in late antiquity Pegasus' soaring flight was interpreted as an allegory of the soul's immortality; in modern times it has been regarded as a symbol of poetic inspiration.

120. a) Eris
The personification of strife, Eris is best known for her part in starting the Trojan War. When she alone of the gods was not invited to the marriage of Peleus and Thetis, she threw among the guests a golden apple inscribed "For the most beautiful". Hera, Athena, and Aphrodite each claimed it, and Zeus assigned the decision to Paris. Paris awarded the apple to Aphrodite, who then helped him win Helen of Troy. In the war that resulted, Hera and Athena remained implacable enemies of Troy.

121. b) Cronus
A male deity, Cronus was worshipped by the pre-Hellenic population of Greece but probably was not widely worshipped by the Greeks themselves; he was later identified with the Roman god Saturn. Son of Uranus (Heaven) and Gaea (Earth), Cronus was the youngest of the 12 Titans. On the advice of his mother he castrated his father with a harpe, thus separating Heaven from Earth.

122. c) Medusa
Medusa, in Greek mythology, is the most famous of the monster figures known as Gorgons. She was usually represented as a winged female creature with a head of hair consisting of snakes. Medusa was the only Gorgon who was mortal; hence her slayer, Perseus, was able to kill her by cutting off her head.

123. d) Psyche
According to Apuleius, the jealous Venus commanded her son Cupid (the god of love) to inspire Psyche with love for the most despicable of men. Instead, Cupid placed Psyche in a remote palace where he could visit her secretly and, by his warning, only in total darkness. One night Psyche lit a lamp and found that the figure at her side was the god of love himself. When a drop of oil from the lamp awakened him, he reproached Psyche and fled. In search of him, Psyche fell into the hands of Venus, who imposed upon her difficult tasks. Finally, touched by Psyche's repentance, Cupid rescued her, and, at his instigation, Jupiter made her immortal and gave her in marriage to Cupid.

124. a) Zoroastrianism
It is the ancient pre-Islamic religion of Iran that survives there in isolated areas and more

prosperously in India, where the descendents of Zoroastrian Iranian (Persian) immigrants are known as Parsis, or Parsees. Founded by the Iranian prophet and reformer Zoroaster in the 6th century BC, this religion, containing both monotheistic and dualistic features, influenced the other major Western religions—Judaism, Christianity, and Islam.

125. c) Michelangelo
Although the Pieta remained mostly a Franco-German theme, its supreme representation is that completed by Michelangelo in 1499 and housed in St. Peter's Basilica in Rome. Influenced by the northern style, Michelangelo draped the figure of Christ across Mary's lap. Through this pyramidal design and the details of his figures, Michelangelo created a scene that displayed at once agony, solemnity, and heroic resignation.

126. c) Pablo Picasso
In late 1906, Picasso started to paint in a truly revolutionary manner. Inspired by Cezanne's flattened depiction of space, and working alongside his friend Georges Braque, he began to express space in strongly geometrical terms. These initial efforts at developing this almost sculptural sense of space in painting are the beginnings of Cubism.

127. b) Pierre-August Renoir
The French painter was originally associated with the Impressionist movement. His early works were typically Impressionist snapshots of real life, full of sparkling colour and light. Renoir had his first attack of rheumatism in 1894, and the attacks became more and more frequent. But in spite of his infirmity, which was more and more constraining, Renoir never ceased to paint.

128. a) Jean-Frederic Bazille
Bazille was an unenthusiastic medical student before his wealthy parents permitted him to study painting. While a student in Paris, he met Monet and Renoir, with whom he worked, travelled, and shared his studio when they could not afford their own. His landscape figures are strangely immobile and have a sculptural, hard-edge quality.

129. b) Pablo Picasso
The Spanish expatriate painter, sculptor, printmaker, ceramicist, and stage designer was one of the greatest and most influential artists of the 20th century and the creator (with Georges Braque) of Cubism. For nearly 80 of his 91 years Picasso devoted himself to an artistic production that contributed significantly to and paralleled the whole development of modern art in the 20th century.

130. a) Paul Cezanne
The French painter was one of the greatest of the Post-Impressionists, whose works and ideas were influential in the aesthetic development of many 20th-century artists and art movements, especially Cubism. Cezanne's art grew out of Impressionism and eventually challenged all the conventional values of painting in the 19th century through its insistence on personal expression and on the integrity of the painting itself.

131. b) Floral
One of the four major schools of floral art in Japan that dates from the Tokugawa period (1603-1868), the Ko school developed the shoka style of the earlier Ikenobo school into a more naturalistic type of arrangement. Calling the arrangements seika rather than shoka, the

Ko school retained the tall, narrow-mouthed type of vase used in the shoka arrangements of the Ikenobo school. The mood of the arrangements was known as nageire, a fresh and spontaneous style that adheres only loosely to the classical rules of structure.

132. b) Buddhist meditation
The school of Chinese painting was inspired by the "meditative" school of Buddhism called, in Chinese, Ch'an (Japanese: Zen). Although Ch'an originated in China with an Indian monk, Bodhidharma, it came to be the most Chinese of Buddhist schools. The ideals of the school later frequently found expression in a special kind of art, typically of broad surfaces of ink monochrome that suggest the sudden, intuitive, and individual awareness—without the secondary aid of either teacher or sacred text—that comes to the Ch'an devotee in moments of illumination.

133. b) Stone sculpture
Henry Moore's stone figures constitute the major 20th-century manifestation of the humanist tradition in sculpture. Much of his work is monumental, and he was particularly well known for a series of reclining nudes. Among his major commissions were sculptures for UNESCO headquarters in Paris (1957-58), for the Lincoln Center in New York City (1963-65), and for the East Building of the National Gallery of Art, Washington, D.C. (1978).

134. c) Expressionistic
El Greco was a master of Spanish painting, whose highly individual dramatic and expressionistic style met with the puzzlement of his contemporaries but gained newfound appreciation in the 20th century. He also worked as a sculptor and as an architect.

135. c) Woodrow Wilson
The memorial (6,000 ft [1,829 m]) is located in the Black Hills of southwestern South Dakota, U.S. Huge sculptures of the heads of presidents George Washington, Thomas Jefferson, Abraham Lincoln, and Theodore Roosevelt are carved in granite on the northeast side of Mt. Rushmore. The four heads, each about 60 ft high, represent, respectively, the nation's founding, political philosophy, preservation, and expansion and conservation.

136. b) Jazz dance
This social jazz dance was highly popular in the 1920s and frequently revived. Characterized by its toes-in, heels-out twisting steps, it was performed as a solo, with a partner, or in a group. Charleston music is in quick 4/4 time with syncopated rhythms. In the basic step the knees are bent, then straightened, as the ft pivot in and out. Weight is shifted from one leg to another, the free leg being kicked out from the body at an oblique angle. The basic step is often interspersed with strenuous movements, such as forward and backward kicks while travelling forward.

137. a) *Dhikr*
There is one outstanding example of pure dance: that of the whirling dervishes, an art that has been practised for more than seven centuries. The procedure is part of a Muslim ceremony called the *dhikr*, the purpose of which is to glorify God and seek spiritual perfection. The dervishes sit in a circle listening to music. Then, rising slowly, they move to greet the *shaykh*, or master, and begin to revolve rhythmically. The rhythm accelerates, and they whirl faster and faster. In

this way they enter a trance in an attempt to lose their personal identities and to attain union with the Almighty. Later they may sit, pray, and begin all over again. The *dhikr* ceremony always ends with a prayer and a procession.

138. c) Hat cheo
It is generally (though not always) played out-of-doors in the forecourt of a village communal house. It is basically satirical in intent. Performances are given by amateur touring groups whose acting is realistic, rather than stylized. The popular theatre repertoire includes plays with historical and legendary themes, social satires, and farces.

139. d) Greece
It was described by Lucian (*c.* AD 125-190) and is still danced today in many varieties in the Greek islands. Traditionally, it was danced by segregated lines of men and women, a youth leading the line of girls; lines now are frequently mixed. The dancers in the chain maintain a simple fundamental step, but the leader improvises, often breaking away from the line.

140. d) Swag
The distinction is sometimes made between a swag and a festoon by limiting the former to festoons entirely made up of folds of cloth. The ends of the swag are sometimes held by carved animals, such as bulls or lions, or they may simply be tied into bows with the ribbon ends hanging down.

Cinco de Mayo is celebrated by the Mexicans as an important symbolic victory for the country's independence against colonial invaders.

The Korean peninsula was settled by nomadic tribes from Manchuria and Siberia, who over time developed into the Korean people of today.

Did You Know?

Geography

1. b) Eratosthenes of Cyrene
The Greek perception of the Earth was highly advanced: the philosophers Pythagoras and Aristotle believed it to be a sphere, and the Pythagorean Philolaus taught that it revolved around a central fire. In the 3rd century BC Eratosthenes of Cyrene, who wrote *Geographica*, employed ingenious reasoning and measurements to produce a remarkably accurate calculation of the circumference of the Earth.

2. a) *Geography*
Strabo was the Greek geographer and historian whose *Geography* has numerous quotations from technical literature which provide a remarkable account of the state of Greek geographical science, as well as of the history of the countries it surveys.

3. c) Bernhardus Varenius
A major figure in the revival of geographic learning in Europe, Varenius's scholarly general geography remained the accepted standard authority for more than a century. After studying medicine, Varenius was attracted to geography by his acquaintance with geographers. In 1649 he published *Descriptio Regni Japoniae* ("Description of the Kingdom of Japan"), which included a Latin translation of an account of Siam (Thailand) and excerpts on religion in Africa. *Geographia generalis* (1650), his best-known work, not only was a systematic geography on a scale not previously attempted but also contained a scheme for special, now known as regional, geography.

4. a) *The Physical Geography of the Sea*
Maury Matthew Fontaine, a U.S. naval officer, pioneer hydrographer, was one of the founders of oceanography. In 1842, Maury was placed in charge of the Depot of Charts and Instruments, out of which grew the U.S. Naval Observatory and Hydrographic Office. To gather information on maritime winds and currents, Maury distributed to captains specially prepared logbooks from which he compiled pilot charts, enabling ships to shorten the time of sea voyages. In 1848 he published maps of the main wind fields of the Earth. Provided with worldwide information, Maury was able to produce charts of the Atlantic, Pacific, and Indian oceans. He also prepared a profile of the Atlantic seabed, which proved the feasibility of laying a transatlantic telegraph cable. In 1855 he published *The Physical Geography of the Sea*.

5. b) Carl Ritter
Viewing geography as an empirical science, Carl Ritter, the German geographer, maintained that its methodology required proceeding from one observation to the next, not from opinion or hypothesis to observation. Though he was convinced that there were laws of geography, he appeared to attach no particular importance to establishing them clearly. He stressed, instead, the importance of utilizing all the sciences to delineate the nature of geography, which was, in his view, unique.

6. b) Krakatoa
The Krakatoa winds are a layer of winds that encircle the Earth in the lower stratosphere, at

altitudes from about 20 to 40 km (12 to 25 miles), between latitudes 15° N and 15° S. They blow at velocities of about 25 to 50 m per second (55 to 110 miles per hour). They are alternately easterly and westerly, reversing about every 13 months. Their name comes from their role in transporting dust thrown into the atmosphere by the explosion (1883) of Krakatoa, a volcanic island in Indonesia.

7. c) Richard Burton

The English scholar-explorer and Orientalist (1821-1890) reached Ujiji, on the lake's eastern shore, in 1858, in his quest with John Hanning Speke for the source of the Nile River. They suffered almost every kind of hardship Africa could inflict. When they reached Lake Tanganyika, Burton was so ill with malaria he could not walk, and Speke was virtually blind.

8. a) Amazon River

The total length of the river—measured from the headwaters of the Ucayali-Apurimac river system in Peru—is about 6,400 km (4,000 miles). Its westernmost source is high in the Andes Mountains, within 161 km (100 miles) of the Pacific Ocean, and its mouth is in the Atlantic Ocean.

9. b) Grand Canyon

It lies in the southwestern portion of the Colorado Plateau, which is a large area of the southwestern United States consisting essentially of horizontal, layered rocks, and lava flows. The broad, intricately sculptured chasm of the canyon contains between its outer walls a multitude of imposing peaks, buttes, gorges, and ravines. It ranges in width from about 0.2 to 29 km (0.012-18 miles)

and extends in a winding course from the mouth of the Paria River, near Lees Ferry and the northern boundary of Arizona, to Grand Wash Cliffs, near the Nevada line, a distance of about 446 km (277 miles). Its greatest depths lie more than 1,800 m (about 6,000 ft) below its rim.

10. c) John Hanning Speke

The British explorer correctly identified Lake Victoria as a source of the Nile. On July 30, 1855, he reached the great lake, which he named in honour of Queen Victoria. On a second expedition (1860), he and James Grant mapped a portion of Lake Victoria. On July 28, 1862, Speke found the Nile's exit from the lake and named it Ripon Falls.

11. b) Lake Baikal

It is located in the southern part of eastern Siberia within the republic of Buryatia and Irkutsk oblast (province) of Russia. Lake Baikal is 20-25 million years old, as well as the deepest continental body of water, having a maximum depth of 1,620 m (5,315 ft). Its area is some 31,588 sq km (12,200 sq miles) and it is also the world's largest freshwater lake by volume, containing about one-fifth of the fresh water on the Earth's surface. Into Lake Baikal flow more than 330 rivers and streams, the largest of which include the Selenga, Barguzin, Upper (Verkhnyaya) Angara, Chikoy, and Uda.

12. c) Lakuga

A tributary of the Lualaba River in eastern Congo (Kinshasa), the Lakuga River issues from the western shore of Lake Tanganyika at Kalemie, Congo, and flows 320 km (200 miles) west to the Lualaba River 40 km

(25 miles) north of Kabalo. There are low-grade coal deposits along its tributaries, north of Kalemie and Moluba (former Greinerville).

13. d) Roald Amundsen
When the Norwegian explorer left Norway in June 1910, no one but his brother knew that he was heading for the South Pole instead of the North. He sailed the *Fram* directly from the Madeira Islands to the Bay of Whales, Antarctica, along the Ross Sea. The base he set up there was 100 km (60 miles) closer to the pole than the Antarctic base of the English explorer Robert Falcon Scott, who was heading a rival expedition with the same goal. Amundsen set out with 4 companions, 52 dogs, and 4 sledges on Oct. 19, 1911, and, after encountering good weather, arrived at the South Pole on December 14.

14. a) Playa
It is found in interior desert basins and adjacent to coasts within arid and semiarid regions, periodically covered by water that slowly filtrates into the ground water system or evaporates into the atmosphere, causing the deposition of salt, sand, and mud along the bottom and around the edges of the depression. Playas (Spanish: shore or beach) are among the flattest known landforms. Their slopes are generally less than 0.2 metre per kilometre. When filled with only a few centimetres of water, many kilometres of surface may be inundated. It is the process of inundation that develops and maintains the near-perfect flatness so characteristic of these arid-region landforms.

15. b) Lincoln Ellsworth
Fascinated with polar air exploration, Ellsworth, the American explorer, engineer, and scientist, financed and accompanied two such expeditions with the Norwegian explorer Roald Amundsen. On the first (1925) they reached latitude 87°44′N in two amphibian planes. The following year Ellsworth and the Italian explorer Umberto Nobile made the first crossing of the North Polar Basin in the dirigible *Norge*—a 5,463-km (3,393-mile) journey from Spitsbergen to Alaska that won worldwide acclaim. In 1931 Ellsworth made an 1,300-km (800-mile) canoe trip through central Labrador and later that year, for the American Geographical Society, made flights over Franz Josef Land and Novaya Zemlya—Arctic islands north of the Soviet Union.

16. b) Lake Tanganyika
It is the longest freshwater lake in the world (660 km [410 miles]) and the second deepest (1,436 m [4,710 ft]) after Lake Baikal in Russia. Comparatively narrow, varying in width from 16 to 72 km (10 to 45 miles), it covers about 12,700 sq miles (32,900 sq km) and forms the boundary between Tanzania and Congo (Kinshasa). Lake Tanganyika is situated on the line dividing the floral regions of eastern and western Africa, and oil palms, which are characteristic of the flora of western Africa, grow along the lake's shores. Rice and subsistence crops are grown along the shores, and fishing is of some significance. Hippopotamuses and crocodiles abound, and the bird life is varied.

17. c) Francisco de Orellana
The Spanish soldier is said to have given the river its name after reporting pitched battles with tribes of female warriors, whom he likened to the Amazons of Greek mythology. Although the name Amazon is conventionally employed for the entire river, in Peruvian and

Brazilian nomenclature it properly is applied only to sections of it. In Peru, the upper main stream down to Iquitos (Peru) is called Maranon (Portuguese: Maranhao), and from there to the Atlantic it is called Amazonas. In Brazil the name Solimoes is used from Iquitos to the mouth of the Negro River and Amazonas only from the Negro to the sea.

18. a) Isthmus
Unquestionably the two most famous are the Isthmus of Panama, connecting North and South America, and the Isthmus of Suez, connecting Africa and Asia. Isthmuses are of great importance in plant and animal geography because they offer a path for the migration of land plants and animals between the two land masses they connect.

19. a) 0° and 30° N-S
Trade winds are very steady winds that blow westward and toward the equator from the subtropical high-pressure belts at latitudes near 30° N and 30° S toward the intertropical convergence zone. It is stronger and more consistent over the oceans than over land and produces fairly clear skies that make trade-wind islands popular tourist resorts. Its average speed is about 5 to 6 m per second (11 to 13 miles per hour). The trade winds were named by the crews of ships that depended on the winds during westward ocean crossings.

20. c) Pampas
It is the vast plain extending westward across central Argentina from the Atlantic coast to the Andean foothills, bounded by the Gran Chaco (north) and Patagonia (south). It has a gradual slope from northwest to southeast, from about 500 m (1,640 ft) above sea level at

Mendoza to 106 m (66 ft) at Buenos Aires. Apart from a few sierras in the northwest and south, most of the region appears perfectly flat. Several smaller plains in other parts of South America, such as the desert of northern Chile, are also referred to by the term pampas.

21. c) Floodplain
They are produced by lateral movement of a stream and by overbank deposition; therefore they are absent where downcutting is dominant. Any erosional widening of one bank is approximately equalled by deposition on the opposite side of the channel in the form of bar development along the inside of meander bends. Thus, the simplest floodplain is made up of a strip of sinuous scrolls immediately adjacent to the stream.

22. a) Seamount
Smaller submarine volcanoes are called sea knolls, and flat-topped seamounts are called guyots. The sides of larger seamounts generally are concave upward and rarely slope more than 14°; smaller seamounts lack this concavity and can have sides as steep as 35°. In plan, seamounts tend to be elliptical or elongate, possibly because the lavas are extruded from linear rifts in the seafloor. A linear cluster of seamounts may result when several are fed by lava extruded from a single linear rift. Most Pacific seamounts occur in linear clusters or elongate groups of 10 to 100.

23. d) Angel Falls
They are located in the Guiana Highlands in Bolivar State, southeastern Venezuela, on the Churun River, 260 km (160 miles) southeast of Ciudad Bolivar. The cataract drops 979 m (3,212 ft) and is 150 m (500 ft) wide at the base. It leaps from a flat-topped plateau,

Auyan-Tepui ("Devils Mountain"), barely making contact with the sheer face. The falls, discovered in 1935, were named for James Angel, an American adventurer.

24. b) Lake Superior

The lakes drain roughly from west to east, emptying into the Atlantic Ocean. Except for Lakes Michigan and Huron, their altitudes drop with each lake, usually causing a progressively increasing rate of flow. Lake Superior, bordered by Ontario, the Upper Peninsula of Michigan, Wisconsin, and Minnesota, is the northernmost and westernmost lake and can be considered the headwater of the system.

25. c) Mudrocks

In terms of volume, mudrocks are by far the most important variety of sedimentary rock, probably constituting nearly 80 percent of the Earth's sedimentary rock column. Shale refers specifically to mudrocks that regularly exhibit lamination or fissility or both. Mudrocks are also loosely referred to as both lutites and pelites and as argillaceous sedimentary rocks.

26. d) Tien Shah

Stretching about 2,500 km (1,500 miles) from west-southwest to east-northeast, it mainly straddles the border between China and Kyrgyzstan and bisects the ancient territory of Turkistan. It is about 480 km (300 miles) wide in places at its eastern and western extremities but narrows to about 354 km (220 miles) in width at the centre. The Tien Shan also includes the Chu-Ili Mountains and the Qaratau Range, which extend far to the northwest into the Kazakstan lowlands. The total area of the Tien Shan is about 1,000,000 sq km (386,000 sq miles).

27. c) Flint Ridge Cave System

The caverns are interconnected to a great extent, and some of them have been explored. Flint Ridge is a plateau capped by resistant sandstone and shale layers, underlain by hundreds of ft of limestone. Acidic water has eaten into the limestone without affecting the overlying sandstone and shale, producing the underground caves. Prominent features within the caverns include extensive sulphate mineral formations, stalactites, stalagmites, and archaeological artefacts.

28. b) Aurora

Called aurora borealis, or northern lights, in the Northern Hemisphere and aurora australis, or southern lights, in the Southern Hemisphere, they are caused by the interaction of energetic particles (electrons and protons) from outside the atmosphere with atoms of the upper atmosphere. Such interaction occurs in zones surrounding the Earth's magnetic poles. During periods of intense solar activity, auroras occasionally extend to the middle latitudes. Auroras take many forms, including luminous curtains, arcs, bands, and patches. The uniform arc is the most stable form of aurora, sometimes persisting for hours without noticeable variation.

29. b) River terrace

A terrace results from any hydrological or climatic shift that causes renewed downcutting. It generally has a flat top made up of sedimentary deposits and a steep fore edge, and it may be the remains of an old floodplain, cut through by the river and left standing above the present floodplain level. Another type of terrace is cut into bedrock and may have a thin veneer of alluvium, or sedimentary deposits. In paired terraces, the terrace features on each side of a valley correspond.

30. d) Tidal bore
Travelling upstream about two or three times as fast as the normal tidal current, a bore usually is characterized by a well-defined front of one or several waves, often breaking, followed by the bore's main body, which rises higher than the water level at its front. The height of the bore is greater near the banks of a river than at midstream. Because of momentum, some bores continue to move upstream for about one-half hour after high water. Not arising in estuaries, tidal bores are formed at a position a short distance upstream, where the river channel has become sufficiently narrow or shallow to concentrate the momentum of the rising tide. Bores occur at spring tides and at several tides preceding and following spring tides but never at neap tides.

31. a) Kuroshio
The temperature and salinity of Kuroshio water are relatively high for the region, about 68° F (20° C) and 34.5 parts per thousand, respectively. Only about 400 m (1,300 ft) deep, the Kuroshio travels at rates ranging between 50 and 300 cm (20 and 120 inches) per second. Flowing past Taiwan (Formosa) and the Ryukyu Islands, the current skirts the east coast of Kyushu, where, during the summer, it branches west and then northeast through the Korea Strait to parallel the west coast of Honshu in the Sea of Japan as the Tsushima Current.

32. d) Cumulonimbus
Meteorologists classify clouds primarily by their appearance. The 10 main cloud families are divided into three groups on the basis of altitude. High clouds, which are found at mean heights of 13 to 5 km (45,000 to 16,500 ft), are, from highest to lowest, cirrus, cirrocumulus, and cirrostratus. Middle clouds, 7 to 2 km (23,000 to 6,500 ft), are altocumulus, altostratus, and nimbostratus. Low clouds, 2 to 0 km (6,500 to 0 ft), are stratocumulus, stratus, cumulus, and cumulonimbus.

33. c) Canada and Russia
China is the largest of all Asian countries and has the largest population of any country in the world. Occupying nearly the entire East Asian landmass, it stretches for about 5,000 km (3,100 miles) from east to west and 5,470 km (3,400 miles) from north to south and covers an area of about 9,572,900 sq km (3,696,100 sq miles), which is approximately one-fourteenth of the land area of the Earth. Among the major countries of the world, China is surpassed in area only by Russia and Canada, and it is almost as large as the whole of Europe.

34. c) El Nino
This event is associated with adverse effects on fishing, agriculture, and local weather from Ecuador to Chile and with far-field climatic anomalies in the equatorial Pacific and occasionally in Asia and North America as well. The name El Nino (Spanish: "The Christ Child"), was originally used during the 19th century by the fishermen of northern Peru in reference to the annual flow of warm equatorial waters southward around Christmas time. Peruvian scientists later noted that more

intense changes occurred at intervals of several years and were associated with catastrophic seasonal flooding along the normally arid coast, while the thermal anomalies lasted for a year or more. The more unusual episodes gained world attention during the 20th century, and the original annual connotation of the name was replaced by that of the anomalous occurrence.

35. a) China
Within China's boundaries exists a highly diverse and complex country. Its topography encompasses the highest and one of the lowest places on Earth, and its relief varies from nearly impenetrable mountainous terrain to vast coastal lowlands. China's climate ranges from extremely dry, desertlike conditions in the northwest to tropical monsoon in the southeast, and the country has the greatest contrast in temperature between its northern and southern borders of any nation in the world. The annual range of temperature between the extreme south and north is about 86° F (48° C).

36. c) Lake Michigan
The third largest of the five Great Lakes of North America, Lake Michigan is the only one wholly within the U.S. Bordered by the states of Michigan (east and north), Wisconsin (west), Illinois (southwest), and Indiana (southeast), it connects with Lake Huron through the Straits of Mackinac in the north.

37. b) Queensland
Cape York Peninsula lies in the northernmost extremity of Australia, projecting into Torres Strait between the Gulf of Carpentaria (west) and the Coral Sea (east). From its tip at Cape York it extends southward in Queensland for

about 800 km (500 miles), widening to its base, which spans 650 km (400 miles) from Cairns (east) to the Gilbert River (west).

38. c) Igneous
Granite is a coarse- or medium-grained intrusive igneous rock that is rich in quartz and feldspar. It is the most common plutonic rock of the Earth's crust, formed by the cooling of magma (silicate melt) at depth.

39. a) Indian Ocean
The subantarctic island lies about 1,900 km (1,200 miles) southeast of Cape Town and 19 km (12 miles) north-northeast of Marion Island and covers an area of 47 sq km (18 sq miles). Discovered in January 1772 by the French explorer Marion du Fresne, the island was given its present name by the British navigator James Cook, who explored the area in 1776. In the 19th and 20th centuries it was frequented by whaling ships and seal hunters. South Africa claimed the island in 1947, annexing it in 1948.

40. b) Oceanic ridge
The submarine mountain chain extends approximately to 80,000 km (50,000 miles) through all the world's oceans. Ridges separate the oceans into distinct basins and may or may not be seismically active. The seismically active oceanic ridge is approximately 60,000 km (37,200 miles) long and extends down the axis of the entire Atlantic Ocean, passing midway between Africa and Antarctica and turning north to the centre of the Indian Ocean, where it branches, the main ridge continuing midway between Australia, New Zealand, and Antarctica to cross the east side of the Pacific Basin, running all the way to the mouth of the Gulf of California.

The name Timur Lenk signified Timur the Lame, a title of contempt used by his Persian enemies, which became Tamburlaine, or Tamerlane, in Europe.

Euripides' only known public activity was his service on a diplomatic mission to Syracuse in Sicily.

Did You Know?

41. a) United States of America
Tornadoes strike in many areas of the world, but nowhere are they as frequent or as fierce as in the United States. More than 1,100, for example, were reported there during 1973 alone. Direct comparisons of relative tornado frequencies in various countries are biased because observational data are often lacking in sparsely settled regions. It appears, however, that Australia, where several hundred per year have been reported, has the dubious honour of second place. Other countries reporting tornadoes include, but are not limited to, Great Britain, Canada, China, France, Germany, The Netherlands, Hungary, India, Italy, Japan, and even Bermuda and the Fiji Islands.

42. c) Iraq
The easternmost country of the Arab world, it is located at about the same latitude as the southern United States. Called Mesopotamia ("Land Between the Rivers") in classical times, the region's extensive alluvial plains gave rise to the world's earliest civilizations. It became known as Iraq in the 7th century. Modern Iraq was created in the aftermath of World War I and gained independence in 1932.

43. a) Strait of Hormuz
The strait is 55 to 95 km (35 to 60 miles) wide and separates Iran (north) from the Arabian Peninsula (south). It contains the islands of Qeshm (Qishm), Hormuz, and Hengam (Henjam) and is of great strategic and economic importance, especially as oil tankers collecting from various ports on the Persian Gulf must pass through the strait.

44. b) Margarita Island
Discovered by Christopher Columbus in 1498, the island became known for its pearls. Through the centuries, settlements on the island were besieged by Indians (in reprisal for slave raids on the mainland) and by British pirates and Dutch forces. Its traders rendered assistance to the revolutionists in the struggle for independence from Spain. Simon Bolivar used the island as a base of operations in 1816, and the Spanish general Pablo Morillo was driven from its shores in 1817.

45. b) Cylindrical
Introduced in 1569 by Gerardus Mercator, it is often described as a cylindrical projection, but it must be derived mathematically. The meridians are equally spaced, parallel vertical lines, and the parallels of latitude are parallel, horizontal straight lines, spaced farther and farther apart as their distance from the Equator increases. This projection is widely used for navigation charts, because any straight line on a Mercator-projection map is a line of constant true bearing that enables a navigator to plot a straight-line course.

46. a) Wadi
A dry channel lying in a semiarid or desert area and subject to flash flooding during seasonal or irregular rainstorms. Such transitory streams, rivers, or creeks are noted for their gullying effects, especially for their rapid rates of erosion, transportation, and deposition. There have been reports of up to 2 m (8 ft) of deposition in 60 years and like amounts of erosion during a single flood event.

47. a) Atlantic Ocean
A cool, coastal desert, the Namib desert extends for 1,900 km (1,200 miles) along the Atlantic coast from Namibe in Angola southward across Namibia to the Olifants

River in the Cape Province of South Africa. It reaches inland 129-161 km (80 to 100 miles) to the foot of the Great Escarpment. The southern portion merges with the Kalahari on the plateau atop the escarpment. Its name is derived from the Nama language, implying "an area where there is nothing".

48. a) Loess
An unstratified, geologically recent deposit of silty or loamy material, Loess is usually buff or yellowish brown in colour and is chiefly deposited by the wind. Loess is a sedimentary deposit composed largely of silt-size grains that are loosely cemented by calcium carbonate. It is usually homogeneous and highly porous and is traversed by vertical capillaries that permit the sediment to fracture and form vertical bluffs. The word loess, with connotations of origin by wind-deposited accumulation, is of German origin and means "loose".

49. a) Monsoon
Any of a type of major wind system that seasonally reverses its direction—for example, one that blows for approximately six months from the northeast and six months from the southwest. The most prominent examples of such seasonal winds occur in southern Asia and in Africa. Monsoonal tendencies also are apparent along the Gulf Coast of the United States and in central Europe, as well as in various other areas.

50. a) Caldera
It is a large bowl-shaped volcanic depression more than 1 km (0.6 miles) in diameter and rimmed by infacing scarps. Calderas usually, if not always, form by the collapse of the top of a volcanic cone or group of cones because of

removal of the support formerly furnished by an underlying body of magma (molten rock).

51. a) Lake Superior
The deepest lake (mean depth 148 m [487 ft]), Lake Superior, lies at an altitude of 183 m (600 ft) above sea level, and discharges into Lake Huron through the St. Marys River at an average rate of 2,141 cu m (75,600 cu ft) per second.

52. a) Utah
A stretch of barren salt flats, it covers about 260 sq km (100 sq miles) in Tooele county, northwestern Utah, U.S. The flats, part of the Great Salt Lake Desert, are a remnant of the bed of an ancient lake formed about 30,000 years ago late in the Pleistocene Epoch and named for B.-L.-E. de Bonneville, an explorer and fur trader. The site of Bonneville Speedway, the extremely level, smooth flats are as solid as concrete by the summer's end and are ideally suited for speed trials; several world automobile and motorcycle speed and endurance records have been established there since 1935.

53. a) Tibet
This great massif occupies about one-fourth of the whole country. A large part of the plateau lies at elevations above 3,900-4,600 m (13,000-15,000 ft). The border ranges of the plateau are even higher, with individual peaks rising to heights of 7,000-7,900 m (23,000-26,000 ft).

54. c) Cape Horn
It is a steep, rocky headland on Hornos Island, Tierra del Fuego Archipelago, Magallanes region, southern Chile. Located off the southern tip of mainland South America,

The legend of the Trojan War is the most notable theme from ancient Greek literature and forms the basis of Homer's *Iliad*.

Blaise Pascal of France and Gottfried Wilhelm Leibniz of Germany invented mechanical digital calculating machines during the 17th century.

Did You Know?

Cape Horn was named Hoorn for the birthplace of the Dutch navigator Willem Corneliszoon Schouten, who rounded it in 1616. False Cape Horn (Falso Cabo de Hornos), on Hoste Island, 56 km (35 miles) northwest, is sometimes mistaken for it. Navigation of the rough waters around the Cape is hazardous. The climate is windy and cold year-round.

55. b) Subtropics and the temperate
The descending air in the subtropical high-pressure belts diverges near the surface; the air that does not flow equatorward flows eastward and poleward as the midlatitude westerlies. These extend to great altitudes and contain jet streams, high-velocity air currents around the 10-km (6-mile) level in both hemispheres. Poleward of 60° N and 60° S, the winds generally blow westward and equatorward as the polar easterlies. In the northern polar regions, where water and land are interspersed, the polar easterlies give way in summer to variable winds.

56. c) Arabian Sea
The Arabian Sea is bounded to the east by India, to the north by Pakistan and Iran, and to the west by the Arabian Peninsula and the Horn of Africa. It is located north of an imaginary line connecting Cape Comorin at the southern tip of India to Xaafuun (Hafun) Point, a peninsula on the eastern coast of Somalia. To the north, the Gulf of Oman connects the Arabian Sea with the Persian Gulf via the Strait of Hormuz. To the west, the Gulf of Aden connects it with the Red Sea via the Strait of Bab el-Mandeb. Nations bordering the sea include India, Pakistan, Iran, Oman, Yemen, and Somalia.

57. c) Turkmenistan
A great sandy region in Central Asia, Karakum Desert occupies about 70 percent of the area of Turkmenistan. The Turkmen Karakum is approximately 350,000 sq km (135,000 sq miles) in area, extending some 800 km (500 miles) from west to east and 480 km (300 miles) from north to south.

58. b) Copenhagen
It is located on the islands of Zealand and Amager. A small village existed on the site of the present city by the early 10th century. In 1167 Bishop Absalon of Roskilde built a castle on an islet off the coast and fortified the town with ramparts and a moat. In 1445 Copenhagen was made the capital of Denmark and the residence of the royal family. In the civil and religious conflicts of the Protestant Reformation, the town was often sacked.

59. c) Bend in a river or stream
An extreme U-bend in a stream, usually occurring in a series, meanders are most often formed in alluvial materials (stream-deposited sediments) and thus freely adjust their shapes and shift downstream according to the slope of the alluvial valley. A meandering channel commonly is about one and one-half times as long as the valley, and it exhibits pools in the meander bends and riffles in the reaches between the meanders. The length of a meander generally ranges from seven to ten times the channel width.

60. a) Bandar-e-Abbas
The "Port of Abbas" was established in 1623 by Shah Abbas I to replace the city of Hormuz, which had been captured by the Portuguese in about 1514. During the 17th

Did You Know?

Sunflowers are looked upon as weeds when growing in cultivated fields or on grazing land of the Great Plains of North America but as wild flowers in uncultivated valleys. The sunflower also is a crop plant cultivated for its seeds; in some places it is a garden flower.

century it was the main port of Persia, but it lost this status in the 18th century to the rival port of Bushehr (Bandar-e Bushehr). From about 1793 Bandar-e Abbas was under lease to the rulers of Muscat, but in 1868 Iran cancelled the contract and resumed direct control.

61. b) Alaska
A volcanic peak of the Aleutian Range, it is about 930 km (580 miles) southwest of Anchorage, on the west side of Pavlof Bay, near the southwestern tip of the Alaska Peninsula, southwestern Alaska, U.S. Pavlof is one of the tallest volcanoes in Alaska (2,515 m [8,250 ft]). It is also one of the most consistently active, having had more than 40 eruptions recorded since 1760.

62. d) Philippines
Called the world's most perfect cone, the volcano has a base 130 km (80 miles) in circumference and rises to 2,421m (7,943 ft) from the shores of Albay Gulf. Popular with climbers and campers, it is the centre of the Mayon Volcano National Park. There are large abaca plantations on its lower slopes. There have been more than 30 eruptions recorded since 1616. Its most destructive eruption was in 1814, when the town of Cagsawa was buried.

63. b) Mount Etna
An active volcano on the east coast of Sicily, the name comes from the Greek Aitne, from *aitho*, "I burn". Etna is the highest active volcano in Europe, its topmost elevation being more than 3,200 m (10,000 ft). Like other active volcanoes, its height varies: in 1865, for example, the volcanic summit was 52 m (170 ft) higher than it was in the late 20th century.

Etna covers an area of 1,600 sq km (600 sq miles); its base has a circumference of about 150 km (93 miles).

64. d) Deep, sunken river valley drowned by the sea
A funnel-shaped estuary that occurs at a river mouth and is formed by the submergence of the lower portion of the river valley. Generally occurring along a rugged coast perpendicular to a mountain chain, many rias were formed by the rise in sea level after the melting of the vast continental glaciers. Rias are commonly very irregular and may have several branching tributaries; they usually are the major drainage systems of the adjacent areas. Their widening funnel shape and steadily increasing depth seaward usually cause an exaggerated tidal effect within the estuary.

65. b) Portugal
An archipelago of volcanic origin in the North Atlantic Ocean, Madeira Island belongs to Portugal and comprises two inhabited islands, Madeira and Porto Santo, and two uninhabited groups, the Desertas and the Selvagens. The islands are the summits of mountains that have their bases on an abyssal ocean floor. Administratively they form the autonomous region of Madeira. The islands have a combined land area of 794 sq km (306 sq miles).

66. b) Margarita Island
An island in the Caribbean Sea, 19 km (12 miles) north of the Peninsula de Araya in northeastern Venezuela, it is also known as the Isle of Pearls. Margarita is the largest of 70 islands comprising Nueva Esparta state. In reality two islands joined by a low, narrow isthmus, Margarita is about 65 km (40 miles)

long, covers an area of 1,072 sq km (414 sq miles), and has a coastline of 319 km (198 miles), with many natural harbours. The island is generally low, but the highest elevation, in the Cerros (mountains) del Macanao, reaches 760 m (2,493 ft).

67. b) Alexander von Humboldt
The German naturalist and explorer was a major figure in the classical period of physical geography and biogeography—areas of science now included in the earth sciences and ecology. With his book *Kosmos* he made a valuable contribution to the popularization of science. The Humboldt Current off the west coast of South America was named after him.

68. c) Lake Titicaca
Lying at 3,810 m (12,500 ft) above sea level in the Andes Mountains of South America, astride the border between Peru to the west and Bolivia to the east, Titicaca is the second largest lake of South America (after Maracaibo). It covers some 8,300 sq km (3,200 sq miles) and extends in a northwest-to-southeast direction for a distance of 190 km (120 miles). In 1862 the first steamer to ply the lake was prefabricated in England and carried in pieces on muleback up to the lake. Today vessels make regular crossings from Puno, on the Peruvian shore, to the small Bolivian port of Guaqui.

69. d) Central Asia
The great desert and semidesert region of Central Asia stretches across vast lands in the Mongolian People's Republic and the Inner Mongolia autonomous ch'u (region) of China. The Gobi occupies a large arc-shaped area oriented east-west that is approximately 1,600

km (1,000 miles) long, 480 to 965 km (300 to 600 miles) wide, and concave to the north. Its total area is about 1,300,000 sq km (500,000 sq miles).

70. c) Chile
The cool, arid region in northern Chile, the desert is 1,000 to 1,100 km (600 to 700 miles) long from north to south. Its limits are not exact, but it lies mainly within Antofagasta and Atacama administrative regions between the south bend of the Loa River and the mountains separating the Salado-Copiapo drainage basins. To the north, the desert continues into the region of Tarapaca and to the border of Peru.

71. a) Dome-shaped hill with an ice core
A pingo is formed in a permafrost area when the hydrostatic pressure of freezing groundwater causes the upheaval of a layer of frozen ground. Pingos may be up to 90 m (about 300 ft) high and over 800 m (about 2600 ft) across and are usually circular or oval. The core, which may be only slightly smaller than the pingo itself, consists of a lens of clear, injected ice.

72. a) Greenland
The island's major physical feature is its massive ice sheet, which is second only to Antarctica's in size. The ice sheet has an average thickness of 1,500 m (5,000 ft), reaches a maximum of about 3,000 m (10,000 ft), and covers more than 1,813,000 sq km (700,000 sq miles), or nearly 85 percent of Greenland's total land area.

73. b) Arctic Ocean
Centring approximately on the North Pole, the Arctic Ocean and its marginal seas (the

Chukchi, East Siberian, Laptev, Kara, Barents, White, Greenland, and Beaufort; some oceanographers also include the Bering and Norwegian Seas) are the least-known basins and bodies of water in the world ocean owing to their remoteness, hostile weather, and perennial or seasonal ice cover.

74. b) Mariana trench
A trench is any long, narrow, steep-sided depression in the ocean bottom in which maximum oceanic depths (approximately 7,300 to 11,000 m [24,000 to 36,000 ft]) occur. Mariana Trench lies east of the Mariana Islands in the western North Pacific Ocean.

75. d) Nile
The longest river of Africa and of the world, the Nile rises in highlands south of the equator and drains into the Mediterranean Sea. The Nile River basin covers about one-tenth of the area of the African continent. The Nile's remotest headstream rises as the Kagera River in the eastern African lakes region of Burundi and flows northward, passing through or forming part of the boundaries of Tanzania, Rwanda, and Uganda before entering Lake Victoria from the west.

76. c) Arctic Ocean
Those conducting oceanic research generally recognize the existence of three major oceans, the Pacific, Atlantic, and Indian. As an approximation, the Arctic Ocean may be regarded as an estuary of the Atlantic Ocean. The major circulation into and from the Arctic Basin is through a single deep channel, the Fram Strait, which lies between the islands of Spitsbergen and Greenland.

77. a) Bering Strait
Although the mean inflow seems to be driven by a slight difference in sea level between the North Pacific and Arctic oceans, a large source of variability is induced by the wind field, primarily large-scale atmospheric circulation over the North Pacific.

78. c) Antarctica
The unique weather and climate of Antarctica provide the basis for these appellations. By far the coldest continent, Antarctica has winter temperatures that range from -128.6° F (-89.2° C), the world's lowest recorded temperature, measured at Vostok Station (Russia) on July 21, 1983, on the high inland ice sheet to -76° F (-60° C) near sea level. Temperatures vary greatly from place to place, but direct measurements in most places are generally available only for summertime.

79. c) Strait of Gibraltar
The channel lies between southernmost Spain and northwesternmost Africa. It is 58 km (36 miles) long and narrows to 8 miles (13 km) in width between Point Marroqui (Spain) and Point Cires (Morocco). The strait's western extreme is 43 km (27 miles) wide between the capes of Trafalgar (north) and Spartel (south), and the eastern extreme is 23 km (14 miles) wide between the Pillars of Hercules—which have been identified as the Rock of Gibraltar (north) and Mount Hacho, just east of Ceuta, a Spanish enclave in Morocco (south). The strait is an important gap, averaging 365 m (1,200 ft) in depth in the arc formed by the Atlas Mountains of North Africa and the high plateau of Spain.

It is believed that *Homo erectus* used wood for fire at least 750,000 years ago. The oldest evidence of the use of wood for construction, found at the Kalambo Falls site in Tanzania, dates from some 60,000 years ago.

A well-known English Elizabethan bed is the Great Bed of Ware (Victoria and Albert Museum, London), which is 3.33 m (10 feet 11 inches) square.

Did You Know?

80. d) Cuba
The capital, major port, and leading commercial centre of Cuba, Havana also constitutes one of Cuba's 14 provinces. Located on the island's north coast, Havana is the largest city in the Caribbean region and has one of the great treasuries of historic colonial preserves in the Western Hemisphere. Prior to 1959, when Fidel Castro came to power, it was a mecca for tourists from the United States, who were drawn by the city's many attractions, which included climate and nightlife in addition to history.

81. d) Baas Strait
The channel separates Victoria, Australia, from the island of Tasmania on the south. Baas Strait's maximum width is 240 km (150 miles), its depth is 50-70 m (180-240 ft). King Island and the Indian Ocean lie at its western extremity, and the Furneaux Group is at its eastern end. Banks Strait is the southeastern opening to the Tasman Sea.

82. a) Reelfoot Lake
The shallow lake lies on the boundary between Lake and Obion counties in northwestern Tennessee, U.S.A. In the upheaval, land on the east side of the Mississippi River sank, creating a depression that the Mississippi rushed in to fill.

83. a) Russia
With an area of 17,075,400 sq km (6,592,800 sq miles), Russia is the world's largest country, covering almost twice the territory of either the United States or China. It ranks sixth in the world in population, following China, India, the United States, Indonesia, and Brazil. The great majority of the people are Russians,

but there also are some 70 smaller national groups living within its borders.

84. b) Rocky
A large tributary of the Mississippi River, the Arkansas River rises in the Sawatch Range of the Rocky Mountains near Leadville in central Colorado, U.S., and flows generally east-southeastward for 2,350 km (1,460 miles) through Kansas, Oklahoma, and Arkansas before entering the Mississippi 64 km (40 miles) northeast of Arkansas City, Arkansas. It has a total fall of 3,475 m (11,400 ft), and its drainage basin covers 417,000 sq km (161,000 sq miles).

85. d) Lake Huron
A channel connecting Lake Michigan (west) and Lake Huron (east), the Straits of Mackinac form an important waterway between the Upper and Lower peninsulas of Michigan, U.S. Spanned by the Mackinac Bridge and underwater oil pipelines, the straits are 6 km (4 miles) wide and approximately 48 km (30 miles) long and include the passage between several islands in northwestern Lake Huron. Discovered by Jean Nicolet in 1634, the straits played a prominent role in the fur trade and defence of the upper Great Lakes and Canada.

86. a) California
The San Andreas fault is a major fracture of the Earth's crust, trending northwestward through southern and northern California, U.S., for 1,050 km (650 miles) and passing seaward in the vicinity of San Francisco. Movement along this transform fault is of the strike-slip type and is characterized by occasional large earthquakes originating near the surface along the path of the fault.

Did You Know?

The main reason people are addicted to nicotine, and that rats will push a lever to inject themselves with it, is that nicotine causes the release of a large amount of the neurotransmitter dopamine in the parts of the brain normally associated with pleasure, according to Alan Leshner, director of the National Institute on Drug Abuse.

87. b) Panama Canal

As early as the 16th century, the Spanish recognized the advantages of a canal across the Central American isthmus. Eventually, two routes came to be considered, one through Panama and the other through Nicaragua. Impetus for selecting the route through Panama increased with the construction (by the United States) of the Panama Railroad in the mid-19th century, which closely followed the eventual route of the canal.

88. c) Kilauea

Located on southeastern Hawaii Island, Hawaii, U.S., it is the central feature of Hawaii Volcanoes National Park. Kilauea ("Much Spreading") is an elongated dome built of lava eruptions from a central crater and from lines of craters extending along east and southwest rifts, or fissures.

89. d) A water-bearing stratum

In hydrology, an aquifer is a rock layer that contains water and releases it in appreciable amounts. The rock contains water-filled pore spaces, and, when the spaces are connected, the water is able to flow through the matrix of the rock. An aquifer also may be called a water-bearing stratum, lens, or zone.

90. c) The water in them is confined and under pressure

An artesian well is a man-made spring from which water flows under natural pressure without pumping. It is dug or drilled wherever a gently dipping, permeable rock layer (such as sandstone) receives water along its outcrop at a level higher than the level of the surface of the ground at the well site. At the outcrop the water moves down into the aquifer (water-bearing layer) but is prevented from leaving it by impermeable rock layers (such as shale) above and below it. Pressure from the water's weight (hydrostatic pressure) forces water to the surface of a well drilled down into the aquifer; the pressure for the steady upflow is maintained by the continuing penetration of water into the aquifer at the intake area.

91. b) Deflation

In geology, deflation is the erosion of loose material from flat areas of dry, uncemented sediments such as those occurring in deserts, dry lake beds, floodplains, and glacial outwash plains. Clay and silt-sized particles are picked up by turbulent eddies in wind and may be carried for hundreds of kilometres; they later settle to form loess deposits.

92. d) Mississippi

The river drains with its major tributaries an area of approximately 3,100,000 sq km (1,200,000 sq miles), or about one-eighth of the entire continent. It lies entirely in the United States. Rising in Lake Itasca in Minnesota, it flows almost due south across the continental interior, collecting the waters of its major tributaries, the Missouri and the Ohio, approximately halfway along its journey to the Gulf of Mexico.

93. a) Plateau of Tibet

It is a vast, high plateau in Central Asia and part of China in which the Tibet Autonomous Region, Tsinghai province, western Szechwan province, and southern Uighur Autonomous Region of Sinkiang are located. It is a region of tangled mountains that rise 4,000 to 5,000 m (13,000 to 15,000 ft).

94. d) Bushveld

Savanna vegetation is found in Africa, South America, India, the Myanmar-Thailand region, Madagascar, and Australia. African savanna grasses are either high grasses (1.5 to 4.5 m [5 to 15 ft] tall) or short grasses (30 cm [about 1 foot] tall). The trees in African savanna are usually thorny and small-leaved; many are species of acacia. Groups of trees such as palms or cactuslike Euphorbia species and single trees such as baobabs are also common.

95. c) Mt. Koussi
The mountain (3,415 m [11,204 ft]) is situated 176 km (109 miles) north-northwest of Faya in the Tibesti massif, northwestern Chad. It is an extinct volcano with a crater approximately 19 km (12 miles) wide and 1,200 m (4,000 ft) deep.

96. b) Indonesia
Krakatoa is on Pulau (island) Rakata in the Sunda Strait between Java and Sumatra, Indonesia. Its eruption in 1883 was one of the most catastrophic in history. Sometime within the past 1,000,000 years, the volcano built a cone-shaped mountain composed of flows of volcanic rock alternating with layers of cinder and ash. From its base, 300 m (1,000 ft) below sea level, the cone projected about 6,000 ft above sea level. Later, the mountain's top was destroyed, forming a caldera or bowl-shaped depression, 4 miles (6 km) across.

97. d) Flinders Island
The first permanent white settlement was made in Tasmania in 1803. The whites treated the Aborigines as subhumans, seizing their hunting grounds, depleting their food supply, attacking the women, and killing the men. Tasmanian attempts to resist were met with the superior weaponry and force of the

Europeans. Between 1831 and 1835, in a final effort at conciliation and to prevent the extermination of the approximately 200 remaining Tasmanians, the Aborigines were removed to Flinders Island.

98. b) David Livingstone
The Zambezi, in south central Africa, was not known at all until, in the mid-19th century, the Scottish missionary-explorer David Livingstone crossed the Kalahari from the south, found Lake Ngami, and, hearing of populous areas farther north, came upon the river in midcourse. On a great exploratory journey from 1852 to 1856, the main purpose of which was to expose the slave trade, he first travelled upstream, crossed the watershed between the tributaries of the upper Zambezi and those of the lower Congo, and reached the west coast at Luanda, Angola. From there a year's march brought him back to his starting point near the falls that the Africans called "smoke does sound" but that Livingstone prosaically renamed the Victoria Falls.

99. c) Volga
The continent's longest, and the principal waterway of western Russia, Volga river's basin, sprawling across about two-fifths of the European part of Russia, contains almost half of the entire population of the Russian Republic. The Volga's immense economic, cultural, and historic importance—along with the sheer size of the river and its basin—ranks it among the world's great rivers.

100. c) Belize
The coral reef is second in size to the Great Barrier Reef of Australia and the largest of its kind in the Northern and Western

---

Did You Know?

Using data collected from satellites, scientists have been watching parts of the Earth's crust bounce back slowly after being loaded down with massive ice sheets eons ago during the last Ice Age.

Ice cream evolved from flavoured ices that were popular with the Roman nobility in the 4th century BC.

hemispheres. Extending for more than 290 km (180 miles) along the Carribean coast of Belize, it maintains an offshore distance ranging from about 300 m (1,000 ft) in the north to 40 km (25 miles) in the south, except at Rocky Point, where it meets the shoreline.

101. a) Chain of volcanoes
A nearly continuous chain of volcanoes that surrounds the Pacific Ocean, it passes along the west coast of North and South America, from the Aleutian Islands to the south of Japan, and from Indonesia to the Tonga Islands, and to New Zealand. The Pacific Basin is underlain by separate lithospheric plates that diverge from one another and that are being subducted beneath the margins of the basin at different rates. This Circum-Pacific chain of volcanoes (often called the Ring of Fire) and the mountain ranges associated with it owe their formation to the repeated subduction of oceanic lithosphere beneath the continents and the islands that surround the Pacific Ocean.

102. c) Qatar
A country on the western coast of the Persian Gulf, occupying a peninsula of Arabia, Qatar projects northward into the gulf for about 180 km (100 miles) and has a maximum width of 90 km (50 miles). Its 56 km (35 miles) of land boundaries meet those of Saudi Arabia and the United Arab Emirates, and it has 560 km (350 miles) of coastline. The capital city is Doha (Ad-Dawhah) on the east coast.

103. d) Pyrenees
A mountain chain of southwestern Europe, the Pyrenees stretches 430 km (270 miles) from the shores of the Mediterranean Sea on the east to the Bay of Biscay of the Atlantic Ocean on the west. It has a maximum width of about 160 km (100 miles) at its centre. The permanently snow-capped central Pyrenees includes the highest point—the Aneto Peak at 3,404 m (11,169 ft).

104. d) Timor Sea
It is an arm of the Indian Ocean, lying southeast of the island of Timor, Indonesia, and northwest of Australia. A maximum depth of more than 3,300 m (10,800 ft) is reached in the Timor Trough in the north, but more than half of the sea has a depth of less than 650 ft (200 m). The Timor Sea is the site of an important oil field.

105. c) Algae
The discolouration of seawater is caused by dynoflagellates (phylum Protozoa), during periodic blooms (or population increases). Toxic substances released by these organisms into the water may be lethal to fish and other marine life. Red tides, or red waters, occur worldwide in warm seas. The red tide along the Northumberland coast in England in 1968 was the cause of the death of many sea birds. Similar red tides, caused by Gonyaulax polyedra, have occurred off the California and Portuguese coasts.

106. c) U.S.A.
Puerto Rico is a commonwealth in free association with the United States; its residents are U.S. citizens. According to the constitution of 1952, executive power resides in the governor, who is elected directly for a term of four years. In addition, Puerto Rico is represented in the U.S. Congress by a nonvoting resident commissioner who is directly elected for a four-year term. The

United States is responsible for the commonwealth's defence.

107. c) Australia

An island in the Indian Ocean, south of the island of Java and northwest of Australia, it is administered as an external territory of Australia. The main settlement and chief port is at Flying Fish Cove on the northeastern part of the island. First sighted in 1615 by Richard Rowe, master of the Thomas, the island was named on Christmas Day 1643 by Captain William Mynors of the British East India Company.

108. b) Tanzania

The wildlife refuge is best known for its huge herds of plains animals (especially gnu [wildebeests], gazelles, and zebras), and it is the only place in Africa where vast land-animal migrations still take place. The park, an international tourist attraction, was added to the UNESCO World Heritage List in 1981.

109. c) Cave

It is found in the island of Capri near the southern entrance to the Bay of Naples, Napoli province, in southern Italy. Stone artefacts have been found in one of the caves with which the rocky shores of Capri abound; the most notable of these is the Blue Grotto (Grotta Azzurra), rediscovered in 1826 and accessible only by boat. Sunlight entering through the water that fills most of the entrance gives it an extraordinary blue light, whence its name.

110. b) Indian Ocean

It is the fourth largest island in the world—after Greenland, New Guinea, and Borneo—with a surface area of 587,041 sq km (226,658 sq miles). Located in the southwestern Indian Ocean, it is separated from the African coast by the 400-km- (250-mile-) wide Mozambique Channel.

111. a) Egypt

The arid Libyan Desert (Eastern Saharan) basin in northwestern Egypt, the Qattara depression covers about 18,100 sq km (7,000 sq miles) and contains salt lakes and marshes. It descends to 133 m (435 ft) below sea level. During World War II, because it was impassable to military traffic, the depression formed a natural anchor at the southern end of the British defence lines at El-Alamein against the final advance of Field Marshal Rommel's German army in July 1942. In the late 1970s oil deposits were discovered in the southern part of the depression.

112. b) Black Sea

The Sea of Azov is an inland sea situated off the southern shores of Ukraine and Russia. It forms a northern extension of the Black Sea, to which it is linked on the south by the Kerch Strait. The Sea of Azov is about 340 km (210 miles) long and 135 km (85 miles) wide and has an area of about 37,600 sq km (14,500 sq miles). Into the Sea of Azov flow the great Don and Kuban rivers and many lesser ones such as the Mius, the Berda, the Obitochnaya, and the Yeya.

113. a) Myanmar and Thailand

The Isthmus of Kra is the narrow neck of southern Myanmar and Thailand, connecting the Malay Peninsula to the Asian mainland. The isthmus lies between the Gulf of Thailand to the east and the Andaman Sea to the west. It is 40-48 km (25-30 miles) wide at its

Did You Know?

The cooking of soup is as ancient as the devising of vessels to hold liquid; before the development of pots that could withstand the direct heat of a fire, soups were cooked by dropping hot stones into the liquid.

narrowest point, between Chumphon and Kra Buri (both in Thailand). Kra Buri, for which it was named, is at the head of the Pakchan River estuary, an inlet of the Andaman Sea.

114. a) James Cook

Between July 1772 and July 1775 Cook made what ranks as one of the greatest sailing ship voyages, with a small former Whitby ship, the *Resolution*, and a consort ship, the *Adventure*. He found no trace of Terra Australis, though he sailed beyond latitude 70° S in the Antarctic, but he successfully completed the first west-east circumnavigation in high latitudes, charted Tonga and Easter Island during the winters, and discovered New Caledonia in the Pacific and the South Sandwich Islands and South Georgia Island in the Atlantic.

115. d) Murray River

Although the river has a total catchment area of 1,072,905 sq km (414,253 sq miles), its average annual discharge is only 0.89 cu m (31 cu ft) per second, and in places it has dried up on at least three occasions. Named after Colonial Secretary Sir George Murray, the river rises on The Pilot (a mountain), near Mount Kosciusko in southeastern New South Wales. It flows west and northwest, passes through Hume Reservoir above Albury, and forms most of the boundary between New South Wales and Victoria.

116. c) Cook Strait

The strait separates the North and South islands of New Zealand. Treacherous currents and fierce storms present serious hazards to navigation, and travel from Wellington (North Island) to Blenheim (South Island) is chiefly by rail ferry and air. Communications and electric-power cables follow the strait's floor.

117. b) Africa

The Cape of Good Hope is a rocky promontory at the southern end of Cape Peninsula, South Africa. It was first sighted by the Portuguese navigator Bartolomeu Dias in 1488. One historical account says that Dias named it Cape of Storms and that John II of Portugal renamed it Cape of Good Hope (because its discovery was a good omen that India could be reached by sea from Europe); other sources attribute its present name to Dias himself.

118. c) California

The Redwood National Park in the northwestern corner of California, U.S., was established in 1968, and designated a World Heritage site in 1980. Preserving virgin (old-growth) groves of ancient redwood trees, including the world's tallest tree, the park also features 64 km (40 miles) of scenic coastline. Redwoods are the tallest living trees; they often exceed 90 m (300 ft) in height, and one has reached 112.1 m (367.8 ft). Their trunks reach typical diameters of 3 to 6 m (10 to 20 ft) or more, measured above the swollen bases. The redwood tree takes 400 to 500 years to reach maturity, and some trees are known to be more than 1,500 years old.

119. d) Zimbabwe

It is bordered on the north by Zambia, on the northeast and east by Mozambique, on the south by South Africa, and on the southwest and west by Botswana, and its extreme western corner touches Namibia. The capital is Harare (formerly Salisbury).

There are no reptiles in the Arctic Zone owing to the absence of frost-free winter refuges, but one amphibian, the wood frog, does penetrate just north of the tree line in Arctic Canada.

The helicopter was one of the earliest apparatus conceived for flying.

Did You Know?

120. b) Wladimir Koppen

The German botanist-climatologist developed the most popular (but not the first) of these vegetation-based classifications. Koppen's classification is based on a subdivision of terrestrial climates into five major types, which are represented by the capital letters A, B, C, D, and E. Each of these climate types, except for B, is defined by temperature criteria. Type B designates climates in which the controlling factor on vegetation is dryness (rather than coldness).

121. c) Philadelphia

The fourth largest city in the United States and the largest in Pennsylvania, Philadelphia displays many characteristics of a small town. Its many trees, parks, and other open spaces and its quiet pace of life reflect in various ways the genteel Quaker heritage bestowed on the city by its founder, William Penn. Nearly everywhere are dignified reminders of the colonial and revolutionary city and of Benjamin Franklin, a Philadelphian by adoption, who left his imprint on innumerable ongoing institutions.

Did You Know?

At the court of Montezuma, the Aztec ruler of Mexico, in 1519, Hernan Cortes was served xacoati, a bitter cocoa-bean drink, which he introduced to Spain. Sweetened, flavoured with cinnamon and vanilla, and served hot, the beverage remained a Spanish secret for almost a hundred years before its introduction to France.

History

1. c) Nepal
The British conquest of India in the 19th century posed a serious threat to Nepal—which expected to be another victim—and left the country with no real alternative but to seek an accommodation with the British to preserve its independence. This was accomplished by the Rana family regime after 1860 on terms that were mutually acceptable.

2. a) Tan'gun
The mythological first king of the Koreans, he was the grandson of Hwanin, the creator, and the son of Hwanung, who fathered his child by breathing on a beautiful young woman. Tangun reportedly became king in 2333 BC.

3. b) Borobudur
A massive Buddhist monument in central Java, Indonesia, 26 miles (42 km) northwest of Yogyakarta. The Borobudur monument combines the symbolic forms of the *stupa* (a Buddhist commemorative mound usually containing holy relics), the temple mountain (based on Mount Meru of Hindu mythology), and the *mandala* (a mystic Buddhist symbol of the universe, combining the square as Earth and the circle as heaven). The style of Borobudur was influenced by Indian Gupta and post-Gupta art. The monument was designated a UNESCO World Heritage site in 1991. Borobudur was constructed between about AD 778 and 850, under the Shailendra dynasty. It was buried under volcanic ash from about AD 1000 and overgrown with vegetation until discovered by the English lieutenant governor, Thomas Stamford Raffles, in 1814.

4. d) Hong Kong
Hong Kong developed initially on the basis of its excellent natural harbour. It is a special administrative region of China located to the east of the Pearl River (Chu Chiang) estuary on the south coast of China.

5. c) Ferdinand Marcos
The Philippine lawyer and politician, as head of state from 1966 to 1986, established an authoritarian regime in the Philippines that came under criticism for corruption and for its suppression of democratic processes. Marcos fled the country on February 25, 1986, at the urging of the United States, and went into exile in Hawaii.

6. a) Kim Il Sung
Originally called Kim Song Ju, the communist was the leader of North Korea from 1948 until his death in 1994. He was the nation's premier from 1948 to 1972, chairman of its dominant Korean Workers' (Communist) Party from 1949, and president and head of state from 1972.

7. b) Pol Pot
Originally called Saloth Sar, the Khmer political leader's totalitarian regime (1975-79) imposed severe hardships on the people of Cambodia. His radical communist government forced the mass evacuations of cities, killed or displaced millions of people, and left a legacy of brutality and impoverishment.

8. c) The Dalai Lama
The Potala Palace is an immense religious and administrative complex situated atop Mar-po-ri (Red Mountain), 425 feet (130 m)

The number of deaths due to small pox in the 20th century represents more deaths during this time period than all the military and civilian casualties of wars, all those who died from AIDS, and all the lives lost due to the 1918 swine flu pandemic.

The sawfish, the only animal with true teeth outside its mouth, uses the teeth on both sides of its snout to slash its prey.

Did You Know?

above the Lhasa River valley in Lhasa, Tibet Autonomous Region, China. Within it the Potrang Karpo (the White Palace) once served as the seat of the Tibetan government and the main residence of the Dalai Lama; from the mid-18th century it was used as a winter palace. Potrang Marpo (the Red Palace) houses several chapels, sacred statues, and the tombs of eight Dalai Lamas. It remains a major pilgrimage site for Tibetan Buddhists.

9. d) Singapore
The British East Indian administrator and founder of the port city of Singapore (1819) was largely responsible for the creation of Britain's Far Eastern empire. He was knighted in 1816. On the morning of Jan. 29, 1819, he landed on the shore of a sparsely populated island off the southern tip of Malaya and, risking imminent collision with the Dutch, established by treaty the port of Singapore.

10. c) Adam's Peak
A mountain in southwestern Sri Lanka (Ceylon), 2,243 m (7,360 ft) high and 11 miles (18 km) northeast of Ratnapura, Adam's Peak is located in the Sri Lanka hill country. Its conical summit terminates in an oblong platform about 22 m by 7 m (74 ft by 24 ft), on which there is a large hollow resembling the print of a human foot, 1m 63 cm (5 ft 4 in) by 76 cm (2 ft 6 in). The depression is venerated alike by Buddhists, Muslims, and Hindus, who regard it as the footprint of the Buddha, Adam, and Shiva, respectively. Many pilgrims of all faiths visit the peak every year. Heavy chains on the mountain's southwestern face, said to have been placed there by Alexander the Great, mark the route to the summit.

11. b) Zahir Shah
Last king of Afghanistan from 1933 to 1973, Zahir Shah provided an era of stable government to his country. In a bloodless coup on July 17, 1973, Zahir Shah was deposed. The leader of the coup, General Mohammad Daud Khan (the king's brother-in-law), proclaimed Afghanistan a republic with himself as its president. Zahir Shah formally abdicated on Aug. 24, 1973.

12. b) Benigno Aquino
Aquino was the chief opposition leader during the era of martial law in the Philippines (1972-81) under President Ferdinand E. Marcos. Two years after martial law was lifted in the Philippines, he flew home, intending to campaign in promised elections. He was shot in the head while leaving the airplane at Manila Airport under security guard.

13. a) Mohammad Reza Shah Pahlavi
The Shah of Iran from 1941 to 1979, Pahlavi maintained a pro-Western foreign policy and fostered economic development in Iran. Widespread dissatisfaction among the lower classes, the Shiite clergy, the bazaar merchants, and students led, in 1978, to the growth of support for the Ayatollah Ruhollah Khomeini, a Shiite religious leader living in exile in Paris. Rioting and turmoil in Iran's major cities brought down four successive governments; on Jan. 16, 1979, the Shah left the country, and Khomeini assumed control. Although the Shah did not abdicate, a referendum resulted in the declaration, on April 1, 1979, of an Islamic republic in Iran.

14. b) Yom Kippur War
On Oct. 6, 1973, the Jewish holy day of Yom Kippur (thus "Yom Kippur War"), Israel was

---

Human hair grows at a rate of about 13 mm (0.5 inch) per month.

South America and Australia have no wild oxen.

Bambuti, a group of pygmies of the Ituri Forest of eastern Congo (Kinshasa), are the shortest group of pygmies in Africa, averaging under 4 feet 6 inches (137 cm) in height.

attacked by Egypt across the Suez Canal and by Syria on the Golan Heights. The Arab armies showed greater aggressiveness and fighting ability than in the previous wars, and the Israeli forces suffered heavy casualties. The Israeli army, however, pushed its way into Syrian territory and encircled the Egyptian Third Army by crossing the Suez Canal and establishing forces on its west bank. Israel and Egypt signed a ceasefire agreement in November and, on Jan. 18, 1974, they signed peace agreements.

15. c) Sarawak
A historic state that is now a part of Malaysia, Sarwak comprises the northwestern part of the island of Borneo and is bounded by the British protectorate of Brunei and Sabah (Malaysia) on the north and by Indonesian Borneo (Kalimantan) on the east and south. Sarawak was ruled by the Brooke Raj (1841-1946), a dynasty of British rajas, for a century.

16. c) The Gang of Four
These most powerful members of a radical political elite were convicted for implementing the harsh policies directed by Communist Party chairman Mao Zedong during the Cultural Revolution of the 1960s and early 1970s. The group included Mao's third wife, Jiang Qing, and Wang Hongwen, Zhang Chunqiao, and Yao Wen-yuan.

17. d) Prophet Muhammad
The Hashimite kings are any of the Arab descendants, either direct or collateral, of the prophet Muhammad, from among whom came the family that created the 20th-century Hashimite dynasty headed by the king of Jordan.

18. b) North and South Korea
The 38th parallel of latitude in East Asia roughly demarcates North and South Korea. The line was chosen by US military planners at the Potsdam Conference, in July 1945, as an army boundary, north of which the USSR was to accept the surrender of the Japanese forces in Korea and south of which the Americans were to accept the Japanese surrender. The line was intended as a temporary division of the country, but the onset of the Cold War led to the establishment of a separate US-oriented regime in South Korea under Syngman Rhee and a communist regime in North Korea under Kim Il-sung.

19. c) Zulfikar Ali Bhutto
The Pakistani statesman, president (1971-73), and prime minister (1973-77), was a popular leader who was overthrown and executed by the military. The government was seized by General Mohammad Zia-ul-Haq, the army chief of staff, on July 5, 1977. Soon afterward Bhutto was imprisoned. He was sentenced to death (March 18, 1978) on the charge of having ordered the assassination of a political opponent in 1974; after an appeal to a higher court, Bhutto was hanged, despite appeals for clemency from several world leaders.

20. c) Charles Barry
In 1835 a design competition was held for the new Houses of Parliament building, also called Westminster Palace, to replace the one destroyed by fire in 1834. Barry won the contest in 1836, and the project occupied him for the rest of his life. With the help of Augustus Welby Northmore Pugin, Barry

Vultures are widely distributed in temperate and tropical regions but absent from Australia and most oceanic islands.

Charon is the only known natural satellite of Pluto. It is unusually close to the planet and so had been obscured by the glare of its light.

Did You Know?

designed a composition ornamented in the Gothic Revival style and featuring two asymmetrically placed towers. The complex of the Houses of Parliament (1837-60) is Barry's masterpiece.

21. c) Anwar el-Sadat
The Egyptian army officer and politician was president of Egypt from 1970 until his death. He was assassinated by extremists while reviewing a military parade commemorating the Arab-Israeli war of October 1973.

22. c) Golda Meir
She was a founder and the fourth prime minister (1969-74) of the State of Israel. Meir was elected to the Knesset (Israeli parliament) in 1949 and served in that body until 1974. She was appointed foreign minister in 1956. Shortly after retiring from the Foreign Ministry in January 1966, she became secretary general of the Mapai Party and supported Prime Minister Levi Eshkol in intraparty conflicts. After Israel's victory in the Six-Day War (June 1967) against Egypt, Jordan, and Syria, Golda Meir helped merge Mapai with two dissident parties into the Israel Labour Party. Upon Eshkol's death in 1969, Meir became prime minister. She resigned as prime minister in April 1974.

23. b) Bhutan
In 1953 a national assembly known as the Tshogdu was established in Bhutan through the king's initiative. It has 151 members who are elected by village headmen or are chosen by the king and the country's official Buddhist monastic order. The Tshogdu meets twice a year and passes legislation enacted by the king.

24. c) Israel
The Knesset ("Assembly") is the unicameral parliament of Israel and supreme authority of that state. The first Knesset opened in Jerusalem on Feb. 16, 1949, and on the same day elected Chaim Weizmann (1874-1952) the first president of Israel.

25. c) Timur
The mausoleum in Samarkand, now in Uzbekistan, of the 14th-century Mongol conqueror Timur, or Tamerlane, still survives though it has suffered from time and earthquakes. It consists of a chapel crowned with a dome, enclosed by a wall, and fronted by an archway. The interior walls are covered with elegant turquoise arabesques and inscriptions in gold.

26. b) Yi Sun-shin
The Korean admiral and national hero's naval victories were instrumental in repelling Japanese invasions of Korea in the 1590s. The *Kobukson* is thought to have been the first ironclad battleship in history. Its upper deck was covered with armoured plates to protect its crew, and spikes and knives were attached to the plates to discourage enemies from boarding. The ship's bow was equipped with a dragon head through which cannon could be fired and clouds of smoke could be emitted to obscure the ship's position. Cannon and guns could also be fired from the stern and the sides of the ship.

27. d) Sukarno
He was leader of the Indonesian independence movement and Indonesia's first president (1949-66), who suppressed the country's original parliamentary system in favour of an authoritarian "Guided Democracy" and who attempted to balance the Communists against

the army leaders. He was deposed in 1966 by the army under Suharto.

28. a) Consuls
Rather than restoring their king, the Romans replaced the kingship with two annually elected magistrates called consuls. The two consuls were primarily generals whose task it was to lead Rome's armies in war. In times of military emergency, when unity of command was sometimes necessary, Rome appointed a dictator in place of the consuls, who, however, could not hold supreme military command for longer than six months.

29. c) Angkor Wat
The temple complex was built in the 12th century by King Suryavarman II (reigned 1113-c. 1150) in present-day Cambodia. The city was oriented around a central mountain or pyramid temple (symbolic of Mount Meru, home of the gods) that was an architectural adaptation and completion of the one natural hill in the area, the Phnom Bakheng. In a similar manner, the central structure of each temple reflected the position of Mount Meru.

30. a) Revolutionary
Emiliano Zapata was a Mexican revolutionary, champion of agrarianism, who fought in guerrilla actions during and after the Mexican Revolution (1911-17). In the course of his campaigns, Zapata distributed lands taken from the haciendas, which he frequently burned without compensation. He often ordered executions and expropriations, and his forces did not always abide by the laws of war. But underneath his picturesque appearance—drooping moustache, cold eyes, big sombrero—was a passionate man with simple ideals that he tried to put into practice. The Zapatistas avoided battle by adopting guerrilla tactics. They farmed their land with rifles on their shoulders, went when called to fight, and returned to their ploughs at the end of a battle or skirmish.

31. b) Auschwitz
Located near the industrial town of Oswieecim in Galicia, southern Poland, the Auschwitz group of camps—I, II, and III— was one of the main sites used by the Nazis to carry out their "final solution", the annihilation of European Jews. Auschwitz was designated a UNESCO World Heritage site in 1979.

32. d) Franklin Roosevelt
He led the United States through two of the greatest crises of the 20th century: the Great Depression and World War II. In so doing, he greatly expanded the powers of the federal government through a series of programmes and reforms known as the New Deal, and he served as the principal architect of the successful effort to rid the world of German National Socialism and Japanese militarism.

33. a) Mukden
The final land battle of the land war was fought at Mukden in late February and early March 1905, between Russian forces totalling 330,000 men and Japanese totalling 270,000. After long and stubborn fighting and heavy casualties on both sides, the Russian commander, General A.N. Kuropatkin, broke off the fighting and withdrew his forces northward from Mukden, which fell into the hands of the Japanese.

Eddie Eagen, boxer and bobsledder, was the only athlete to win gold medals at both the Summer and Winter Olympics.

The first Tarzan story appeared in 1912, followed in 1914 by *Tarzan of the Apes.*

The English term cafe, borrowed from the French, derives ultimately from the Turkish *kahve,* meaning coffee.

Did You Know?

34. c) Zaire
Congo was known as Zaire, an attempt by then-ruler Mobutu Sese Seko to return to the source of the nation's identity and authenticity. After Mobutu's overthrow in 1997, however, the name of the country before 1971, the Democratic Republic of the Congo, was restored. "Zaire" is a variation of traditional African names for great rivers and specifically the Congo River, whose basin lies almost entirely within the republic. The river was named during the colonial period for the kingdom of the Kongo people, who inhabit the area along the river's mouth on the Atlantic Ocean.

35. b) Mary I
Also called Mary Tudor, she was the first queen to rule England (1553-58) in her own right. She was known as Bloody Mary for her persecution of Protestants in a vain attempt to restore Roman Catholicism in England.

36. d) Russia
In 1904 Japanese ships attacked the Russian fleet at Port Arthur without warning. In the Russo-Japanese War (1904-05) that followed, Japanese arms were everywhere successful; the most spectacular victory occurred in the Tsushima Strait, where the ships of Admiral Togo Heihachiro destroyed the Russian Baltic fleet. But the war was extremely costly in Japanese lives and treasure, and Japan was relieved when U.S. President Theodore Roosevelt offered to mediate a peace settlement.

37. d) Prime Minister of Great Britain
Benjamin Disraeli was a British statesman and novelist who was twice prime minister (1868, 1874-80) and who provided the Conservative Party with a twofold policy of Tory democracy and imperialism.

38. a) Elizabeth I
She was queen of England (1558-1603) during a period, often called the Elizabethan Age, when England asserted itself vigorously as a major European power in politics, commerce, and the arts.

39. a) Victoria
Victoria ascended the throne on June 20, 1837, at the age of eighteen. On Feb. 10, 1840, she married her cousin, Prince Albert. He was titled Prince Consort, but he had the greatest influence on Victoria's decisions. In essence, she turned power over to him.

40. d) Albion
It was used by ancient Greek geographers from the 4th century BC and even earlier, who distinguished "Albion" from Ierne (Ireland) and from smaller members of the British Isles. The Greeks and Romans probably received the name from the Gauls or the Celts. The name Albion has been translated as "white land"; and the Romans explained it as referring to the chalk cliffs at Dover (Latin *albus,* "white").

41. a) Seretse Khama
The first president of Botswana (1966-80), after the former Bechuanaland protectorate gained independence from Great Britain, Khama promoted his ideal of a multiracial democracy. He achieved free universal education in Botswana and sought to diversify and strengthen the country's economy. He was reelected to successive terms and served as president of Botswana until his death.

Did You Know?

The first cafe is said to have opened in 1550 in Constantinople.

The first so-called hot-dog stand, selling sausages as a sandwich on what was to become the standard long hot-dog bun, was opened at Coney Island, New York, in 1916.

Frankfurters are named for Frankfurt am Main, Germany, the city of their origin, where they were sold and eaten at beer gardens.

42. b) Edward William Stafford

Landowner and statesman, he served three times as prime minister of New Zealand (1856-61, 1865-69, 1872). The son of a landed Irish family, Stafford was elected superintendent of Nelson province (1853) and representative from Nelson to the General Assembly (1855). Stafford's next ministry (1865-69) was primarily concerned with the problem of New Zealand's dependence on British troops. Stafford's third ministry lasted less than a month (Sept. 6 to Oct. 4, 1872).

43. b) Kent

In 597 the monk Augustine led a mission from Rome to Kent; Kent was the first English kingdom to be converted to Christianity. The Christian church provided another unifying influence, overriding political divisions, although it was not until 669 that the church in England acknowledged a single head.

44. b) Clement Attlee

Labour won 393 seats, almost double the Conservative total of 213 and far more than it had expected. On July 26, 1945, as soon as the results were clear, Churchill resigned and Attlee became prime minister.

45. a) April 1949

The North Atlantic Treaty Organization was developed to implement the North Atlantic Treaty, which came into force on Aug. 24, 1949. It sought to establish a military counterweight to the Soviet military presence in post-World War II eastern Europe. NATO continued thereafter as the primary collective-defence agreement of the Western powers in opposition to communist forces in Europe.

46. b) Charles I

Charles was shy and physically deformed. He had a speech defect that made his pronouncements painful for him and his audiences alike. Charles had not been raised to rule. His childhood had been spent in the shadow of his brother, Prince Henry, who had died in 1612, and Charles had little practical experience of government. He was introverted and clung tenaciously to a few intimates.

47. b) French Revolution

The revolutionary movement shook France between 1787 and 1799 and reached its first climax there in 1789. Although historians disagree on the causes of the Revolution, the following reasons are commonly adduced: (1) the increasingly prosperous elite of wealthy commoners—merchants, manufacturers, and professionals, often called the bourgeoisie—resented its exclusion from political power and positions of honour; (2) the peasants were acutely aware of their situation and were less and less willing to support the anachronistic and burdensome feudal system; (3) the Philosophes, who advocated social and political reform, had been read more widely in France than anywhere else; (4) French participation in the War of Independence had driven the government to the brink of bankruptcy; and (5) crop failures in much of the country in 1788, coming on top of a long period of economic difficulties, made the population particularly restless.

48. b) Marie Antoinette

Queen consort of King Louis XVI of France (1774-93), Marie Antoinette was known to be frivolous, imprudent, and prodigal. An enemy of reform, she contributed to the popular unrest that led to the Revolution and to the overthrow of the monarchy in August 1792. Popular hatred of the Queen provided impetus to the insurrection that overthrew the monarchy on Aug. 10, 1792. Marie Antoinette spent the remainder of her life in Parisian prisons. Louis XVI was executed on orders from the National Convention in January 1793, and the Queen was brought before the Revolutionary tribunal on Oct. 14, 1793, and guillotined two days later.

49. b) A political group
The most famous political group of the French Revolution, the club became identified with extreme equalitarianism and violence, which led the Revolutionary government from mid-1793 to mid-1794. The Jacobins originated as the Club Breton at Versailles. The group was reconstituted as the Society of the Friends of the Constitution, but it was commonly called the Jacobin Club because its sessions were held in a former convent of the Dominicans, who were known in Paris as Jacobins. Its purpose was to protect the gains of the Revolution against a possible aristocratic reaction.

50. b) Britain
In the period 1760 to 1830 the Industrial Revolution was largely confined to Britain. Aware of their head start, the British forbade the export of machinery, skilled workers, and manufacturing techniques. The British monopoly could not last forever, especially since some Britons saw profitable industrial opportunities abroad, while continental European businessmen sought to lure British know-how to their countries.

51. a) Arnold Toynbee
Although used earlier by French writers, the term Industrial Revolution was first popularized by the English economic historian Arnold Toynbee (1852-83) to describe England's economic development from 1760 to 1840. His lectures on the economic history of the Industrial Revolution in Britain proved widely influential. The collection of his lectures, published posthumously as *The Industrial Revolution* in 1884, was one of the first economic histories of Britain's industrial development in the 18th and 19th centuries.

52. a) February Revolution
In the first stage of the Russian Revolution of 1917, the monarchy was overthrown and replaced by the Provisional Government. This government, intended as an interim stage in the creation of a permanent democratic-parliamentary polity for Russia, was in turn overthrown by the Bolsheviks in October (November, new style) of the same year. The October (November) Revolution, sometimes called the Bolshevik Revolution, established the Soviet Communist government in Russia.

53. d) Trinity
The plutonium weapon was fired at 5:29:45 AM (local time) on July 16, 1945, at the Alamogordo Bombing Range in south central New Mexico. The test produced an energy, or yield, equivalent to 21,000 tons of TNT.

54. c) Mao Zedong
The Cultural Revolution was launched by Chinese Communist Party chairman Mao Zedong during his last decade in power (1966-76) to renew the spirit of the Chinese

revolution. Mao ultimately adopted four goals for the cultural revolution: to replace his designated successors with leaders more faithful to his current thinking; to rectify the Chinese Communist Party; to provide China's youths with a revolutionary experience; and to achieve some specific policy changes to make the educational, health care, and cultural systems less elitist.

55. b) George Washington
An American general and commander-in-chief of the colonial armies in the American Revolution (1775-83), Washington's administration of the government was marked by the caution, the methodical precision, and the sober judgment that had always characterized him. He regarded himself as standing aloof from party divisions. He had a firm belief that the United States must insist on its national identity, strength, and dignity.

56. b) George Washington
Formerly called the Executive Mansion, the White House is the official residence of the president of the United States at 1600 Pennsylvania Avenue in Washington, D.C. The White House and its landscaped grounds occupy 18 acres (7.2 hectares) of ground. The main building has been the home of every U.S. president since John Adams, the second president of the United States, and is the oldest federal building in the capital.

57. c) Theodore Roosevelt
In 1791 a public competition was held to choose the most suitable design for a presidential residence in the newly designated capital city of Washington. The Irish-American architect James Hoban of Philadelphia won the commission with his plan for a Georgian

mansion in the Palladian style. By 1809 it was already called the "White House" because its white-grey sandstone contrasted strikingly with the red brick of nearby buildings. In 1902, President Theodore Roosevelt adopted "White House" as the building's official name.

58. b) Grover Cleveland
The 22nd and 24th president of the United States (1885-89 and 1893-97), Cleveland distinguished himself as one of the few truly honest and principled politicians of the Gilded Age. His view of the president's function as primarily that of blocking legislative excesses made him quite popular during his first term, but that view cost him public support during his second term when he steadfastly denied a positive role for government in dealing with the worst economic collapse the nation had yet faced.

59. a) Dolley Madison
American First Lady and wife of James Madison, fourth U.S. president, Dolley's legendary charm, warmth, and ingenuity contributed to her considerable popularity. When British troops occupied and burned Washington, D.C., in August 1814, Dolley Madison acted quickly in salvaging a Gilbert Stuart portrait of George Washington and many important state documents before fleeing.

60. d) Rutherford Hayes
He was the first president to hold office (1877-81) by decision of an extraordinary commission appointed to rule on contested electoral ballots. An economic depression and Northern disenchantment with Reconstruction policies in the South combined to give Hayes's Democratic

It has been estimated that if the oceans of the world were completely dried up they would yield at least 4.5 million cu miles of rock salt, about 14.5 times the bulk of the entire continent of Europe above the high-water mark.

The Dead Sea, which covers an area of 394 sq miles (1,020 sq km), contains approximately 12,650,000,000 tons of salt.

Did You Know?

opponent, Samuel J. Tilden, a popular majority, and early returns indicated a Democratic victory in the electoral college as well. However, Hayes's campaign managers challenged the validity of the returns from South Carolina, Florida, and Louisiana, and as a result two sets of ballots were submitted from the three states. On March 2, 1877, a special Electoral Commission voted to award all the contested electoral votes to Hayes, who was thus elected with 185 electoral votes to Tilden's 184. The result was greeted with outrage and bitterness by some Northern Democrats, who thereafter referred to Hayes as "His Fraudulency".

61. a) John F. Kennedy
Nominated on the first ballot, he balanced the Democratic ticket by choosing Lyndon B. Johnson as his running mate. In his acceptance speech Kennedy declared, "We stand on the edge of a New Frontier."

62. c) John F. Kennedy
He was the youngest man ever elected up to that time to the presidency of the United States. Kennedy was also the first Roman Catholic to to be elected to the post. His administration lasted 1,037 days. From the onset he was concerned with foreign affairs. In his memorable inaugural address he called upon Americans "to bear the burden of a long twilight struggle...against the common enemies of man: tyranny, poverty, disease, and war itself."

63. b) Henry Bacon
The stately monument in Washington, D.C. honours President Abraham Lincoln and "the virtues of tolerance, honesty, and constancy in the human spirit". Designed by Henry Bacon on a plan similar to that of the Parthenon in Athens, the structure includes 36 columns of Colorado marble surrounding the building, one for each state that comprised the Union in Lincoln's time. The colossal seated statue of Lincoln, composed of Georgia white marble and resting on a pedestal of Tennessee marble, was designed by Daniel Chester French and carved by the Piccirilli brothers of New York; it dominates the interior and looks eastward across a reflecting pool at the Washington Monument and Capitol.

64. a) Imposition of poll tax
Also called Wat Tyler's Rebellion, its immediate cause was the imposition of the unpopular poll tax, which brought to a head the economic discontent that had been growing since the middle of the century. The rebellion drew support from several sources and included well-to-do artisans and villeins as well as the destitute. Probably the main grievance of the agricultural labourers and urban working classes was the Statute of Labourers (1351), which attempted to fix maximum wages during the labour shortage following the Black Death.

65. b) Thomas Jefferson
Draftsman of the Declaration of Independence, Jefferson was the first secretary of state (1789-94), second vice president (1797-1801), and the third president of the United States (1801-09). An early advocate of total separation of church and state, he also was the founder and architect of the University of Virginia and the most eloquent American proponent of individual freedom as the core meaning of the American Revolution.

66. b) John Adams and Thomas Jefferson
Jefferson could not attend the celebrations of the 50th anniversary of the proclamation of the Declaration of Independence because of illness. His old friend John Adams was nearing death in Massachusetts. Both wanted badly to live until the 50th anniversary of the day that symbolized the central endeavour and achievement of their lives. They succeeded. Jefferson passed away in his bed at Monticello at about half-past noon on July 4, 1826. His last conscious words, uttered the preceding evening, were, "Is it the Fourth?" More remarkably, up in Quincy on that same day his old rival and friend also managed to die on schedule. John Adams passed away later in the afternoon. His last words, "Thomas Jefferson still lives", were wrong at the moment but right for the future, since Jefferson's complex legacy was destined to become the most resonant and controversial touchstone in all of American history.

67. c) James Madison
He was the fourth president of the United States (1809-17) and one of the founding fathers of his country. At the Constitutional Convention (1787) he influenced the planning and ratification of the U.S. Constitution and collaborated with Alexander Hamilton and John Jay in the publication of *The Federalist Papers.* As a member of the new House of Representatives, he sponsored the first 10 amendments to the Constitution.

68. a) Ronald Reagan
The son of a shoe salesman, Reagan graduated from Eureka College, Illinois, in 1932. He then became a radio sports announcer in Iowa. In 1937, he began a long career as a motion-picture actor, eventually appearing in about 50 films, notably including *Knute*

Rockne—All American (1940), *Kings Row* (1942), and *The Hasty Heart* (1950).

69. b) Reinhard Heydrich
He masterminded the fake "Polish" attack on the Gleiwitz radio transmitter that provided Hitler with a pretext for invading Poland on Sept. 1, 1939. Heydrich also organized the Einsatzgruppen, mobile killing squads that murdered almost one million Soviet and Polish Jews in the occupied territories. On July 31, 1941, Hermann Goring commissioned Heydrich to carry out a "final solution of the Jewish question", authorizing him to take all organizational and administrative measures necessary for the extermination of the Jews. Less than a year later, two Free Czech agents bombed and shot him while he was riding in his car without an armed escort.

70. c) Martin Van Buren
Eighth president of the United States (1837-41), Buren was one of the founders of the Democratic Party. He was known as the "Little Magician" because of his reputed cunning and skill as a politician.

71. c) James Abram Garfield
On July 2, 1881, after only four months in office, the 20th president of the United States (March 4-Sept. 19, 1881), Garfield was shot at the railroad station in Washington, D.C., by Charles J. Guiteau, a disappointed office seeker. For 80 days the president lay ill and performed only one official act—the signing of an extradition paper. The president passed away on September 19.

72. a) William Henry Harrison
The ninth president of the United States, Harrison's successful Indian campaigns, while

a territorial governor and army officer, thrust him into the national limelight and led to his election in 1840. He was the first chief executive to die in office, after only one month's service.

73. a) Benjamin Franklin
With the pseudonym Richard Saunders, Benjamin Franklin (1706-1790) was an American printer and publisher, author, inventor and scientist, and diplomat. Next to George Washington, Franklin was possibly the most famous 18th-century American. By 1757 he had made a small fortune, established the Poor Richard of his almanacs (written under his pseudonym) as an oracle on how to get ahead in the world, and become widely known in European scientific circles for his reports of electrical experiments and theories. He was then just at the beginning of a long career as a politician, in the course of which he would be chief spokesman for the British colonies in their debates with the king's ministers about self-government and would have a hand in the writing of the Declaration of Independence, the securing of financial and military aid from France during the American Revolution, the negotiation of the treaty by which Great Britain recognized its former 13 colonies as a sovereign nation, and the framing of the Constitution, which for more than two centuries has been the fundamental law of the United States of America.

74. c) Emma Lazarus
The American poet and essayist is best known for her sonnet "The New Colossus", written to the Statue of Liberty. "The New Colossus" remains a most moving and eloquent expression of an American ideal: "Give me your tired, your poor," the sonnet concludes,

"Your huddled masses yearning to breathe free, / The wretched refuse of your teeming shore. / Send these, the homeless, tempest-tost to me, / I lift my lamp beside the golden door!"

75. a) Adolf Hitler
Leader of the National Socialist (Nazi) Party (from 1920/21) and dictator of Germany (1933-45), Hitler (1889-1945) was officially chancellor (*Kanzler*) from Jan. 30, 1933, and, after President Paul von Hindenburg's death, assumed the twin titles of *Fuhrer* and chancellor (Aug. 2, 1934).

76. c) Abraham Lincoln
Among American heroes, Lincoln continues to have a unique appeal for his fellow countrymen and also for people of other lands. This charm derives from his remarkable life story—the rise from humble origins, the dramatic death—and from his distinctively human and humane personality as well as from his historical role as saviour of the Union and emancipator of the slaves. His relevance endures and grows especially because of his eloquence as a spokesman for democracy.

77. b) *Mein Kampf*
The political manifesto *Mein Kampf* was Adolf Hitler's only complete book. It was published in two volumes in 1925 and 1927, with an abridged edition appearing in 1930. By 1939 it had sold 5,200,000 copies and had been translated into 11 languages.

78. a) Fourteen Points
On Jan. 8, 1918, President Wilson, in his address to the joint session of the United States Congress, formulated under 14 separate

heads his ideas of the essential nature of a post-World War I settlement. On Oct. 3-4, 1918, Prince Maximilian of Baden, the German imperial chancellor, sent a note, via Switzerland, to President Wilson, requesting an immediate armistice and the opening of peace negotiations on the basis of the Fourteen Points.

79. b) League of Nations
The organization for international cooperation was established at the end of World War I. During the war influential groups in the U.S. and Britain had urged the creation of such a body, and U.S. President Woodrow Wilson strongly favoured the idea as a means of preventing another destructive world conflict. A league covenant, embodying the principles of collective security (joint action by League members against an aggressor), arbitration of international disputes, reduction of armaments, and open diplomacy, was formulated and subscribed to by the Allies at the Paris Peace Conference (1919).

80. c) Erwin Rommel
The German field marshal (1891-1944) is best known for his spectacular victories as commander of the Afrika Korps in World War II. In February 1941, Rommel was appointed commander of the German troops dispatched to aid the all but defeated Italian army in Libya. The deserts of North Africa became the scene of his greatest successes—and of his defeat at the hands of a vastly superior enemy. In the North African theatre of war, the "Desert Fox", as he came to be called by both friend and foe because of his audacious surprise attacks, acquired a formidable reputation, and soon Hitler, impressed by such successes, promoted him to field marshal.

81. d) Woodrow Wilson
An American scholar and statesman, Woodrow Wilson (1856-1924) led his country into World War I. Later, he seized the initiative on war aims with his Fourteen Points speech of January 8, 1918, in which he promised a liberal, nonpunitive peace and a league of nations. Determined to keep those promises, Wilson made the controversial decision to go in person to the Paris Peace Conference. The final product, the Treaty of Versailles, was signed on June 28, 1919. The treaty's financial and territorial terms severely compromised Wilson's aims, but those were offset by its inclusion of the Covenant of the League of Nations, which he believed would adjust international differences and maintain peace.

82. b) Hermann Goering
He was a leader of the Nazi Party and one of the primary architects of the Nazi police state in Germany. Goering's sole concern in the Reichstag was to stultify the democratic system, which the Reichstag ostensibly represented up to March 1933. Goering used his position as minister of the interior in Prussia, Germany's largest and most influential state, to Nazify the Prussian police and establish the Gestapo, or secret political police. He also established concentration camps for the "corrective treatment" of difficult opponents.

83. b) Benito Mussolini
He was Italy's youngest prime minister (1922-43) till then and the first of 20th-century Europe's fascist dictators. Anxious to demonstrate that he was not merely the leader of Fascism but also the head of a united Italy, he presented to the king a list of ministers, a

majority of whom were not members of his party. He made it clear, however, that he intended to govern authoritatively. He obtained full dictatorial powers for a year; and in that year he pushed through a law that enabled the Fascists to secure a majority in the Chamber. The elections in 1924, though undoubtedly fraudulent, secured his personal power.

84. c) Heinrich Himmler
He was a highly effective administrator and a ruthless and adroit power seeker who was slavishly devoted to Hitler. He combined a penchant for philosophical mysticism with a cold-blooded, fanatical adherence to the Nazi racist ideology, with the result that he was the prime architect of the Holocaust. More than any other individual, Himmler was the man who created the network of state terror by which the Third Reich suppressed its opposition, eliminated its internal enemies, and compelled obedience from the German citizenry.

85. a) Graf (Count) von Stauffenberg
The most stalwart conspirator in the July plot, he personally carried out the assassination attempt. Stauffenberg succeeded in placing a bomb in Hitler's headquarters at Rastenburg (July 20, 1944), which, however, failed to kill the dictator. A planned simultaneous coup in Berlin likewise miscarried.

86. b) Otto Von Bismarck
The prime minister of Prussia (1862-1890), Bismarck was the founder and first chancellor (1871-90) of the German Empire. Once the empire was established, he actively and skillfully pursued pacific policies in foreign affairs, succeeding in preserving the peace in Europe for about two decades. But his greatest achievement, the German Empire, only survived him by 20 years. Although he had united Germany in one sense, he had failed to create an internally unified people.

87. c) James Madison
Reentering the Virginia legislature in 1784, he persuaded the states-rights advocate John Tyler to sponsor the calling of the Annapolis Convention of 1786, which, aided by Madison's influence, produced the Constitutional Convention of 1787. There his Virginia, or large-state, Plan, put forward through Governor Edmund Randolph, furnished the basic framework and guiding principles of the Constitution, earning him the title of father of the Constitution. Madison believed keenly in the value of a strong government in which power was well controlled because it was well balanced among the branches.

88. a) North Atlantic Treaty Organization
The organization was developed to implement the North Atlantic Treaty, signed on April 4, 1949 (and entered into force on August 24, 1949), which sought to establish a military counterweight to the Soviet military presence in post-World War II eastern Europe. NATO continued thereafter as the primary collective-defence agreement of the Western powers in opposition to communist forces in Europe. Its members include Belgium, Canada, the Czech Republic, Denmark, France, Germany (or West Germany, 1955-90), Greece, Hungary, Iceland, Italy, Luxembourg, The Netherlands, Norway, Poland, Portugal, Spain, Turkey, the United Kingdom, and the United States. All

Did You Know?

The platypus finds its food chiefly in underwater mud; it consumes daily nearly its own weight in crustaceans, fishes, frogs, mollusks, tadpoles, and earthworms.

The first known ventriloquist as such was Louis Brabant, valet to the French king Francis I in the 16th century.

were original signatories except Greece and Turkey, which joined in February 1952, West Germany, which joined in May 1955, Spain, which joined in May 1982, and the Czech Republic, Hungary, and Poland, which joined in March 1999. France withdrew from the integrated military command of NATO in 1966, though it remained a member of the organization.

89. c) United Nations

This international organization was established by charter on Oct. 24, 1945. Its primary purpose, therefore, is to maintain international peace and security. The United Nations (UN) became the successor to the League of Nations and absorbed much of the latter's administrative and physical apparatus when it was disbanded in 1946.

90. b) Winston Churchill

The Iron Curtain refers to the political, military, and ideological barrier erected by the Soviet Union after World War II to seal off itself and its dependent eastern European allies from open contact with the West and other noncommunist areas. The term Iron Curtain had been in occasional and varied use as a metaphor since the 19th century, but it only came to prominence after it was used by the former British prime minister Winston Churchill in a speech at Fulton, Missourie, U.S., on March 5, 1946.

91. a) World War I

The First World War was an international conflict that in 1914-18 embroiled most of the nations of Europe along with Russia, the United States, the Middle East, and other regions. The war pitted the Central Powers—mainly Germany, Austria-Hungary, and Turkey—against the Allies—mainly France, Great Britain, Russia, Italy, Japan, and, from 1917, the United States. It ended with the defeat of the Central Powers. The war was virtually unprecedented in the slaughter, carnage, and destruction it caused.

92. c) Sino-Japanese War

The conflict between Japan and China (1894-95) marked the emergence of Japan as a major world power and demonstrated the weakness of the Chinese Empire. The war grew out of conflict between the two countries for supremacy in Korea.

93. a) 1961

Between 1949 and 1961, about 2.5 million East Germans had fled from East to West Germany, including steadily rising numbers of skilled workers, professionals, and intellectuals. Their loss threatened to destroy the economic viability of the East German state. In response, East Germany built a barrier to close off East Germans' access to West Berlin (and hence West Germany). This barrier, the Berlin Wall, was first erected on the night of Aug. 12-13, 1961, as the result of a decree passed on August 12 by the East German Volkskammer ("Peoples' Chamber"). The original wall, built of barbed wire and cinder blocks, was subsequently replaced by a series of concrete walls that were topped with barbed wire and guarded with watchtowers, gun emplacements, and mines. On November 9, 1989, the East German government opened the country's borders with West Germany (including West Berlin), and openings were made in the Berlin Wall through which East Germans could travel freely to the West. The wall henceforth ceased to function as a political barrier between East and West Germany.

The hippopatamus' thick hide secretes a reddish, oily substance that protects the skin in water and in dry conditions. This has led to the myth that the animal sweats blood.

The Treaty of Versailles reduced the population and territory of Germany by about 10 percent.

Did You Know?

94. a) Harry Truman

In June 1950 military forces of communist North Korea suddenly plunged southward across the 38th parallel boundary in an attempt to seize noncommunist South Korea. Truman, the 33rd president of the United States (1945-1953) did not ask Congress for a declaration of war. Instead, he sent to South Korea, with UN sanction, U.S. forces under General Douglas Mac Arthur to repel the invasion.

95. a) Axis Powers

The alliance originated in a series of agreements between Germany and Italy, followed by the proclamation of an "axis" binding Rome and Berlin (Oct. 25, 1936) and then by the German-Japanese Anti-Comintern Pact against the Soviet Union (Nov. 25, 1936). The connection was strengthened by a full military and political alliance between Germany and Italy (the Pact of Steel, May 22, 1939), and the Tripartite Pact signed by all three powers on Sept. 27, 1940.

96. b) Japan

The surprise aerial attack (Dec. 7, 1941) on the U.S. naval base at Pearl Harbor on Oahu Island, Hawaii, by the Japanese precipitated the entry of the United States into World War II. The attack climaxed a decade of worsening relations between the United States and an increasingly expansionist and militaristic Japan. Though Japan continued to negotiate with the United States up to the day of the Pearl Harbor attack, the government of Prime Minister Tojo Hideki decided on war.

97. b) The General Assembly

It is the only body in which all UN members are represented. Through its deliberative, supervisory, financial, and elective functions, the General Assembly occupies a central position in the operation of the United Nations. Its primary significance is as a deliberative body: the assembly may discuss any issue and make recommendations within the scope of the Charter or concerning any other UN body (as long as the issue is not concurrently before the Security Council).

98. a) Francis Ferdinand

The Austrian archduke was the eldest son of the archduke Charles Louis, who was the brother of the emperor Francis Joseph. The death of the heir apparent, the archduke Rudolf, in 1889, made Francis Ferdinand next in succession to the Austro-Hungarian throne after his father, who died in 1896. In June 1914, he and his wife were assassinated by the Serb nationalist Gavrilo Princip at Sarajevo; a month later World War I began with Austria's declaration of war against Serbia.

99. a) Operation Overlord

As the tide of battle in World War II began to turn in favour of the Allies, U.S. Gen. Dwight D. Eisenhower had the task of forming the largest invasion fleet in history in order to effect an amphibious landing on the northern coast of France. A huge armada had been assembled, including 1,200 fighting ships, 10,000 planes, 4,126 landing craft, 804 transport ships, and hundreds of amphibious and other special purpose tanks. Delayed 24 hours by bad Channel weather, the invasion began before dawn on June 6 with units of the U.S. 82nd and 101st Airborne divisions making night landings near the town of Sainte-Mere-Eglise, while British commando units captured key bridges and knocked out Nazi communications.

Did You Know?

The modern machine gun, which had been developed in the 1880s and 1890s, was a reliable belt-fed gun capable of sustained rates of extremely rapid fire; it could fire 600 bullets per minute with a range of more than 1,900 m (1,000 yards).

The Royal Air Force (RAF), the world's first separate air service, was brought into active existence by a series of measures taken between October 1917 and June 1918.

100. c) International Court of Justice
It is the principal judicial organ of the United Nations. The court's origins precede the League of Nations. The idea for the first international court arose at The Hague, Netherlands, in 1899, to regulate principles for arbitration of international disputes. This institution adopted its present name with the foundation of the United Nations in 1945. The seat of the World Court is The Hague.

101. b) William II
The German emperor (kaiser) and king of Prussia from 1888 to the end of World War I in 1918 was known for his frequently militaristic manner as well as for his vacillating policies. World War I began as an attempt to save Austria-Hungary from collapse; it was transformed into a world conflict by Germany. During the war, although nominally supreme commander, he did not attempt to resist his generals when they kept its conduct in their own hands.

102. a) German-Soviet Nonagression Pact
The pact was concluded a few days before the beginning of World War II, dividing eastern Europe into German and Soviet spheres of influence. The Soviet Union had been repeatedly ignored in its attempts to enter into a collective-security agreement with Britain and France against Nazi Germany. By early 1939 the Soviets faced the prospect of resisting German military expansion in eastern Europe virtually alone, and so they began searching about for a change of policy. On May 3, 1939, the Soviet Foreign Minister V.M. Molotov began negotiations with the Nazi foreign minister, Joachim von Ribbentrop. The end result of the German-Soviet negotiations was the Nonaggression Pact, which was dated August 23 and was signed by Ribbentrop and Molotov in the presence of Stalin, in Moscow.

103. c) The United Nations Peacekeeping Force
In peacekeeping missions, UN troops are placed in situations of conflict to defuse tensions and are deployed only in situations in which all parties to the conflict in question have agreed on their emplacement. The UN troops are to remain neutral and use force only for self-defence purposes. Peacekeeping missions have generally been used after a stalemate in fighting has been reached or after allied states have agreed to place joint pressure on those in conflict to reach a ceasefire. As a result, UN peacekeeping has most often been used to contain extant conflicts rather than to prevent the outbreak of wars. UN peacekeeping troops, called "blue helmets", have served throughout the world, most extensively in the Middle East.

104. d) Jean-Baptist-Point Du Sable
A black pioneer trader, Du Sable settled on the shore of Lake Michigan at the mouth of the Chicago River. His loyalty to the French and the Americans led to his arrest in 1779 by the British, who took him to Fort Mackinac. From 1780 to 1783 or 1784 he managed for his captors a trading post called the Pinery on the St. Clair River in present-day Michigan, after which he returned to the site of Chicago. Though he moved to Missouri, his 20-year residence on the shores of Lake Michigan had established his title as Father of Chicago.

The English Channel probably derives its current English name (in general use since the early 18th century) from the designation "canal" in Dutch sea atlases of the late 16th century. Earlier names had included Oceanus Britannicus and the British Sea, and the French have regularly used La Manche (in reference to the sleevelike coastal outline) since the early 17th century.

Did You Know?

105. c) Frederick Jackson Turner

The single most influential interpretation of the American past, the "frontier thesis" proposed that the distinctiveness of the United States was attributable to its long history of "westering". Turner's penetrating analyses of American history and culture were powerfully influential and changed the direction of much American historical writing.

106. c) Francis Drake

In 1577, Drake was chosen to lead an expedition intended to pass around South America through the Strait of Magellan and to explore the coast that lay beyond. He set sail in December and reached the Brazilian coast in the spring of 1578. He entered the Strait on Aug. 21, 1578. Before sailing westward he sailed north to seek the Northwest Passage back into the Atlantic but the bitterly cold weather defeated him. In his search for a passage around the north of America he was the first European to sight the west coast of what is now Canada. In July 1579 he sailed west across the Pacific. He went to the Philippines and the Moluccas. Two years after being to the Strait of Magellan, Drake returned to the Atlantic. He brought his ship to the Plymouth Harbour on Sept. 26, 1580.

107. d) Tet offensive

On Jan. 30, 1968, the North Vietnamese and Viet Cong launched a massive surprise offensive during the Tet (lunar New Year) Vietnamese festival. They attacked 36 major South Vietnamese cities and towns. The offensive had an important strategic effect, because it convinced a number of Americans that, contrary to their government's claims, the insurgency in South Vietnam could not be crushed and the war would continue for years to come.

108. a) Bartolomeu Dias

The Portuguese king John II ordered Dias to find the southern limit of Africa. Dias's fleet is now usually supposed to have left in August 1487 moving along the coast for most of the way. After Jan. 6, 1488, he was prevented by storms from proceeding along the coast and sailed south out of sight of land for several days. When he again turned to port, no land appeared, and it was only on sailing north that he sighted land on February 3. He had thus rounded the Cape without having seen it. It was now clear that the Cape route could help to reach India, and Dias turned back. He sighted the Cape itself in May.

109. b) Diogo Cao

The Portuguese navigator and explorer set up a stone pillar at the mouth of the Congo river to mark Portuguese overlordship of the area. Sailing a short way upstream, he found that the inhabitants along the banks appeared willing to trade. He then travelled southward along the present Angola coast and erected a second pillar at Cape Santa Maria (Monte Negro). On a second voyage (1485-86) he reached Cape Cross, now in Namibia.

110. a) The White House

Formerly (1818-1902) Executive Mansion, it was the official residence of the president of the United States. The main building has been the home of every U.S. president since John Adams.

111. a) United States of America

The Constitution is the fundamental law of the U.S. federal system of government and a

---

Did You Know?

Sports arenas, racetracks, and public swimming pools of the present day owe their origin to the ancient Romans (though certain precedents can be found in Crete and Greece). The design of arenas and tracks has been scarcely altered from the Colosseum and Circus Maximus.

Many animals engage in play, but *Homo sapiens* is the only animal to have invented sports.

landmark document of the Western world. It is the oldest written national constitution in operation. The Constitution defines the principal organs of government and their jurisdictions and the basic rights of citizens. The Constitution was written during the summer of 1787, ostensibly to amend the Articles of Confederation, the country's first written constitution. The new Constitution was submitted for ratification to the 13 states on Sept. 28, 1787, and after the ninth state had ratified it in June 1788, Congress set March 4, 1789, as the date for the new government to commence proceedings, and their adoption was certified on Dec. 15, 1791.

112. c) Henry Knox
He became active in the colonial militia and in 1775 joined the Continental Army at Cambridge, Massachusetts. He was commissioned a colonel and placed in charge of the artillery. He became secretary of war (1785) in the government under the Articles of Confederation and was carried over into President Washington's first Cabinet (1789).

113. b) A merchant and navigator
The name America is derived from that of the Italian merchant and navigator Amerigo Vespucci, one of the earliest European explorers to the New World. Although at first the term America was applied only to the southern half, the designation soon was applied to the entire landmass; those portions that widened out north of the Isthmus of Panama became known as North America, and those that broadened to the south became known as South America.

114. b) United States of America
The Treaty of Paris (1898), concluding the Spanish-American War, was signed by representatives of Spain and the United States in Paris. It transferred Philippine sovereignty from Spain to the United States but was not recognized by Filipino leaders, whose troops were in actual control of the entire archipelago except the capital city of Manila. Although an end to the insurrection was declared in 1902, sporadic fighting continued for several years thereafter.

115. b) Democratic Party
In the United States, the Democratic Party has historically represented organized labour, minorities, and progressive reformers. The party's traditional symbol is the donkey, and its theme song, since the 1930s, has been "Happy Days Are Here Again".

116. a) James Earl Ray
Ray had been a small-time crook, a robber of gas stations and stores, who had served time in prison, once in Illinois and twice in Missouri, and received a suspended sentence in Los Angeles. He escaped from the Missouri State Penitentiary on April 23, 1967; and in Memphis, Tennessee, a year later, on April 4, 1968, from a window of a neighbouring rooming house, he shot Martin Luther King, Jr., who was standing on the balcony of a motel room.

117. c) Margaret Thatcher
The British Conservative politician and prime minister (1979-90), Thatcher was Europe's first woman prime minister. At the time of her resignation she was also Britain's longest-serving prime minister since 1827. The Conservatives' decisive victory in the general

Amelia Bloomer's reformed trousers for women did not become fashionable, but they were adopted by women gymnasts and sea bathers.

Except at militaristic Sparta, Greek girls rarely participated in sports of any kind. Women were excluded from the Olympic Games even as spectators (except for the priestess of Demeter).

Did You Know?

elections of 1979, which elevated her to the prime ministry, was thought partly to have resulted from her denunciation of trade-union-induced chaos in the previous winter's strikes.

118. b) Conservative Party

Formally called National Union Of Conservative And Unionist Associations in the United Kingdom, the Conservative Party is the heir, and in some measure the continuation, of the old Tory Party. The name Conservative was first used as a description of the party by John Wilson Croker writing in the *Quarterly Review* of Jan. 1, 1830.

119. d) James Monroe

He was the fifth president of the United States (1817-25). The chief events of his calm and prosperous administration were the First Seminole War (1817-18); the acquisition of the Floridas from Spain (1819-21); the Missouri Compromise (1820), by which the first conflict over slavery under the Constitution was peacefully settled; recognition of the new Latin American states, former Spanish colonies, in Central and South America (1822); and—most intimately connected with Monroe's name—the enunciation, in the presidential message of Dec. 2, 1823, of the Monroe Doctrine, which has profoundly influenced the foreign policy of the United States.

120. a) Robert Peel

The British prime minister (1834-35, 1841-46), Peel, was by nature quick-tempered, courageous, stubborn, and often autocratic. With a first-class intellect, an exact memory, and great capacity for work, he was a superb administrator and an outstanding parliamentary debater. Though he has an unchallenged place as founder of the modern Conservative Party, his political outlook was formed in the pre-reform era. He regarded ministers of the crown as servants of the state rather than as mouthpieces for sectional or party views.

121. c) United States of America

The flag of the United States of America, or star-spangled banner, consists of white stars (50 from July 4, 1960) on a blue canton, with a field of 13 alternate stripes, 7 red and 6 white. The 50 stars stand for the 50 states of the Union, and the 13 stripes stand for the original 13 states. In 1818, Congress enacted legislation pertaining to a new flag, requiring that henceforth the stripes should remain 13, that the number of stars should always match the number of states, and that any new star should be added on the July 4 following a state's admission. This has been the system ever since.

122. b) Winston Churchill

The British statesman, orator, and author as prime minister (1940-45, 1951-55) led his country during World War II from the brink of defeat to victory. A gifted journalist, biographer and historian of classic proportions, an amateur painter of talent, an orator of rare power, a soldier of courage and distinction, Churchill, by any standards, was a man of rare versatility. As a wartime leader, at the peak of his powers, he united in a harmonious whole his liberal convictions about social reform, his deep conservative devotion to the legacy of his nation's history, his unshakeable resistance to tyranny from the right or from the left, and his capacity to look beyond Britain to the larger Atlantic community and the ultimate unity of Europe.

Did You Know?

Gregory Peck gave up training in medicine to pursue his interests in the acting profession in the early 1940s.

Originally, gymnasiums were public institutions where only male athletes over the age of 18 received training for competition in the public games of that time (as opposed to the palaestrae, which were private schools where boys were trained in physical exercises).

123. d) Kokura
The second atom bomb, a duplicate of the plutonium-239 implosion assembly tested in Trinity and nicknamed Fat Man, was to be dropped on Kokura on August 11; a third was being prepared in the United States for possible use in late August or early September. To avoid bad weather, the schedule was moved up two days to August 9. The B-29, named *Bock's Car*, spent 10 minutes over Kokura without sighting its aim point; it then proceeded to the secondary target of Nagasaki, where, at 11:02 a.m. local time, the weapon was air-burst at 1,650 feet with a force later estimated at 21 kilotons.

124. a) Henry Fitzhenry
The second son of King Henry II of England, he was regarded, after the death of his elder brother, William, in 1156, as his father's successor in England, Normandy, and Anjou. On June 14, 1170, the young Henry was crowned king (theoretically to rule in association with his father) at Westminster by Archbishop Roger of York. York's officiation, usurping a prerogative of the archbishop of Canterbury, exacerbated the dispute between the latter, namely, Thomas Becket, and Henry II, which ended with Becket's murder six months later. Crowned again on Aug. 27, 1172 (this time with Margaret), the Young King received no share of his father's power. (He was nevertheless called by contemporaries and by certain later chroniclers King Henry III.)

125. b) Patrick Henry
A brilliant orator and a major figure of the American Revolution, he was independent Virginia's first governor (serving 1776-79, 1784-86). At the second Virginia Convention, on March 23, 1775, in St. John's Church, Richmond, he delivered the speech that assured his fame as one of the great advocates of liberty. Convinced that war with Great Britain was inevitable, he presented strong resolutions for equipping the Virginia militia to fight against the British and defended them in a fiery speech with the famed peroration, "I know not what course others may take, but as for me, give me liberty or give me death."

126. a) Henrietta Anne
She was the English princess and duchesse d'Orleans, a notable figure at the court of her brother-in-law King Louis XIV of France. In 1670 she went to England and played a vital role in the secret negotiations with Charles II that led to the Treaty of Dover, allying England and France against the Dutch.

127. c) Neville Chamberlain
He was prime minister from May 28, 1937, to May 10, 1940. On three occasions in September 1938, Chamberlain went to Germany in efforts to prevent the outbreak of a general European war over Hitler's demand that Czechoslovakia cede the Sudetenland to Germany. By the Munich Agreement of September 30, he and Premier Edouard Daladier of France granted almost all of Hitler's demands and left Czechoslovakia defenceless. He returned to England a popular hero, speaking of "peace with honour" (echoing an earlier prime minister, Benjamin Disraeli) and "peace in our time".

128. a) John Major
British politician and public official, Major was prime minister of the United Kingdom from 1990 to 1997. Major's first years in office coincided with the longest economic

recession (1990-93) in Britain since World War II. His government became increasingly unpopular despite an economic recovery in the mid-1990s that combined steady growth and drastically falling unemployment with low levels of inflation.

129. a) Clement Attlee
British Labour Party leader from 1935 to 1955 and prime minister from July 26, 1945, to Oct. 26, 1951, Atlee presided over the establishment of the welfare state in Great Britain and over the most important step—the granting of independence to India—in the conversion of the British Empire into the Commonwealth of Nations. During Attlee's tenure, independence within the Commonwealth was granted to India, a measure that established the separate nation of Pakistan.

130. a) Anthony Eden
British foreign secretary in 1935-38, 1940-45, and 1951-55, Eden was prime minister from 1955 to 1957. On Oct. 27, 1951, after Churchill and the Conservative Party had been returned to power, Eden again became foreign secretary and also was designated deputy prime minister. In 1954 he helped to settle the Anglo-Iranian oil dispute, to resolve the quarrel between Italy and Yugoslavia over Trieste, to stop the Indochina War, and to establish the Southeast Asia Treaty Organization (SEATO).

131. c) James I
He was the king of Scotland (as James VI) from 1567 to 1625 and the first Stuart king of England from 1603 to 1625. James was a strong advocate of royal absolutism, and his conflicts with an increasingly self-assertive Parliament set the stage for the rebellion

against his successor, Charles I. James's rule of Scotland was basically successful as he was able to rule Scotland almost as absolutely as Elizabeth ruled England.

132. b) Edward III
During the 1330s England gradually drifted into a state of hostility with France. Contributory causes were France's new king Philip VI's support of the Scots and Edward's alliance with the Flemish cities. In January 1340 he assumed the title of king of France. But his pretensions to the French crown gradually became more important, and the persistence with which he and his successors urged them made stable peace impossible for more than a century. This was the struggle famous in history as the Hundred Years' War.

133. b) William Kirkcaldy
From 1550 to 1556 Kirkcaldy served in France as a secret agent for England. He returned to Scotland in 1557. When Mary Stuart assumed control of the government in 1561, Kirkcaldy at first cooperated with her regime. But later he joined with the Protestant lords against the ruling couple of Mary and James Hepburn.

134. a) General Assembly
The Secretariat is headed by the secretary-general, who is appointed for a five-year term by the General Assembly on the recommendation of the Security Council. In addition to being the chief administrative officer of the United Nations, the secretary-general has important political functions, being specifically charged with bringing before the organization any matter that threatens international peace and security.

135. c) Food and Agriculture Organization
FAO was established in October 1945 and was the first permanent specialized agency of the United Nations to be founded after World War II. The goal of the FAO is to achieve world food security and ensure physical and economic access to food in all countries. The organization also assists countries through research, training, development, and field missions.

136. c) Alexander Hamilton Stephens
A politician who served as vice-president of the Confederate States of America during the American Civil War (1861-65), Stephens was called "Little Ellick" by his colleagues because he weighed only about 100 pounds. Stephens was admitted to the bar in 1834. Though plagued by infirmities, he rose steadily in politics, serving in the Georgia House of Representatives (1837-41), the state Senate (1842-43), the U.S. House of Representatives (1843-59 and 1873-82), and as governor of Georgia (1882-83).

137. b) Maintenance of international peace and security
This is the primary function of the United Nations. Chapter 6 of the Charter provides for the pacific settlement of disputes, through such means as negotiation, mediation, arbitration, and/or judicial decisions. When pacific settlement fails, the goal of collective security—whereby the security of each member is assured by all, and aggression against one would be met by the resistance of all—underlies the provisions in Chapter 7 for coercive measures, including economic and military sanctions, against an aggressor.

138. c) Stockholm
A growing concern with environmental issues led the General Assembly to organize the UN Conference on the Human Environment in Stockholm in 1972. This led to the creation of the UN Environment Programme (UNEP) that same year. UNEP has worked on such problems as cleaning up the Mediterranean; protecting water resources; combating deforestation, desertification, and drought; and phasing out the production of ozone-depleting chemicals.

139. d) General Assembly
The United Nations has played a major role in defining, codifying, and expanding the realm of international law. The International Law Commission, established by the General Assembly in 1947, is the primary institution responsible for developing and codifying international law. The commission and assembly have influenced international law in several domains, including laws of war, law of the sea, treaty law, and human rights law.

140. d) Namibia
In 1988, with Namibian independence and Cuban troop departures from neighbouring Angola implicitly linked, South Africa finally agreed to withdraw from Namibia. The following year a UN force supervised elections and assisted in repatriating refugees. Namibia gained formal independent status in 1990.

141. b) James Gavin
The Army commander he parachuted with combat troops during World War II. He commanded the parachute assault section of the division during the Normandy Invasion on June 6, 1944. His division later fought in Germany until the surrender in 1945. After

the war Gavin was chief of staff of the 5th Army and of allied forces in southern Europe, and commanding general of the U.S.

142. d) Abraham Lincoln
The edict, issued by U.S. President Abraham Lincoln on Jan. 1, 1863, freed the slaves of the Confederate states in rebellion against the Union. Lincoln had declared that he meant to save the Union as best he could—by preserving slavery, by destroying it, or by destroying part and preserving part. Just after the Battle of Antietam (Sept. 17, 1862) he issued his proclamation calling on the revolted states to return to their allegiance before the next year, otherwise their slaves would be declared free men. No state returned, and the threatened declaration was issued on Jan. 1, 1863.

143. a) Elba
The island is located off the west coast of Italy, in the Tyrrhenian Sea. Elba has an area of 223 sq km (86 sq miles) and is the largest island of the Tuscan Archipelago. It is famous as Napoleon's place of exile in 1814-15. Napoleon's chief residence, the Mulini Palace, overlooks the sea near Portoferraio, Elba's chief town, on the north coast. His summer residence, Villa San Martino, lies 6 km (4 miles) southwest and contains a museum and a collection of engravings.

144. c) Napoleon Bonaparte
French general, First Consul (1799-1804), and emperor of the French (1804-1814/15), Napoleon is one of the most celebrated personages in the history of the West. He revolutionized military organization and training; sponsored the Napoleonic Code, the prototype of later civil-law codes; reorganized education; and established the long-lived Concordat with the papacy.

Literature

1. d) Yorkshire
James Herriot, the Scottish-born veterinarian and writer, charmed millions of fans around the world with his humorous fictionalized reminiscences of his life as a rural veterinarian in the Yorkshire Dales, particularly in the years just before and after World War II.

2. c) *Daddy-Long-Legs*
First serialized in the *Ladies' Home Journal*, the story became a best-seller when published in book form. It was a successful stage play (1914) in Webster's own adaptation, and a popular Mary Pickford silent film (1919). *Daddy-Long-Legs* was not only a successful piece of fiction but also a stimulus to reform the institutional treatment of orphans. In 1914 Webster published *Dear Enemy*, a sequel to *Daddy-Long-Legs* and also a best-seller.

3. b) Isaac Asimov
He began contributing stories to science-fiction magazines in 1939 and in 1950 published his first book, *Pebble in the Sky*. His trilogy of novels, *Foundation, Foundation and Empire,* and *Second Foundation* (1951-53), recounts the collapse and rebirth of a vast interstellar empire in the universe of the future.

4. b) Charles Perrault
One of the earliest and most enduring classics of children's literature was Charles Perrault's fairy-tale collection entitled *Contes de ma mère l'oye* (1697), which was translated into English in 1729 as *Tales of Mother Goose*. Among its classic stories are "Cinderella", "Little Red Riding Hood", "The Sleeping Beauty", and "Puss in Boots".

5. d) Beatrix Potter
The English author of children's books created Peter Rabbit, Jeremy Fisher, Jemima Puddle-Duck, Mrs. Tiggy-Winkle, and other animal characters. The tiny books, which she designed so that even the smallest children could hold them, combined a deceptively simple prose, concealing dry north-country humour, with illustrations in the best English watercolour tradition.

6. b) Richard Wright
The novelist and short-story writer was among the first black American writers to protest white treatment of blacks, notably in his novel *Native Son* (1940) and his autobiography, *Black Boy* (1945). The latter is a moving account of Wright's childhood and young manhood in the South. *Black Boy* chronicles the extreme poverty of his childhood, his experience of white prejudice and violence against blacks, and his growing awareness of his interest in literature.

7. c) *Renga*
The *renga* form began as the composition of a single *tanka* (a traditional five-line poem) by two people and was a popular pastime from ancient times, even in remote rural areas. The *Kin'yo-shu* (c. 1125) was the first Imperial anthology to include *renga,* which was at the time simply *tanka* composed by two poets, one supplying the first three lines of five, seven, and five syllables and the other the last two of seven syllables each. The first poet often gave obscure or even contradictory details to make it harder for the second to complete the poem intelligibly and, if

possible, inventively. The standard length of a *renga* was 100 verses, although there were variations.

8. c) Oliver Goldsmith
The English essayist, poet, novelist, dramatist, and eccentric's play *She Stoops to Conquer* has outlived almost all other English comedies from the early 18th to the late 19th century by virtue of its broadly farcical horseplay and vivid, humorous characterizations.

9. d) Iio Sogi
He was a Buddhist monk and the greatest master of *renga* (linked verse), the supreme Japanese poet of his age. Sogi's own selection of his best work shows him at his most ingenious in the aristocratic tradition; but his modern reputation is based on the deeply moving vein found in his simpler and more personal poems.

10. c) Kakinomoto Hitomaro
The poet has been venerated by the Japanese since earliest times. Among his surviving works are poems in the two major Japanese poetic forms of his day–*tanka* and *choka*. All of the poems accepted as indisputably authored by Hitomaro (61 *tanka* and 16 *choka*), as well as a large number of others attributed to him, are to be found in the *Man'yo-shu*, the first and largest of Japan's anthologies of native poetry. These poems, together with notes by the compilers, are the chief source for information on his life, about which very little is known. Hitomaro achieved in his poems a splendid balance between the homely qualities of primitive song and the more sophisticated interests and literary techniques of a new age.

11. c) Dionysius Thrax
Thrax's grammar of Western tradition dealt only with word morphology. He called grammar "the acquaintance with (or observation of) what is uttered by poets and writers", using a word meaning a less general form of knowledge than what might be called "science". His typically Alexandrian literary goal is suggested by the headings in his work: pronunciation, poetic figurative language, difficult words, true and inner meanings of words, exposition of form classes, literary criticism. Dionysius defined a sentence as a unit of sense or thought, but it is difficult to be sure of his precise meaning.

12. c) Arthur Koestler
The Hungarian-born British novelist, journalist, and critic was best known for his novel *Darkness at Noon* (1940). Published in 30 languages, it is the penetrating story of an old-guard Bolshevik who, during Stalin's purge trials of the 1930s, first denies, then confesses to, crimes that he has not committed. Specifically dealing with the plight of an aging revolutionary who can no longer condone the excesses of the government he helped put in power, the novel is an examination of the moral danger inherent in a system that sacrifices means to an end.

13. c) Gnaeus Naevius
The titles of two *praetextae* by Naevius are known, *Romulus* and *Clastidium,* the latter celebrating the victory of Marcus Claudius Marcellus in 222 BC and probably produced at his funeral games in 208. Naevius produced half a dozen tragedies and more than 30 comedies, many of which are known only by their titles. Some were translated from Greek plays, and, in adapting them, he created the

Latin *fabula palliata* (from *pallium,* a type of Greek cloak), perhaps being the first to introduce song and recitative, transferring elements from one play into another, and adding variety to the metre.

14. a) Quintus Ennius

An epic poet, dramatist, and satirist, he was the most influential of the early Latin poets. His epic *Annales,* a narrative poem telling the story of Rome from the wanderings of Aeneas to the poet's own day, was the national epic until it was eclipsed by Virgil's *Aeneid.* Ennius was at home in three languages: Oscan, his native tongue; Greek, in which he was educated; and Latin, the language of the army with which he served in the Second Punic War. Only some 600 lines of the *Annales* survive. Ennius excelled in tragedy. Titles survive of 19 plays adapted from the Greek, mostly Euripides.

15. c) Aeschylus

Aeschylus wrote approximately 90 plays, including satyr plays as well as tragedies; of these, about 80 titles are known. Only seven tragedies have survived entire. One account, perhaps based on the official lists, assigns Aeschylus 13 first prizes, or victories; this would mean that well over half of his plays won, since sets of four plays rather than separate ones were judged.

16. d) *Shih Ching*

The anthology consists of temple, court, and folk songs, and was given a definitive form somewhere around the time of Confucius (551-479 BC). But its 305 songs are believed to range in date from the beginning of the Chou dynasty to the time of their compiling. The *Shih Ching* ("Classic of Poetry") is generally accounted the third of the Five Classics (*Wu Ching*) of Confucian literature, the other four of which are: the *I Ching* ("Classic of Changes"), the *Shu Ching* ("Classic of History"), the *Li chi* ("Record of Rites"), and the *Ch'un-ch'iu* ("Spring and Autumn") annals. The poems of the *Shih Ching* were originally sung to the accompaniment of music; and some of them, especially temple songs, were accompanied also by dancing.

17. a) *Koenig Rother*

A medieval German romance (*c.* 1160), it combines elements from German heroic literature (without the grimness of the older tales) with Orientalisms derived from the Crusades. In the story, the young king Rother sends 12 envoys to the Byzantine emperor in Constantinople to ask his daughter's hand, but before the envoys leave, Rother takes a harp and plays three tunes, which they are to listen for if in danger. After their arrival, the emperor throws the envoys in prison, so Rother sets out, assuming the name Dietrich. He rescues the envoys and carries off the princess. Her father, however, sends a cunning *Spielmann* (minstrel) after them, who then tricks the princess into returning. To get her back, Rother has to undertake a second series of adventures.

18. a) Ulfilas

A Christian bishop and missionary, he evangelized the Goths. Ulfilas's outstanding contribution to writing is his invention of the Gothic alphabet, which he devised from Greek (primarily) and Latin. For the first time in the Germanic world, writing could be used for the propagation of ideas. He coined a Germanic Christian terminology, some of which is still in use. Before 381 he translated parts of the Bible from Greek to Gothic. He reportedly wrote many sermons and interpretations in Gothic, Greek, and Latin, and some extant Arian writings have been ascribed to him.

19. b) George Orwell
Born in Bengal, India, Orwell decided to follow family tradition and went to Burma as assistant district superintendent in the Indian Imperial Police. He served in a number of country stations. He recounted his experiences and his reactions to imperial rule in his novel *Burmese Days* and in two brilliant autobiographical sketches, "Shooting an Elephant" and "A Hanging", classics of expository prose.

20. d) Miguel de Cervantes Saavedra
A Spanish novelist, playwright, and poet, Cervantes is the creator of *Don Quixote* (1605). Cervantes was a great experimenter. He tried his hand in all the major literary genres save the epic. He was a notable short-story writer, and a few of those in his collection of *Novelas exemplares* ("Exemplary Tales") attain a level close to that of *Don Quixote*, on a miniature scale.

21. c) Aleksandr Pushkin
The Russian poet, novelist, dramatist, and short-story writer has often been considered his country's greatest poet. Pushkin's use of the Russian language is astonishing in its simplicity and profundity. His novel in verse, *Yevgeny Onegin*, was the first Russian work to take contemporary society as its subject and pointed the way to the Russian realistic novel of the mid-19th century. Translated into all the major languages, his works are regarded both as expressing most completely Russian national consciousness and as transcending national barriers.

22. a) William Butler Yeats
The Irish poet, dramatist, and prose writer is one of the greatest English-language poets of the 20th century. Yeats received the Nobel Prize for Literature in 1923. In 1917 Yeats published *The Wild Swans at Coole*.

23. a) Herbert George Wells
The English novelist, journalist, sociologist, and historian is also known for such comic novels as *Tono-Bungay* and *The History of Mr. Polly*. As a creative writer his reputation rests on the early science-fiction books and on the comic novels. In his science fiction, he took the ideas and fears that haunted the mind of his age and gave them symbolic expression as brilliantly conceived fantasy made credible by the quiet realism of its setting. In the comic novels, though his psychology lacks subtlety and the construction of his plots is often awkward, he shows a fund of humour and a deep sympathy for ordinary people.

24. a) Hugo Gernsback
The American inventor and publisher was largely responsible for the establishment of science fiction as an independent literary form. In 1908 he founded *Modern Electrics* (later absorbed by *Popular Science*), a pioneer magazine for radio enthusiasts. In 1926 Gernsback began publishing *Amazing Stories,* one of the first magazines devoted exclusively to what he referred to as "scientifiction". The stories were often crudely written, but the very existence of the magazine and its successors, including *Wonder Stories,* encouraged the development and refinement of the genre. His

contribution was later recognized with the establishment of the annual Hugo Award for the best science fiction novel.

25. a) *Lord of the Flies*
William Golding's first published novel was *Lord of the Flies* (1954; film 1963 and 1990), the story of a group of schoolboys isolated on a coral island who revert to savagery.

26. d) Ernest Hemingway
The American novelist and short-story writer was awarded the Nobel Prize for Literature in 1954. Hemingway was noted for the intense masculinity of his writing. His succinct and lucid prose style exerted a powerful influence on American and British fiction in the 20th century.

27. c) Alan Alexander Milne
An English humorist, Milne was the originator of the immensely popular stories of Christopher Robin and his toy bear, Winnie-the-Pooh. His most popular works were the two sets of stories about the adventures of Christopher Robin and his toy animals— Pooh, Piglet, Tigger, Kanga, Roo, Rabbit, Owl, and Eeyore—as told in *Winnie-the-Pooh* (1926) and *The House at Pooh Corner* (1928).

28. a) *The Wind in the Willows*
Written by Kenneth Grahame, the book is one of the English classics of children's literature. Its animal characters—principally Mole, Rat, Badger, and Toad—combine captivating human traits with authentic animal habits.

29. a) Emily Bronte
The English novelist and poet produced but one novel, *Wuthering Heights* (1847), a highly imaginative novel of passion and hate set on the Yorkshire moors. The record of her life is extremely meagre, for she was silent and reserved and left no correspondence of interest.

30. a) Robert Cawdrey
In 1604 at London appeared the first purely English dictionary to be issued as a separate work, entitled *A Table Alphabeticall, conteyning and teaching the true writing and understanding of hard usuall English wordes, borrowed from the Hebrew, Greeke, Latine,* or *French &c.*, by Robert Cawdrey, who had been a schoolmaster at Oakham, Rutland, about 1580, and in 1604 was living at Coventry.

31. d) *The Catcher in the Rye*
Like Holden Caulfield, the hero of *The Catcher in the Rye,* Salinger grew up in New York City. The humour and colourful language of *The Catcher in the Rye* place it in the tradition of Mark Twain's *Adventures of Huckleberry Finn* and the stories of Ring Lardner, but its hero, like most of Salinger's child characters, views his life with an added dimension of precocious self-consciousness.

32. a) Doctor
Conan Doyle practised medicine until 1891 after graduating from the University of Edinburgh. The character of Sherlock Holmes, who first appeared in *A Study in Scarlet* (1887), partly derives from a teacher at Edinburgh noted for his deductive reasoning.

33. b) Erle Stanley Gardner
The American author and lawyer wrote nearly 100 detective and mystery novels that sold more than 1,000,000 copies each, making him easily the best-selling American writer of his

time. His best-known works centre on the lawyer-detective, Perry Mason.

34. d) *Animal Farm*
In 1944 Orwell finished the book, a political fable based on the story of the Russian Revolution and its betrayal by Joseph Stalin. In this book a group of barnyard animals overthrow and chase off their exploitative human masters and set up an egalitarian society of their own. Eventually the animals' intelligent and power-loving leaders, the pigs, subvert the revolution and form a dictatorship whose bondage is even more oppressive and heartless than that of their former human masters.

35. d) *The Poor Man and the Lady*
In 1867-1868 he wrote the class-conscious novel *The Poor Man and the Lady*, which was considered sympathetically by three London publishers but never published. Hardy was advised to write a more shapely and less opinionated novel.

36. c) Alexandre Pere Dumas
He was one of the most prolific and most popular French authors of the 19th century. Without ever attaining indisputable literary merit, Dumas succeeded in gaining a great reputation first as a dramatist and then as a historical novelist, especially for such works as *The Count of Monte Cristo* and *The Three Musketeers*. The latter is story of the fortunes and exploits of three of them, Athos, Porthos, and Aramis.

37. c) Sherlock Holmes
The fictional character was created in 1887 by the English writer Arthur Conan Doyle; Sherlock Holmes became the prototype for the modern mastermind detective. A slim, nervously intense, hawk-nosed man, he uses purely scientific reasoning to solve crimes and can make the most startling deductions from trivial details and bits of physical evidence overlooked by others.

38. c) Spanish Civil War
The harvest of Hemingway's considerable experience of Spain in war and peace was the novel *For Whom the Bell Tolls* (1940). Set during the Spanish Civil War, it tells of Robert Jordan, an American volunteer, who is sent to join a guerrilla band behind the Nationalist lines in the Guadarrama Mountains. Through dialogue, flashbacks, and stories, Hemingway offers telling and vivid profiles of the Spanish character and unsparingly depicts the cruelty and inhumanity stirred up by the civil war.

39. d) Nathaniel Hawthorne
The American novelist and short-story writer was a master of the allegorical and symbolic tale. One of the greatest fiction writers in American literature, he is best-known for *The Scarlet Letter* (1850) and *The House of the Seven Gables* (1851).

The latter is a sombre study in hereditary sin based on the legend of a curse pronounced on Hawthorne's own family by a woman condemned to death during the witchcraft trials. The greed and arrogant pride of the novel's Pyncheon family down the generations is mirrored in the gloomy decay of their seven-gabled mansion, in which the family's enfeebled and impoverished poor relations live.

40. d) Washington Irving
Called the "first American man of letters", Irving is best known for the short stories "The

Legend of Sleepy Hollow" and "Rip Van Winkle". They have been called the first American short stories. They are both Americanized versions of German folktales. The main character of "Rip Van Winkle" is a henpecked husband who sleeps for 20 years and awakes as an old man to find his wife dead, his daughter happily married, and America now an independent country.

41. a) George Eliot
A pseudonym of Mary Ann, or Marian, Cross, nee Evans, the English Victorian novelist developed the method of psychological analysis characteristic of modern fiction. Her major works include *Adam Bede* (1859), *The Mill on the Floss* (1860), *Silas Marner* (1861), *Middlemarch* (1871-72), and *Daniel Deronda* (1876).

42. a) Henry Wadsworth Longfellow
The popular American poet fashioned *The Song of Hiawatha* in1855. Its appeal to the public was immediate. Hiawatha is an Ojibwa Indian who, after various mythic feats, becomes his people's leader and marries Minnehaha before departing for the Isles of the Blessed. Both the poem and its singsong metre have been frequent objects of parody.

43. a) Lucy Maud Montgomery
The Canadian regional romantic novelist is best known for *Anne of Green Gables* (1908), a sentimentalized but often charming story of a spirited, unconventional orphan girl who finds a home with an elderly couple. The book drew on the author's own girlhood experiences and on the rural life and traditions of Prince Edward Island.

44. c) Laura Ingalls Wilder
This American author wrote children's fiction based on her own youth in the American Midwest. Her stories centred on the male unrest and female patience of pioneers in the mid-1800s and celebrated their peculiarly American spirit and independence. In 1932, she published *Little House in the Big Woods*, which was set in Wisconsin. After writing *Farmer Boy* (1933), a book about her husband's childhood, she published *Little House on the Prairie* (1935), a reminiscence of her family's stay in Indian Territory.

45. d) Sylvia Plath
An American poet and novelist, Plath's best-known works are preoccupied with alienation and with death and self-destruction. Her second book, a strongly autobiographical novel titled *The Bell Jar*, was published in 1963 under the pseudonym "Victoria Lucas". The book describes the mental breakdown, attempted suicide, and eventual recovery of a young college girl.

46. c) Edward Albee
An American dramatist and theatrical producer, Albee is best known for his play *Who's Afraid of Virginia Woolf?* (1962), which displays slashing insight and witty dialogue in its gruesome portrayal of married life. In this play a middle-aged professor, his wife, and a younger couple engage one night in an unrestrained drinking bout that is filled with malicious games, insults, humiliations, betrayals, savage witticisms, and painful, self-revealing confrontations. *Virginia Woolf* won immediate acclaim and established Albee as a major American playwright.

In 1953 Twentieth Century-Fox introduced CinemaScope, the process by which a picture is projected on a screen two and a half times as wide as it is high.

The earliest known mental hospitals were established in the Arab world, in Baghdad (AD 918) and in Cairo.

Did You Know?

47. d) Tennessee Williams
The U.S. dramatist's plays revealed a world of human frustration in which sex and violence underlie an atmosphere of romantic gentility. *A Streetcar Named Desire* (1947) won a Pulitzer Prize. It is a study of the mental and moral ruin of Blanche Du Bois, another former Southern belle, whose genteel pretensions are no match for the harsh realities symbolized by her brutish brother-in-law, Stanley Kowalski.

48. c) *Seize the Day*
Bellow is an American novelist whose characterizations of the modern urban man, disaffected by society but not destroyed in spirit, earned him the Nobel Prize for Literature in 1976. *Seize the Day* (1956), a novella, is a unique treatment of a failure in a society where the only success is success.

49. b) A kind of paradox
It is an apparently self-contradictory statement, the underlying meaning of which is revealed only by careful scrutiny. The purpose of a paradox is to arrest attention and provoke fresh thought. The statement "Less is more" is an example. When a paradox is compressed into two words as in "loud silence", "lonely crowd", or "living death", it is called an oxymoron.

50. d) *Twelfth Night*
A play in five acts by William Shakespeare, it is one of his finest comedies. The play pokes gentle fun at wooing and the folly of lovers. Duke Orsino, for example, is in love with the state of being in love, and Lady Olivia's initial vow of isolation to honour her dead brother is exposed as excessive and even self-indulgent. The two positions are contrasted with the mature and sensible attitude of Viola.

51. a) *Anna Karenina*
The novel (1875-77) interweaves the stories of three families, the Oblonskys, the Karenins, and the Levins. In *Anna Karenina*, Tolstoy presents a large-scale obsessive study of feminine psychology that is almost excruciating in its relentless probing.

52. b) Pablo Neruda
A Chilean poet, diplomat, and politician, Neruda was awarded the Nobel Prize for Literature in 1971. *Twenty Love Poems and a Song of Despair* was his second book. It became an instant success and is still one of Neruda's most popular books. The verse in *Twenty Love Poems* is vigorous, poignant, and direct, yet subtle and very original in its imagery and metaphors. The poems express young, passionate, unhappy love perhaps better than any book of poetry in the long Romantic tradition.

53. b) *Sons and Lovers*
One of the most influential English writers of the 20th century, Lawrence's novel *Sons and Lovers* (1913) is a quasi-autobiography. The whole narrative turns Lawrence's own life history into a powerful psychoanalytic study of a young man's Oedipal attraction toward his mother and its consequences on his relations with other women.

54. a) *Pygmalion*
George Bernard Shaw was an Irish comic dramatist, literary critic, and Socialist propagandist. His comedic masterpiece, and certainly his funniest and most popular play, is *Pygmalion* (performed 1913). It was claimed by Shaw to be a didactic drama about phonetics, and its antiheroic hero, Henry Higgins, is a phonetician, but the play is a

Did You Know?

Apart from the human body, the Egyptians mummified sacred animals, birds, reptiles, fishes. Even insects were treated in a similar way, and the meat offerings deposited with the wealthy dead were likewise "preserved".

The Romans never used butter as a food.

humane comedy about love and the English class system. The play is about the training Higgins gives to a Cockney flower girl to enable her to pass as a lady and is also about the repercussions of the experiment's success. *Pygmalion* has been both filmed (1938), winning an Academy Award for Shaw for his screenplay, and adapted into an immensely popular musical, (1956; motion-picture version, 1964).

55. b) Ben Jonson
The English Jacobean dramatist, lyric poet, and literary critic Johnson, is generally regarded as the second most important English dramatist, after William Shakespeare, during the reign of James I. In the play *Every Man In His Humour* (1598), Jonson tried to bring the spirit and manner of Latin comedy to the English popular stage by presenting the story of a young man with an eye for a girl, who has difficulty with a phlegmatic father, is dependent on a clever servant, and is ultimately successful—in fact, the standard plot of the Latin dramatist Plautus.

56. b) Lord Byron
The English Romantic poet and satirist's poetry and personality captured the imagination of Europe. *Don Juan* (1819-24) is a satire in the form of a picaresque verse tale. The first two cantos of *Don Juan* were begun in 1818 and published in July 1819. Byron transformed the legendary libertine Don Juan into an unsophisticated, innocent young man who, though he delightedly succumbs to the beautiful women who pursue him, remains a rational norm against which to view the absurdities and irrationalities of the world.

57. c) *Casino Royale*
Ian Fleming created the character of James Bond, a British secret service agent. James Bond gained tremendous popularity in 20th-century popular fiction. *Casino Royale* (1953) was the first of Fleming's 12 James Bond novels. The novels are packed with violent action, hairbreadth escapes, international espionage, terror, and intrigue.

58. a) William Somerset Maugham
An English novelist, playwright, and short-story writer, Maugham's work is characterized by a clear unadorned style, cosmopolitan settings, and a shrewd understanding of human nature. *Of Human Bondage* (1915) is a semi-autobiographical account of a young medical student's painful progress toward maturity.

59. a) A poetic stanza
A tercet is a unit or group of three lines of verse, usually containing rhyme, as in William Shakespeare's "The Phoenix and the Turtle":
Death is now the phoenix' nest;
And the turtle's loyal breast
To eternity doth rest,…

60. b) Rudyard Kipling
The English short-story writer, poet, and novelist's *The Jungle Books* (1894 and 1895) is a stylistically superb collection of stories linked by poems for children. These books give further proof that Kipling excelled at telling a story but was inconsistent in producing balanced, cohesive novels.

61. d) Gustave Flaubert
Madame Bovary (1857) is a realistic portrayal of bourgeois life. For *Madame Bovary*, Flaubert took a commonplace story of

adultery and made of it a book that will always be read because of its profound humanity. *Madame Bovary*, with its unrelenting objectivity—by which Flaubert meant the dispassionate recording of every trait or incident that could illuminate the psychology of his characters and their role in the logical development of his story—marks the beginning of a new age in literature.

62. a) *The Prelude*
The poem extends the quiet autobiographical mode of reminiscence that Wordsworth had begun in "Tintern Abbey" and traces the poet's life from his school days through his university life and his visits to France, up to the year (1799) in which he settled at Grasmere. It thus describes a circular journey—what has been called a long journey home. But the main events in the autobiography are internal: the poem exultantly describes the ways in which the imagination emerges as the dominant faculty, exerting its control over the reason and the world of the senses alike.

63. a) Hester Prynne
The main character of *The Scarlet Letter* is Hester Prynne, a young married woman who has borne an illegitimate child while living away from her husband in a village in Puritan New England.

64. c) *Great Expectations*
The book is a first-person narration, drawing on parts of Dickens' personality and experience. The hero Pip's mind is explored with great subtlety, and his development through a childhood and youth beset with hard tests of character is traced critically but sympathetically. Various "great expectations"

in the book proved ill founded—a comment as much on the values of the age as on the characters' weaknesses and misfortunes.

65. c) A whale
Moby Dick was published in London in October 1851 and a month later in America. It brought its author neither acclaim nor reward. Basically its story is simple. Captain Ahab pursues the white whale, Moby Dick, which finally kills him. At that level, it is an intense, superbly authentic narrative of whaling. In the perverted grandeur of Captain Ahab and in the beauties and terrors of the voyage of the "Pequod", however, Melville dramatized his deeper concerns: the equivocal defeats and triumphs of the human spirit and its fusion of creative and murderous urges.

66. d) Dr. Faustus
Hero of one of the most durable legends in Western folklore and literature, *Dr. Faustus* is the story of a German necromancer or astrologer who sells his soul to the devil in exchange for knowledge and power.

67. d) Playwrights
The first generation of professional playwrights in England was known collectively as the "university wits". Their nickname identifies their social pretensions, but their drama was primarily middle class, patriotic, and romantic. Their preferred subjects were historical or pseudo-historical, mixed with clowning, music, and love interest.

68. a) *Henry IV*
In the *Henry IV* plays, which are dominated by the massive character of Falstaff and his roguish exploits in Eastcheap, Shakespeare intercuts scenes among the rulers with scenes

among those who are ruled, to create a multifaceted composite picture of national life at a particular historical moment.

69. d) Ben Jonson

Shakespeare's friend and nearest rival, Jonson stands at the fountainhead of what has subsequently been the dominant modern comic tradition. His early plays, particularly *Every Man in His Humour* (1598) and *Every Man Out of His Humour* (1599), with their galleries of grotesques, scornful detachment, and rather academic effect, were patently indebted to the verse satires of the 1590s; they introduced to the English stage a vigorous and direct anatomizing of "the time's deformities" the language, habits, and humours of the London scene.

70. c) William Blake

The English poet, painter engraver, and visionary mystic's hand-illustrated series of lyrical and epic poems, beginning with *Songs of Innocence* (1789) and *Songs of Experience* (1794), form one of the most strikingly original and independent bodies of work in the Western cultural tradition. The songs show the two contrary states of the human soul. The "two contrary states" are: *innocence,* when the child's imagination has simply the function of completing its own growth; and *experience,* when it is faced with the world of law, morality, and repression.

71. c) A form of poetry

A *masnawi* is a series of distichs (couplets) in rhymed pairs (*aa, bb, cc,* and so on) that makes up a characteristic type of Persian verse, used chiefly for heroic, historical, and romantic epic poetry and didactic poetry. The form originated in the Middle Persian period (roughly from the 3rd century BC to the 9th century AD). It became a favourite poetic form of the Persians and of those cultures they influenced. The *masnawi* enabled the poet to develop the thread of a tale through thousands of verses.

72. c) *The Waste Land*

The work expresses with great power the disenchantment, disillusionment, and disgust of the period after World War I. In a series of vignettes, it portrays a sterile world of panicky fears and barren lusts, and of human beings waiting for some sign or promise of redemption.

73. b) Rudyard Kipling

Much of his childhood was unhappy. Kipling was taken to England by his parents at the age of six and was left for five years at a foster home at Southsea, the horrors of which he described in the story "Baa Baa, Black Sheep" (1888).

74. c) Alan Stewart Paton

One of the foremost writers in South Africa, best known for his first novel, Paton's *Cry, the Beloved Country* (1948) is a passionate tale of racial injustice. The book vividly portrays the anguish suffered by an elderly black minister who must come to terms with his faith when his son is convicted of murdering a white man.

75. c) Mississippi River

Huckleberry Finn, by general agreement, is Twain's finest book and an outstanding American novel. Its narrator is Huck, a youngster whose carelessly recorded vernacular speech is admirably adapted to detailed and poetic descriptions of scenes, vivid

The word "telephone", from the Greek roots *tele,* "far", and *phone,* "sound", was applied as early as the late 17th century to the string telephone familiar to children.

The production of iron began in Anatolia about 2000 BC.

Did You Know?

representations of characters, and narrative renditions that are both broadly comic and subtly ironic. Huck, son of the village drunkard, is uneducated, superstitious, and sometimes credulous; but he also has a native shrewdness, a cheerfulness that is hard to put down, compassionate tolerance, and an instinctive tendency to reach the right decisions about important matters. He runs away from his increasingly violent father and, with his companion, the runaway slave Jim, makes a long and frequently interrupted voyage floating down the Mississippi River on a raft.

76. a) *A Portrait of the Artist as a Young Man*
An autobiographical novel, James Joyce's *A Portrait of the Artist* traces the intellectual and emotional development of a young man named Stephen Dedalus and ends with his decision to leave Dublin for Paris to devote his life to art.

77. a) Friedrich Nietzsche
The German classical scholar, philosopher, and critic of culture became one of the most influential of all modern thinkers. His attempts to unmask the motives that underlie traditional Western religion, morality, and philosophy deeply affected generations of theologians, philosophers, psychologists, poets, novelists, and playwrights. He thought through the consequences of the triumph of the Enlightenment's secularism, expressed in his observation that "God is dead", in a way that determined the agenda for many of Europe's most celebrated intellectuals after his death. Although he was an ardent foe of nationalism, anti-Semitism, and power politics, his name was later invoked by Fascists to advance the very things he loathed.

78. c) Tennessee Williams
The U.S. dramatist's plays reveal a world of human frustration in which sex and violence underlie an atmosphere of romantic gentility. In "The Glass Menagerie" Williams portrayed a declassed Southern family living in a tenement. The play is about the failure of a domineering mother, Amanda, living upon her delusions of a romantic past, and her cynical son, Tom, to secure a suitor for Tom's crippled and painfully shy sister, Laura, who lives in a fantasy world with a collection of glass animals.

79. a) Alice Walker
The American writer's novels, short stories, and poems are noted for their insightful treatment of African American culture. Her novels, most notably *The Color Purple* (1982), focus particularly on women.

80. a) *Hamlet*
Claudius was the unscrupulous king of Denmark, stepfather of Prince Hamlet, and second husband to Queen Gertrude in Shakespeare's *Hamlet*. Cunning and politically savvy, Claudius represents blind ambition. Having murdered his brother and seduced and married his sister-in-law, he thinks his only domestic problems are with his weak but unpredictable nephew-stepson, Hamlet. Ultimately, however, Claudius' treacheries bring about the collapse of the kingdom and destroy the royal family.

81. a) Nick Bottom
He is a weaver and the most important of the six "mechanicals" in Shakespeare's comedy *A Midsummer Night's Dream*. Bottom—together with Peter Quince, a carpenter, Francis Flute, a bellows mender, Tom Snout, a tinker, Snug, a

joiner, and Robin Starveling, a tailor—initiates a series of low-comedy antics that contrast with the machinations of the aristocratic lovers. Bottom and the other tradesmen present a performance of the tragedy of Pyramus and Thisbe. In both the planning and the execution, their enactment provides some of the most hilarious and memorable horseplay in all of Shakespeare's comedies.

82. c) Toni Morrison
The novel examines (among other issues) the dynamics of friendship and the expectations for conformity within the community. *Song of Solomon* (1977) is told by a male narrator in search of his identity; its publication brought the American writer to national attention.

83. a) Religious verse
Aside from his name, little is known of Cynewulf; he probably lived in the 9th century in Mercia. Elene, perhaps the best of his poems, describes the mission of St. Helena, mother of the emperor Constantine, to recover Christ's cross. Cynewulf's work is lucid and technically elegant; his theme is the continuing evangelical mission from the time of Christ to the triumph of Christianity under Constantine.

84. a) Julian of Norwich
The celebrated mystic's *Revelations of Divine Love* is generally considered one of the most remarkable documents of mediaeval religious experience. She spent the latter part of her life as a recluse at St. Julian's Church, Norwich.

85. a) O. Henry
The tales of this American short-story writer have romanticized the commonplace—in particular the life of ordinary people in New York City. His stories expressed the effect of coincidence on character through humour, grim or ironic, and often had surprise endings, a device that became identified with his name and cost him critical favour when its vogue had passed.

86. b) Saki
The stories of this Scottish writer and journalist depict the Edwardian social scene with a flippant wit and power of fantastic invention used both to satirize social pretension, unkindness, and stupidity and to create an atmosphere of horror. His short stories and sketches include *Reginald* (1904), *Reginald in Russia* (1910), *The Chronicles of Clovis* (1912), and *Beasts and Super-Beasts* (1914).

87. b) Ayn Rand
The Russian-born American writer, in commercially successful novels, presented her philosophy of objectivism, essentially reversing the traditional Judeo-Christian ethic. *The Fountainhead* (1943), her first best-selling novel, depicts a highly romanticized architect-hero, a superior individual whose egoism and genius prevail over timid traditionalism and social conformism.

88. a) William Congreve
His masterpiece, "The Way of the World" (1700) is a brilliant combination of intricate plotting and incisively humane portraiture.

89. a) William Blake
Blake's efforts were to revise his contemporaries' view of the universe and to construct a new mythology centred not in the

God of the Bible but in Urizen, a figure of reason and law who he believed to be the true deity worshipped by his contemporaries.

90. d) Her father, Otto Frank
Friends who had searched the annex after the family's departure later gave Otto Frank the papers left behind by the Gestapo; among them he found Anne's diary. He had it published in 1947 as *Het Achterhuis* (Eng. trans., *The Diary of a Young Girl*). Precocious in style and insight, it traces her emotional growth amid adversity and records her assertion that "In spite of everything I still believe that people are really good at heart." The diary has been translated into more than 50 languages and has been widely read.

91. b) *Twelfth Night*
One of Shakespeare's finest comedies, *Twelfth Night* precedes the great tragedies and problem plays in order of composition. There is a humorous subplot involving the members of Lady Olivia's household—Feste the jester; Maria; Olivia's uncle, Sir Toby Belch; and Sir Toby's friend, Sir Andrew Aguecheek—who scheme to undermine the high-minded, pompous Malvolio. At the play's end, Malvolio is the only solitary figure among the pairs of happy lovers.

92. a) *Mourning Becomes Electra*
One of O'Neill's masterpieces, *Mourning Becomes Electra*, represents his most complete use of Greek forms, themes, and characters. Based on the Oresteia trilogy by Aeschylus, it was itself three plays in one.

93. d) Sappho
The celebrated lyric poet has been greatly admired in all ages for the beauty of her writing. She is said to exceed all other poets, except Archilochus and Alcaeus, in the history of Greek literature in entering into a close personal relation with the reader.

94. a) Pearl S. Buck
The Good Earth (1931) is a poignant tale of a Chinese peasant and his slave-wife and their struggle upward. The book established Buck as an interpreter of the East to the West and was adapted for stage and screen.

95. c) Emily Dickinson
She experimented with poetic rhythms and rhymes. Almost all her poetry was published posthumously. The subjects of Dickinson's poems, expressed in intimate, domestic figures of speech, include love, death, and nature. The contrast between her quiet, secluded life in the house in which she was born and died and the depth and intensity of her terse poems has provoked much speculation about her personality and personal relationships. Her 1,775 poems and her letters, which survive in almost as great a number, reveal a passionate, witty woman and a scrupulous craftsman who made an art not only of her poetry but also of her correspondence and her life.

96. b) *A Winter's Tale*
One of Shakespeare's final plays, *A Winter's Tale* is a romantic comedy with elements of tragedy. The plot opens with Leontes, the king of Sicilia, entertaining his old friend Polixenes, the king of Bohemia. Leontes jealously mistakes the courtesy between his wife Hermione and Polixenes as a sign of Hermione's adultery with him. The pregnant Hermione is then publicly humiliated and

Did You Know?

The word "spa" is derived from Spa, Belgium, a municipality nestled in the forested hills of the northern Ardennes, filled with mineral springs that have been frequented for their healing powers since the 16th century.

The piles of lava that form Hawaii rise as high as 9,700 m (32,000 ft) above the ocean floor.

thrown in jail, despite her protests of innocence. When the child, a girl, is born, Leontes rejects her out of hand and gives her over to Antigonus, the husband of Hermione's attendant Paulina, who is instructed to abandon the baby in some wild place. Having learned of his mother's mistreatment, Leontes' beloved son Mamillius dies, and Hermione, too, is carried out and reported dead. At the end, all is forgiven, and Hermione, who is seen as a statue, proves to be alive.

97. d) James Fenimore Cooper
The first major U.S. novelist, Cooper was the author of the novels of frontier adventure known as the Leatherstocking Tales, featuring the wilderness scout called Natty Bumppo, or Hawkeye. They include *The Pioneers* (1823), *The Last of the Mohicans* (1826), *The Prairie* (1827), *The Pathfinder* (1840), and *The Deerslayer* (1841).

98. d) The Pulitzer Prize
The prizes, originally endowed with a gift of $500,000 from the newspaper magnate Joseph Pulitzer, are highly esteemed and have been awarded each May since 1917. The awards are made by Columbia University on the recommendation of The Pulitzer Prize Board, composed of judges appointed by the university. The prizes have varied in number and category over the years but currently number 14 prizes in the field of journalism, 6 prizes in letters, 1 prize in music, and 4 fellowships.

99. b) Ken Kesey
In 1959, he volunteered to take part in a government drug research programme that tested a variety of psychoactive drugs. He wrote of his drug-induced experiences for government researchers and from the same experience, wrote his most celebrated novel, *One Flew Over the Cuckoo's Nest.*

100. a) Anton Chekhov
Wood Demon (1888-89), a long-winded and ineptly facetious four-act play, somehow, by a miracle of art, became converted—largely by cutting—into *Dyadya Vanya* (*Uncle Vanya*) one of Chekov's greatest stage masterpieces. The conversion—to a superb study of aimlessness in a rural manor house—took place some time between 1890 and 1896.

101. d) Charlotte Bronte
The English novelist Charlotte Bronte's noted work is *Jane Eyre* (1847), a strong narrative of a woman in conflict with her natural desires and social condition. The novel gave new truthfulness to Victorian fiction. She later wrote *Shirley* (1849) and *Villette* (1853).

Did You Know?

The Turkish bath originated in the Middle East and combines exposure to warm air, then steam or hot-air immersion, massage, and finally a cold-water bath or shower.

The pack ice of the Northern Hemisphere covers an average area of about 10,600,000 sq km (4,100,000 sq miles), filling the Arctic Ocean Basin and adjacent North Atlantic Ocean.

Nobel

1. d) The Swedish Academy
From Stockholm, the Royal Swedish Academy of Sciences confers the prizes for physics, chemistry, and economics, the Karolinska Institute confers the prize for physiology or medicine, and the Swedish Academy confers the prize for literature. The Norwegian Nobel Committee based in Oslo confers the prize for peace. The Nobel Foundation is the legal owner and functional administrator of the funds and serves as the joint administrative body of the prize-awarding institutions, but it is not concerned with the prize deliberations or decisions, which rest exclusively with the four institutions.

2. d) Dynamite
The Swedish chemist, engineer, and industrialist invented dynamite and other, more powerful explosives and also founded the Nobel Prize. Nobel invented dynamite in 1867. By chance, he discovered that nitroglycerin was absorbed to dryness by kieselguhr, a porous siliceous earth, and the resulting mixture was much safer to use and easier to handle than nitroglycerin alone. Nobel named the new product dynamite (from Greek *dynamis,* "power") and was granted patents for it in Great Britain (1867) and the United States (1868). Dynamite established Nobel's fame worldwide and was soon put to use in blasting tunnels, cutting canals, and building railways and roads.

3. c) Penicillin
The Scottish bacteriologist's discovery of penicillin (1928) prepared the way for the highly effective practice of antibiotic therapy for infectious diseases. Fleming shared the Nobel Prize for Physiology or Medicine in 1945 with Ernst Boris Chain and Howard Walter Florey, who both (from 1939) carried Fleming's basic discovery further in the isolation, purification, testing, and quantity production of penicillin.

4. c) Explanation of photoelectric effect
The German-American physicist developed the special and general theories of relativity and won the Nobel Prize for Physics in 1921 for his explanation of the photoelectric effect. Recognized in his own time as one of the most creative intellects in human history, in the first 15 years of the 20th century Einstein advanced a series of theories that proposed entirely new ways of thinking about space, time, and gravitation. His theories of relativity and gravitation were a profound advance over the old Newtonian physics and revolutionized scientific and philosophic inquiry.

5. b) Pierre Curie
The French physical chemist was a co-winner of the Nobel Prize for Physics in 1903. He and his wife, Marie Curie, discovered radium and polonium in their investigation of radioactivity. The French physical chemists, Frederic and Irene Joliot-Curie, husband and wife, who were jointly awarded the 1935 Nobel Prize for Chemistry for their discovery of new radioactive isotopes prepared artificially, were the son-in-law and daughter of Pierre and Marie Curie.

Of the world's known mineral reserves of gold ore, 50 percent is found in South Africa.

Copper was the first nonprecious metal to be wrought by man.

The brick was first produced in a sun-dried form at least 6,000 years ago.

Did You Know?

6. b) Neils Bohr

Aage Niels Bohr, the Danish physicist, shared the 1975 Nobel Prize for Physics with Ben R. Mottelson and James Rainwater for their work in determining the asymmetrical shapes of certain atomic nuclei. Bohr was educated at the University of Copenhagen, where he received his doctorate in 1954. During the 1940s he worked as assistant to his father, Niels Bohr (1922 Nobel Prize for Physics), on the development of the atomic bomb at Los Alamos, New Mexico.

7. c) Jean Paul Sartre

The French novelist and playwright was an exponent of Existentialism—a philosophy acclaiming the freedom of the individual human being. He was awarded the Nobel Prize for Literature in 1964, but he declined it, the reasons being both personal and objective. In a letter to the Swedish Academy, Satre explained that he did not accept official honours and had rejected them earlier too. He added that as a writer if he accepted the award, his personal commitments would be associated with the awarding institution. He believed that a writer should not allow himself to be so associated.

8. a) Boris Pasternak

The Russian poet's novel *Doctor Zhivago* helped win him the Nobel Prize for Literature in 1958 but aroused so much opposition in the Soviet Union that he declined the honour. An epic of wandering, spiritual isolation, and love amid the harshness of the Russian Revolution and its aftermath, the novel became an international best-seller but was circulated only in secrecy and translation in his own land.

9. c) Le Duc Tho

The Vietnamese politician is best known for his part in the ceasefire of 1973, when he served as special adviser to the North Vietnamese delegation to the Paris Peace Conferences in 1968-73. He eventually became his delegation's principal spokesman, in which capacity he negotiated the ceasefire agreement that led to the withdrawal of the last American troops from South Vietnam. It was for this accomplishment that he was awarded the Nobel Peace Prize, which he declined, giving as his reason the present situation in Vietnam. Tho oversaw the North Vietnamese offensive that overthrew the South Vietnamese government in 1975, and he played a similar role in the first stages of Vietnam's invasion of Cambodia in 1978. He remained a member of the Politburo until 1986.

10. a) Dag Hammarskjold

The Swedish economist and statesman served as the second secretary-general of the United Nations (1953-61) and enhanced the prestige and effectiveness of the UN. He was posthumously awarded the Nobel Prize for Peace in 1961. The son of Hjalmar Hammarskjold, prime minister of Sweden (1914-17) and chairman of the Nobel Prize Foundation (1929-47), Dag Hammarskjold studied law and economics at the universities of Uppsala and Stockholm and taught political economy at Stockholm (1933-36). He then joined the Swedish civil service. On April 10, 1953, five months after the resignation of Trygve Lie of Norway as secretary-general, Hammarskjold was elected to the office for a term of five years. In September 1957 he was reelected to another five-year term.

Did You Know?

The lock originated in the Near East; the oldest known example was found in the ruins of the palace of Khorsabad near Nineveh, possibly 4,000 years old.

Electrum, the natural or artificial alloy of gold with at least 20 percent silver, was used to make the first known coins in the Western world.

11. a) Erik Axel Karlfeldt
The Swedish poet, whose essentially regional, tradition-bound poetry was extremely popular, won the Nobel Prize for Literature posthumously in 1931; he had refused it in 1918. Karlfeldt's strong ties to the peasant culture of his rural homeland remained a dominant influence on him all his life. Some of his poems have been published in English translation in *Arcadia Borealis: Selected Poems of Erik Axel Karlfeldt* (1938). In time, even some of his admirers criticized him for employing his gifts so exclusively in the service of a dying local culture.

12. b) Bank of Sweden
In the will he drafted in 1895, Nobel instructed that most of his fortune be set aside as a fund for the awarding of five annual prizes "to those who, during the preceding year, shall have conferred the greatest benefit on mankind". These prizes as established by his will are: the Nobel Prize for Physics (Nobelpriset i Fysik); the Nobel Prize for Chemistry (Nobelpriset i Kemi); the Nobel Prize for Physiology or Medicine (Nobelpriset i Fysiologi eller Medicin); the Nobel Prize for Literature (Nobelpriset i Litteratur); and the Nobel Prize for Peace (Nobels Fredspris). The first distribution of the prizes took place on December 10, 1901, the fifth anniversary of Nobel's death. An additional award, the Prize for Economic Sciences in Memory of Alfred Nobel (Priset i Ekonomisk Vetenskap till Alfred Nobels Minne), was established in 1968 by the Bank of Sweden and was first awarded in 1969.

13. b) Chemistry
The French physicist, famous for her work on radioactivity, was twice a winner of the Nobel Prize. With Henri Becquerel and her husband, Pierre Curie, she was awarded the 1903 Nobel Prize for Physics. She was then sole winner of the 1911 Nobel Prize for Chemistry.

14. a) Third law of thermodynamics
The German scientist was one of the founders of modern physical chemistry. Simply stated, the law postulates that at a temperature above absolute zero, all matter tends toward random motion and all energy tends to dissipate. Nernst also conducted important research on the theory of galvanic cells, the thermodynamics of chemical equilibrium, the properties of vapours at high temperature and of solids at low temperature, and the mechanism of photochemistry. Nernst was also interested in applied science. He invented an improved electric light and an electronically amplified piano. His influential textbook of theoretical chemistry was first published in 1893. In later years he concerned himself chiefly with astrophysical theories.

15. c) King Gustav III
The Swedish Academy was founded by King Gustav III on April 5, 1786, in Stockholm. The goal of the organization was defined as working for the "purity, vigour and majesty" of the Swedish language. This was to be accomplished by such activities as producing a dictionary and grammar of the Swedish language, recognizing the achievements of Swedes in "eloquence and poetry" in annual competitions, and minting an annual coin to honour an eminent Swede. The poetry competitions have not been held frequently, yet the academy awards more than 10 other literary prizes, such as the Swedish Language Prize for scholarship in the language and the Swedish Teaching Prize for inspiring interest in the language and literature of

Sweden in younger generations. Most importantly, the academy awards the Nobel Prize for Literature, as requested by Alfred Nobel in his will.

16. c) Sinclair Lewis

The American novelist and social critic punctured American complacency with his broadly drawn, widely popular satirical novels. He won the Nobel Prize for Literature in 1930. He undertook the writing of *Main Street* as a major effort, assuming that it would not bring him the ready rewards of magazine fiction. Yet its publication in 1920 made his literary reputation. *Main Street* is seen through the eyes of Carol Kennicott, an Eastern girl married to a Midwestern doctor who settles in Gopher Prairie, Minnesota. The power of the book derives from Lewis's careful rendering of local speech, customs, and social amenities. Lewis's other works include *Babbit* (1922), *Arrowsmith* (1925), and *Dodsworth* (1929).

17. a) Serum therapy

Emil von Behring is considered the founder of the science of immunology; the bacteriologist received in 1901 the first Nobel Prize for Physiology or Medicine for his work on serum therapy, especially its application against diphtheria. With the Japanese bacteriologist Kitasato Shibasaburo, he showed that it was possible to provide an animal with passive immunity against tetanus by injecting it with the blood serum of another animal infected with the disease. Behring then applied this technique of antitoxic immunity (a term which he and Kitasato originated) to prevent diphtheria. Administration of diphtheria antitoxin, successfully marketed in 1892, became a routine part of the treatment of the disease.

18. c) Peace

On February 1, the six Nobel Committees—one for each prize category—start their work on the nominations received. Several thousand people are engaged in the committees' efforts to determine the originality and significance of each nominee's contribution, and outside experts are frequently consulted during the process. During September and early October the Nobel Committees submit their recommendations to the Royal Swedish Academy of Sciences and the other prize-awarding institutions. A committee's recommendation is usually but not invariably followed. The deliberations and the voting within these institutions are secret at all stages. The final decision by the awarders must be made by November 15. Prizes may be given only to individuals, except the Peace Prize, which may also be conferred upon an institution.

19. b) Wilhelm Conrad Rontgen

The German physicist was a recipient of the first Nobel Prize for Physics, in 1901, for his discovery of X-rays, which heralded the age of modern physics and revolutionized diagnostic medicine. He took the first X-ray photographs of the interiors of metal objects and of the bones in his wife's hand.

20. a) For work on sugar and purine groups of substances

The German chemist was awarded the Nobel Prize in 1902. Fischer's research on the purines was instituted in 1881. He determined the structures of uric acid, xanthine, caffeine, theobromine, and other related compounds, and he showed that they are all derivatives of a single compound, a nitrogenous base that he named purine. His study of sugars led him to investigate the reactions and substances involved in fermentation; in his investigations of how enzymes break down sugars, Fischer laid the foundations for enzyme chemistry.

21. b) Sully Prudhomme
The French poet was a leading member of the Parnassian movement, which sought to restore elegance, balance, and aesthetic standards to poetry, in reaction to the excesses of Romanticism. In 1865 he began to publish fluent and melancholic verse inspired by an unhappy love affair. *Stances et poemes* (1865) contains his best known poem, *Le vase brise* ("The Broken Vase"). Sully Prudhomme later renounced personal lyricism for the more objective approach of the Parnassians, writing poems attempting to represent philosophical concepts in verse. Two of the best known works in this vein are *La Justice* (1878; "Justice") and *Le Bonheur* (1888; "Happiness").

22. a) Svante August Arrhenius
The physical chemist is best known for his theory that electrolytes are separated, or dissociated, into electrically charged particles, or ions, even when there is no current flowing through the solution. In 1903 he was awarded the Nobel Prize for Chemistry.

23. b) Econometrics
The pioneer Norwegian econometrician and economist was a joint winner of the 1969 Nobel Prize for Economics. Frisch was educated at the University of Oslo, obtaining his Ph.D. in 1926. He was appointed to a specially created professorship at Oslo in 1931, a post he held until his retirement in 1965. Frisch was a pioneer of econometrics—the application of mathematical models in association with statistical techniques to

economic data—and is credited with inventing the term. He was one of the founders of the Econometric Society and, for 21 years, editor of *Econometrica*.

24. a) Jacobus Henricus van't Hoff
The physical chemist received the Nobel Prize for Chemistry in 1901 for work on rates of reaction, chemical equilibrium, and osmotic pressure. In 1874 he and Le Bel, independently of each other, announced a concept that proved to be the cornerstone in the study of the three-dimensional structure (stereochemistry) of organic compounds: the four chemical bonds that carbon can form are directed to the corners of a tetrahedron. This concept helped explain the property of optical rotation.

25. c) Henryk Sienkiewicz
The Polish author of novels, which achieved great popularity, Sienkiewicz was the winner of the Nobel Prize for Literature in 1905. Sienkiewicz's great trilogy of historical novels began to appear in *Slowo* in 1883. It is composed of *Ogniem i mieczem* (1884; *With Fire and Sword*), *Potop* (1886; *The Deluge*), and *Pan Wolodyjowski* (1887-88; *Pan Michael*). Set in the later 17th century, the trilogy describes Poland's struggles against Cossacks, Tatars, Swedes, and Turks, stressing Polish heroism in a vivid style of epic clarity and simplicity. Sienkiewicz's other novels include the widely translated *Quo Vadis?* (1896), a historical novel set in Rome under Nero, which established Sienkiewicz's international reputation.

26. b) Wassily Leontief
The Russian-born American economist has been called the father of input-output analysis

Rodents are the most numerous of existing mammals, both in number of species and number of individuals, and are one of the most diverse of living lineages.

The milk of whales and seals is some 12 times as rich in fats and four times as rich in protein as that of domestic cows but contains almost no sugar.

Did You Know?

in econometrics and won the Nobel Prize for Economic Sciences in 1973. The core of his complex input-output system is a gridlike table showing what individual industries buy from and sell to one another. With the addition of government, consumers, foreign countries, and other elements, there emerges a general outline of the goods and services circulating in a national economy. The input-output method of economic analysis is used in various forms by a large number of industrialized countries for both planning and forecasting.

27. a) Malaria

Ronald Ross's discovery in 1897 of the malarial parasite in the gastrointestinal tract of the *Anopheles* mosquito led to the realization that malaria was transmitted by *Anopheles,* and laid the foundation for combating the disease. Using birds that were sick with malaria, he was soon able to ascertain the entire life cycle of the malarial parasite, including its presence in the mosquito's salivary glands. He demonstrated that malaria is transmitted from infected birds to healthy ones by the bite of a mosquito, a finding that suggested the disease's mode of transmission to humans.

28. c) Paul Anthony Samuelson

The American economist was educated at the University of Chicago and at Harvard, where he obtained his Ph.D. in 1941. He was professor of economics at the Massachusetts Institute of Technology from 1940. Samuelson also served as a government economic adviser on several occasions. Samuelson's *Foundations of Economic Analysis* (1947) provides the foundation for a basic theme of his work, the universal nature of consumer behaviour as the key to economic theory.

29. a) Frederic Passy

A French economist and advocate of international arbitration, Passy's work for peace began during the Crimean War (1853-56). His plea for peace in the periodical *Le Temps* (1867) helped to avert war between France and Prussia over Luxembourg. In the same year he founded the International League for Peace, later known as the French Society for International Arbitration. After the Franco-German War (1870-71) he proposed independence and permanent neutrality for Alsace-Lorraine. As a member of the French Chamber of Deputies (from 1881), he successfully urged arbitration of a dispute between France and The Netherlands concerning the French Guiana-Surinam boundary. He assisted in founding the Inter-Parliamentary Union (1888) and remained active in the peace movement for the rest of his life.

30. a) Theory of electromagnetic radiation

The Dutch physicist was the joint winner, with Pieter Zeeman, of the Nobel Prize for Physics in 1902 for his theory of electromagnetic radiation, which, confirmed by findings of Zeeman, gave rise to Albert Einstein's special theory of relativity. His work in physics was wide in scope, but his central aim was to construct a single theory to explain the relationship of electricity, magnetism, and light.

31. b) Four

The British chemist's discovery of four of the noble gases (neon, argon, krypton, and xenon) earned him the Nobel Prize for Chemistry in 1904. When in 1892 the British physicist Lord Rayleigh asked chemists to explain the difference between the atomic

Corpses have been pickled in vinegar, wine, and stronger spirits: the body of the British admiral Lord Nelson was returned from Trafalgar to England in a cask of brandy.

The first academic department of sociology was created by Albion Small at the University of Chicago in 1892.

weight of nitrogen found in chemical compounds and the heavier free nitrogen found in the atmosphere, Ramsay predicted that nitrogen isolated from the atmosphere was consistently contaminated with a hitherto undiscovered heavy gas. Devising a method that assured the total removal of nitrogen and oxygen from air, Ramsay and Rayleigh found (1894) a chemically inert gaseous element, later called argon, making up nearly 1 percent of the atmosphere. In 1910 Ramsay detected the presence of the last of the noble-gas series, called niton (now known as radon), in the radioactive emissions of radium.

32. a) Research on organic dyes
The German research chemist synthesized indigo (1880) and formulated its structure (1883). Notable among Baeyer's many achievements were the discovery of the phthalein dyes and his investigations of uric acid derivatives, polyacetylenes, and oxonium salts.

33. d) Rudyard Kipling
The English short-story writer, poet, and novelist, Rudyard Kipling is chiefly remembered for his celebration of British imperialism, his tales and poems of British soldiers in India, and his tales for children. He received the Nobel Prize for Literature in 1907. Besides numerous short-story collections and poetry collections such as *The Seven Seas* (1896), Kipling's novels include *The Light That Failed* (1890), *Captains Courageous* (1897), *Kim* (1901), *The Jungle Books* (1894 and 1895), *Puck of Pook's Hill* (1906), and *Rewards and Fairies* (1910).

34. a) Alphonse Laveran
The French physician, pathologist, and parasitologist discovered the cause of malaria in the course of the autopsies he conducted on malaria victims while serving as a military surgeon in Algeria in 1880. He found the causative organism to be a protozoan which he named *Oscillaria malariae,* though it was later renamed *Plasmodium.* Laveran was a powerful influence in developing research in tropical medicine, carrying on fruitful work in trypanosomiasis, leishmaniasis, and other protozoal diseases, as well as his epochal work in malaria. He established the Laboratory of Tropical Diseases at the Pasteur Institute (1907) and founded the Societe de Pathologie Exotique (1908).

35. d) Indian Medical Service
After graduating in medicine (1879), Ross entered the Indian Medical Service and served in the third Anglo-Burmese War (1885). On leave he studied bacteriology in London (1888-89) and then returned to India, where, prompted by Patrick Manson's guidance and assistance, he began (1892) a series of investigations on malaria. In addition to mathematical papers, poems, and fictional works, he wrote *The Prevention of Malaria* (1910).

36. b) Theodore Roosevelt
He was the 26th president of the United States (1901-09) and writer, naturalist, and soldier. He expanded the powers of the presidency and of the federal government in support of the public interest in conflicts between big business and labour and steered the nation toward an active role in world politics, particularly in Europe and Asia. He won the Nobel Prize for Peace for mediating an end to the Russo-Japanese War.

Ginkgo biloba may be the oldest living seed plant; it is regarded by some as one of the wonders of the world.

The ferns constitute an ancient division of vascular plants, some of them as old as the Carboniferous Period (beginning 360 million years ago) and perhaps older.

Did You Know?

37. b) Marie Curie

The Polish-born French physicist is famous for her work on radioactivity and twice a winner of the Nobel Prize. She shared the 1903 Nobel Prize for Physics with Henri Becquerel and Pierre Curie, her husband. Radioactivity was first reported in 1896 by Henri Becquerel for a double salt of uranium and potassium. It was soon found that all uranium compounds and the metal itself were similarly radioactive. In 1898, Marie and Pierre Curie discovered two other strongly radioactive elements, radium and polonium, that occur in nature.

38. c) John Richard Hicks

The English economist made pioneering contributions to the general economic equilibrium theory. Hicks's classic work, *Value and Capital* (1939), helped to resolve basic conflicts between business-cycle theory and the equilibrium theory, which holds that economic forces tend to balance one another rather than simply reflect cyclical trends. Both Hicks and Arrow demonstrated that active forces, not passive ones, strike economic balances when the forces cancel each other out. Their theories were used widely by public and private interests to determine foreign trade, investment policies, and prices.

39. d) Henri Moissan

The French chemist received the 1906 Nobel Prize for Chemistry. He took up the study of fluorine compounds in 1884. Two years later, by electrolyzing a solution of potassium fluoride in hydrofluoric acid, he prepared the highly reactive gas fluorine. He made a full study of the properties of the element and its reactions with other elements. In 1892 Moissan developed the electric arc furnace and used it to prepare numerous new compounds and to vaporize substances previously regarded as infusible.

40. c) Isolation of argon gas

The English physical scientist, John William Strutt Rayleigh, made fundamental discoveries in the fields of acoustics and optics that are basic to the theory of wave propagation in fluids. He received the Nobel Prize in 1904 for his successful isolation of argon, an inert atmospheric gas.

41. d) Phototherapy

Niels Ryberg Finsen, the Danish physician, founder of modern phototherapy (the treatment of disease by the influence of light), received the 1903 Nobel Prize for Physiology or Medicine for the application of light in the treatment of skin diseases.
In 1893 Finsen found that lengthy exposure of smallpox sufferers to the red light formed by exclusion of the violet end of the spectrum prevents the suppuration of the pustules, or formation of characteristic pockmarks. Aware of the bacteria-destroying effects of sunlight, he developed an ultraviolet treatment for lupus vulgaris, a form of skin tuberculosis, which met with great success. Although phototherapy has largely been superseded by other forms of radiation and drug therapy, Finsen's work did much to encourage the radiation therapy then being developed and led to the use of ultraviolet sterilization techniques in bacteriological research.

42. a) Selma Ottilia Lovisa Lagerlof

She was also the first Swedish writer to receive the Nobel Prize for Literature. In 1894 she published a collection of stories, *Osynliga Lankar* (*Invisible Links*), and in 1895 she won a travelling scholarship, gave up teaching, and devoted herself to writing. Her works include *Antikrists mirakler* (1897; *The Miracles of Antichrist*), *En herrgårdssägen* (*Tales of a Manor*), and *Jerusalem,* 2 vol. (1901-02).

43. b) *Gitanjali*

The Bengali poet, short-story writer, song composer, playwright, essayist, and painter was awarded the Nobel Prize for Literature in 1913. Tagore introduced new prose and verse forms and the use of colloquial language into Bengali literature, thereby freeing it from traditional models based on classical Sanskrit. Years of sadness arising from the deaths of his wife and two children between 1902 and 1907 are reflected in his later poetry, which was introduced to the West in *Gitanjali, Song Offerings* (1912). This book contains Tagore's English prose translations of religious poems from several of his Bengali verse collections, including *Gitanjali* (1910).

44. d) Ivan Petrovich Pavlov

The Russian physiologist is known chiefly for his development of the concept of the conditioned reflex. During 1890-1900 especially, and to a lesser extent until about 1930, Pavlov studied the secretory activity of digestion. While working with Heidenhain, he devised an operation to prepare a miniature stomach, or pouch; he isolated the stomach from ingested foods, while preserving its vagal nerve supply. The surgical procedure enabled him to study the gastrointestinal secretions in a normal animal over its lifespan. He wrote *Lectures on the Work of the Digestive Glands* in 1897.

45. b) Woodrow Wilson

He was the 28th president of the United States (1913-21), scholar and statesman best remembered for his legislative accomplishments and his high-minded idealism. Wilson led his country into World War I and became the creator and leading advocate of the League of Nations, for which he was awarded the Nobel Prize. During his second term the Nineteenth Amendment to the U.S. Constitution, giving women the right to vote, was passed and ratified.

46. a) Philipp Lenard

The German physicist was the recipient of the 1905 Nobel Prize for Physics for his research on cathode rays and the discovery of many of their properties. His results had important implications for the development of electronics and nuclear physics. In 1899 he proved that cathode rays are created when light strikes metal surfaces; this phenomenon later became known as the photoelectric effect.

47. d) Gunnar Myrdal

The Swedish economist and sociologist was regarded as a major theorist of international relations and in particular of third world development policies. Myrdal wrote *An American Dilemma: The Negro Problem and Modern Democracy* (1944). In this work, Myrdal presented his theory of cumulative causation, of poverty breeding poverty.

48. a) Non-cellular fermentation

The German biochemist was awarded the 1907 Nobel Prize for Chemistry for demonstrating that the fermentation of carbohydrates results from the action of different enzymes contained in yeast and not the yeast cell itself. He showed that an enzyme, zymase, can be extracted from yeast cells and that it causes sugar to break up into carbon dioxide and alcohol.

The ears of katydids and crickets are found on the first walking legs; those of grasshoppers are on the first segment of the abdomen.

Originally, eau de cologne was a mixture of citrus oils from such fruits as lemons and oranges, combined with such substances as lavender and neroli (orange-flower oil).

Did You Know?

49. a) *Saint Joan*
George Bernard Shaw was an Irish comic dramatist, literary critic, and Socialist propagandist. The canonization of Joan of Arc in 1920 reawakened within Shaw ideas for a chronicle play about her. In the resulting masterpiece, *Saint Joan* (performed 1923), the Maid is treated not only as a Catholic saint and martyr but as a combination of practical mystic, heretical saint, and inspired genius.

50. a) Robert Koch
The German physician, one of the founders of the science of bacteriology, discovered the tubercle bacillus (1882) and the cholera bacillus (1883). Although it was known that tuberculosis was due to an infective agent, the organism had not yet been isolated and identified. On March 24, 1882, Koch announced before the Physiological Society of Berlin that he had isolated and grown the tubercle bacillus, which he believed to be the cause of all forms of tuberculosis. He discovered the cause of amoebic dysentery and the bacilli of two varieties of Egyptian conjunctivitis. Proceeding to India, where cholera is endemic, he discovered the cholera organism and its transmission via drinking water, food, and clothing.

51. c) Austen Chamberlain
The Locarno Pact, concluded by Great Britain, France, Italy, Belgium, and Germany, was the high point of Chamberlain's foreign secretaryship; he lost popularity after the failure of the Geneva Conference on naval limitations (August 1927) and the abortive and needlessly secret Anglo-French disarmament negotiations (July 1928). He left office with Stanley Baldwin's second ministry in June 1929, returned briefly (August–October 1931) as first lord of the admiralty, and then passed the rest of his life as an elder statesman.

52. c) Leonid Vitalyevich Kantorovich
The Soviet mathematician and economist shared the Nobel Prize for work on the optimal allocation of scarce resources. Kantorovich's most famous work is *The Best Use of Economic Resources* (1959). He pioneered the technique of linear programming as a tool of economic planning, having developed a linear programming model in 1939. He used such mathematical techniques to show how the decentralization of decision making in a planned economy ultimately depends on a system in which prices are based on the relative scarcity of resources.

53. d) Albert Abraham Michelson
The German-born American physicist established the speed of light as a fundamental constant and pursued other spectroscopic and metrological investigations. In 1907 he became the first American ever to receive a Nobel Prize in the sciences, for his spectroscopic and metrological investigations. Michelson constructed an interferometer, a device designed to split a beam of light in two, send the parts along perpendicular paths, then bring them back together. The interferometer made it possible for him to determine the width of heavenly objects by matching the light rays from the two sides and noting the interference fringes that resulted. In 1920, using a 20-foot (6-m) interferometer attached to a 100-inch (254-cm) telescope, he succeeded in measuring the diameter of the star Betelgeuse (Alpha Orionis) as 386,160,000 km (300 times the diameter of

the Sun). This was the first substantially accurate determination of the size of a star.

54. d) Theodore William Schultz
The American economist's influential studies of the role of "human capital"—education, talent, energy, and will—in economic development won him a share of the Nobel Prize. Schultz's view of economic development was grounded in the conviction that agricultural development is the indispensable precondition to industrialization. In applying classical economic analysis to agriculture in poor countries he proposed that human capital could be studied in the same terms commonly applied to capital in the usual sense.

55. b) Opthalmology
The Swedish ophthalmologist received the Nobel Prize for his research on the eye as a light-refracting apparatus. Gullstrand contributed to knowledge of the structure and function of the cornea and to research on astigmatism. He improved corrective lenses for use after surgery for cataracts and devised the Gullstrand slit lamp, a valuable diagnostic tool that facilitates detailed study of the eye. Gullstrand's investigations led to a new concept of the theory of optical images.

56. a) Franco Modigliani
The Italian-born American economist and finance educator received the Nobel Prize in 1985 for his pioneering research in several fields of economic theory that had practical applications. One of these was his analysis of personal savings, termed the life-cycle theory. The theory posits that individuals build up a store of wealth during their younger working lives for the purpose of consuming these savings during their own old age, not for

the purpose of passing them on to their descendants.

57. b) James Mcgill Buchanan
The American economist and educator received the Nobel Prize in 1986 for his development of the "public-choice theory", a unique method of analyzing economic and political decision making. Buchanan wrote a number of significant books—both with others and alone—the best known of which is *The Calculus of Consent: Logical Foundations of Constitutional Democracy* (1962), with Gordon Tullock.

58. d) Robert Merton Solow
In the 1950s Solow developed a mathematical model that could show the relative contributions of various factors to producing sustained national economic growth. Contrary to traditional economic thinking, he showed that the rate of technological progress is actually more important than capital accumulation and increases in labour in achieving such growth. The greater efficiency and productivity that result from qualitative improvements such as new machines and improved human skills are thus more important than strictly quantitative investments that result in a greater number of machines and factories. From the 1960s, Solow's studies were influential in persuading governments to channel their funds into technological research and development in order to spur economic growth.

59. d) Ernest Rutherford
The British physicist was awarded the Nobel Prize for Chemistry in 1908. He contributed substantially to the understanding of the disintegration and transmutation of radioactive elements, discovered and named the particles expelled from radium, identified the alpha

The Yangtze is the longest river in Asia flowing for 6,300 km (3,915 miles).

The highest point in the Maya mountains is Victoria Peak, which rises to 1,122 m (3,681 ft).

Did You Know?

particle as a helium atom and with its aid evolved the nuclear theory of atomic structure, and used that particle to produce the first artificial disintegration of elements.

60. b) Developing the colour photographic plate

The French physicist was known for the innovations that resulted from his search for a direct colour-sensitive medium in photography. In 1891 Lippmann revealed a revolutionary colour-photography process, later called the Lippmann process, which utilized the natural colours of light wavelengths instead of using dyes and pigments. He placed a reflecting coat of mercury behind the emulsion of a panchromatic plate. The mercury reflected light rays back through the emulsion to interfere with the incident rays, forming a latent image that varied in depth according to each ray's colour. The development process then reproduced this image, and the result, when viewed, was brilliantly accurate. This direct method of colour photography was slow and tedious because of necessarily long exposure times, and no copies of the original could be made. It never achieved popularity, therefore, but it was an important step in the development of colour photography.

61. a) Carl von Ossietzky

The award to the German journalist and pacifist was interpreted as an expression of worldwide censure of Nazism. Hitler's reply was a decree forbidding Germans to accept any Nobel Prize.

62. a) For developing a method of suturing blood vessels

The French surgeon Alexis Carrel received the Nobel Prize in 1912. Soon after graduating, he became interested in the repair of blood vessels, and he developed a method to suture them together end-to-end with a minimum of stitches. This technique became essential for many surgical operations, including the transplantation of blood vessels and organs.

63. a) Sun valve

The Swedish engineer Nils Dalen won the Nobel Prize for Physics in 1912 for his invention of the automatic sun valve, or Solventil, which regulates a gaslight source by the action of sunlight, turning it off at dawn and on at dusk or at other periods of darkness. It rapidly came into worldwide use for buoys and unmanned lighthouses.

64. d) Heike Kamerlingh Onnes

The Dutch physicist won the Nobel Prize for Physics in 1913 for his work on low-temperature physics and his production of liquid helium. He discovered superconductivity, the almost total lack of electrical resistance in certain materials when cooled to a temperature near absolute zero. Kamerlingh Onnes also demonstrated that the resistance of some electrical conductors disappears suddenly at a temperature near absolute zero (-273° C), and he termed this phenomenon "superconductivity". His systematic researches on superconductivity (begun in 1911) were of extreme importance because of their bearing on the theory of electrical conduction in solids.

65. c) Friends Service Council

The organization was founded in Great Britain in 1927 and committed to foreign work. The American Friends Service Committee (AFSC) was founded by the

Society of Friends (Quakers) in the United States in 1917, initially to provide work overseas for conscientious objectors. Both committees are devoted to peace and humanitarian activities.

66. d) Gary Stanley Becker
The American economist, awarded the Nobel Prize for Economic Sciences in 1992, applied the methods of economics to aspects of human behaviour previously considered more or less the exclusive domain of sociology, anthropology, and demography. The central premise of Becker's writings is that rational economic choices, based on self-interest, govern most aspects of human behaviour, not just the purchasing and investment decisions traditionally regarded as economic behaviour.

67. d) Quantum theory
Planck made many contributions to theoretical physics, but his fame rests primarily on his role as originator of the quantum theory. This theory revolutionized the understanding of atomic and subatomic processes. It constitutes the fundamental theories of 20th-century physics along with Albert Einstein's theory of relativity.

68. a) Gao Xingjian
The Chinese novelist, playwright, translator, and critic won the 2000 Nobel Prize for Literature. Gao Xingjian has lived in France since 1987. His works had been banned in his native country because of their social and political criticism.

69. d) Charles Jules Henri Nicolle
The French bacteriologist received the 1928 Nobel Prize for Physiology or Medicine. At the Pasteur institute in Tunis Nicolle noticed that typhus was very contagious outside the hospital, with sufferers of the disease transmitting it to many people who came into contact with them. Once inside the hospital, however, these same patients ceased to be contagious. Nicolle suspected that the key point in this reversal was that of admission to the hospital, when patients were bathed and their clothes were confiscated. The carrier of typhus must be in the patients' clothes or on their skin and could be removed from the body by washing. The obvious candidate for the carrier was the body louse (*Pediculus humanus humanus*), which Nicolle proved to be the culprit in 1909 in a series of experiments.

70. b) Albert John Luthuli
The Zulu chief, teacher, and religious leader was the president of the African National Congress (1952-60) in South Africa. He was awarded the Nobel Prize in 1960, in recognition of his nonviolent struggle against racial discrimination.

71. a) A nickel-steel alloy
The French physicist Charles Edouard Guillaume's exhaustive studies of ferronickel alloys culminated in the discovery of invar (a nickel-steel alloy). His early studies included exhaustive investigations of the mercury thermometer. From 1890 he focussed his attention on alloys and developed invar and elinvar. Invar's low coefficient of expansion (change in volume caused by change in temperature) and elinvar's low coefficient of elasticity (change in elasticity caused by change in temperature), combined with their low cost, resulted in their widespread use in scientific instruments.

The first historically recorded attempt to divert a lava stream was made at Catania during the eruption of 1669.

The greatest temperature change in 24 hours occurred in Browning, Montana, on January 23, 1916, from 44 degrees above zero to 56 degrees below zero.

Did You Know?

72. b) Christiaan Eijkman

The Dutch physician and pathologist was coawarded, with Frederick Hopkins, the 1929 Nobel Prize for Physiology or Medicine. Eijkman sought a bacterial cause for beriberi. In 1890 polyneuritis broke out among his laboratory chickens. Noticing this disease's striking resemblance to the polyneuritis occurring in beriberi, he was eventually (1897) able to show that the condition was caused by feeding the fowl a diet of polished, rather than unpolished, rice. Eijkman believed that the polyneuritis was caused by a toxic chemical agent, possibly originating from the action of intestinal microorganisms on boiled rice. He maintained this theory even after his successor in Batavia, Gerrit Grijns, demonstrated (1901) that the problem was a nutritional deficiency, later determined to be a lack of vitamin B_1 (thiamine).

73. b) Chemistry and Peace

The American chemist Linus Pauling applied quantum mechanics to the study of molecular structures, particularly in connection with chemical bonding. He received the Nobel Prize for Chemistry in 1954 and the Nobel Prize for Peace in 1962 (the latter in recognition of his efforts on behalf of the international control of nuclear weapons and his campaigns against nuclear testing).

74. c) Atomic nature of matter

The French physicist Jean Perrin's studies of the Brownian motion of minute particles suspended in liquids, verified Albert Einstein's explanation of this phenomenon and thereby confirmed the atomic nature of matter. In 1895 he established that cathode rays are negatively charged particles (electrons). About 1908 Perrin began to study the erratic movement of particles suspended in a liquid. Einstein's mathematical analysis (1905) of this phenomenon suggested that the particles were being jostled by the randomly moving water molecules around them. Using the newly developed ultramicroscope, Perrin carefully observed the manner of sedimentation of these particles and provided experimental confirmation of Einstein's equations.

75. a) Daniel Bovet

The pharmacologist discovered, in 1944, the first antihistamine, pyrilamine (mepyramine), which, in counteracting the effect of histamine, is effective against allergic reactions. In 1947 a search for a synthetic substitute for curare (a muscle relaxant) led to his discovery of gallamine and other muscle relaxants. Among these are derivatives of succinylcholine, whose curare-like action he was the first to recognize. Curare and its synthetic substitutes are used in conjunction with light anaesthesia during surgery to induce muscle relaxation.

76. d) Martin Luther King, Jr.

The eloquent Baptist minister led the Civil Rights Movement in the United States from the mid-1950s until his death by assassination in 1968. His leadership was fundamental to that movement's success in ending the legal segregation of blacks in the South and other portions of the United States. King rose to national prominence through the organization of the Southern Christian Leadership Conference, promoting nonviolent tactics such as the massive March on Washington (1963) to achieve civil rights.

77. d) Frederick Banting and John James Richard Macleod

Banting was a Canadian physician who, with Charles H. Best, was the first to extract the hormone insulin from the pancreas. Banting was awarded a share of the 1923 Nobel Prize for Physiology or Medicine for his achievement. In May 1921 Banting and Best began an intensive effort in the laboratories of the Scottish physiologist J.J.R. Macleod, at the University of Toronto, to isolate the hormone. Banting and Best completed their experiments in 1922. The following year Banting and Macleod received the Nobel Prize, though Macleod had not actually taken part in the research. Angered that Macleod, rather than Best, had received the Nobel Prize, Banting divided his share of the award equally with Best.

78. c) UNICEF
A special programme of the United Nations, it is devoted to aiding national efforts to improve the health, nutrition, education, and general welfare of children. UNICEF was created in December 1946 to provide relief to children in countries devastated by World War II. After 1950 the fund's efforts were directed toward general programmes for the improvement of children's welfare, particularly in less-developed countries as well as those in various emergency situations. The change in the organization's name to the United Nations Children's Fund reflected this shift in function.

79. b) Chandrasekhara Venkata Raman
The Indian physicist's work was influential in the growth of science in India. He was the recipient of the Nobel Prize for Physics in 1930 for the discovery that when light traverses a transparent material, some of the light that is deflected changes in wavelength. This phenomenon is now called Raman scattering and is the result of the Raman Effect. Studying the scattering of light in various substances, in 1928 he found that when a transparent

substance is illuminated by a beam of light of one frequency, a small portion of the light emerges at right angles to the original direction, and some of this light is of different frequencies than that of the incident light. These so-called Raman frequencies are equal to the infrared frequencies for the scattering material and are caused by the exchange of energy between the light and the material.

80. a) Cloud chamber
The Scottish physicist, C.T.R. Wilson received the Nobel Prize for Physics in 1927 for his invention of the radiation detector, the Wilson cloud chamber, that became widely used in the study of radioactivity, X-rays, cosmic rays, and other nuclear phenomena. Wilson believed that in the absence of dust the clouds formed by condensing on ions (charged atoms or molecules) in the air. He experimented and found that radiation left a trail of condensed water droplets in his cloud chamber. Perfected by 1912, his chamber proved indispensable in the study of nuclear physics and eventually led to the development (by Donald A. Glaser in 1952) of the bubble chamber.

81. b) Robert C. Merton
The American economist is known for his work on finance theory and risk management; he is noted especially for his contribution to assessing the value of stock options and other derivatives. Merton shared the Nobel Prize for Economic Sciences in 1997 with Myron S. Scholes, whose option valuation model, the Black-Scholes formula (developed with economist Fischer Black), provided the foundation for much of Merton's work. (Upon his death in 1995, Black became ineligible for the Nobel Prize, which is not awarded posthumously.)

Rahmangs ("Books of routes") contain descriptions of coasts, approaches, and islands, and information on winds, currents, soundings, and navigation by stars.

The Aral Sea derived its name from the Kyrgyz word *Aral-denghiz,* which means Sea of Islands.

Did You Know?

82. b) Richard Zsigmondy

The Austrian chemist received the Nobel Prize for Chemistry in 1925 for research on colloids, which consist of submicroscopic particles dispersed throughout another substance. While employed in a glassworks (1897) Zsigmondy directed his attention to colloidal gold present in ruby glass, and he discovered a water suspension of gold. He theorized that much could be learned about the colloidal state of matter from studying the manner in which the particles scatter light. To facilitate such study, he and Heinrich Siedentopf developed the ultramicroscope (1903), and Zsigmondy used it to investigate various aspects of colloids, including Brownian motion. His work proved particularly helpful in biochemistry and bacteriology.

83. b) Amartya Sen

The Indian economist was awarded the 1998 Nobel Prize for Economic Sciences for his contributions to welfare economics and social choice and for his interest in the problems of society's poorest members. Sen was best known for his work on the causes of famine, which led to the development of practical solutions for preventing or limiting the effects of real or perceived shortages of food.

84. b) Adolf Windaus

The German organic chemist discovered 7-dehydrocholesterol, which is the chemical precursor of vitamin D, and he showed that it is a steroid. He discovered that it is converted into the vitamin when one of its chemical bonds is broken by the action of sunlight. This explained why exposure to sunlight can prevent vitamin D deficiency (rickets) in humans.

85. d) Norman Ernest Borlaug

The American agricultural scientist and plant pathologist was one of those who laid the groundwork of the so-called Green Revolution, the agricultural technological advance that promised to alleviate world hunger. He developed strains of grain that dramatically increased crop yields. Wheat production in Mexico multiplied threefold in the time that he worked with the Mexican government; "dwarf" wheat imported in the mid-1960s was responsible for a 60 percent increase in harvests in Pakistan and India. He also created a wheat-rye hybrid known as triticale. The increased yields resulting from Borlaug's new strains enabled many developing countries to become agriculturally self-sufficient.

86. b) Arthur Harden

The English biochemist was the corecipient, with Hans von Euler-Chelpin, of the 1929 Nobel Prize for Chemistry for work on the fermentation of sugar and the enzyme action involved. His more than 20 years of study of the fermentation of sugar advanced knowledge of intermediary metabolic processes in all living forms. He also pioneered in studies of bacterial enzymes and metabolism.

87. a) Eisaku Sato

Prime minister of Japan between 1964 and 1972, Sato presided over Japan's post-World War II reemergence as a major world power. He was a corecipient of the Nobel Prize for his policies on nuclear weapons, which led to Japan's signing of the Treaty on the Non-proliferation of Nuclear Weapons. As prime minister Sato presided over the continued growth of the Japanese economy and the improvement of Japanese relations with other Asian countries. In 1969 Sato reached an agreement with U.S. President Richard M.

Nixon, for future return of the Ryukyu Islands to Japan, the removal of all nuclear weapons from the area, and the continued maintenance of the U.S.-Japanese Mutual Security Treaty.

88. c) Developments in harnessing nuclear power

The Italian-born American physicist was one of the chief architects of the nuclear age. He developed the mathematical statistics required to clarify a large class of subatomic phenomena; discovered neutron-induced radioactivity; and directed the first controlled chain reaction involving nuclear fission. The Enrico Fermi Award of the U.S. Department of Energy is given in his honour.

89. c) Francis Peyton Rous

The American pathologist found that sarcomas in hens could be transmitted to fowl of the same inbred stock not only by grafting tumour cells but also by injecting a submicroscopic agent extractable from them; this discovery gave rise to the virus theory of cancer causation. Although his research was derided at the time, subsequent experiments vindicated his thesis.

90. a) Peter Camenzind

Hermann Hesse was a German novelist and poet whose main theme deals with man's breaking out of the established modes of civilization to find his essential spirit. With his appeal for self-realization and his celebration of Eastern mysticism, Hesse posthumously became a cult figure to young people in the English-speaking world. Hesse remained in the bookselling business until 1904, when he became a freelance writer and brought out his first novel, *Peter Camenzind*, about a failed and dissipated writer.

91. b) Chemistry

The American biochemist Vincent du Vigneaud won the Nobel Prize for Chemistry in 1955 for the isolation and synthesis of two pituitary hormones: vasopressin, which acts on the muscles of the blood vessels to cause elevation of blood pressure; and oxytocin, the principal agent causing contraction of the uterus and secretion of milk.

92. a) Cosmic radiation

The discoveries in the field of cosmic radiation that Patrick Maynard Stuart Blackett accomplished primarily with cloud-chamber photographs, revealed the way in which a stable atomic nucleus can be disintegrated by bombarding it with alpha particles (helium nuclei). Although such nuclear disintegration had been observed previously, his data explained this phenomenon for the first time and were useful in explaining disintegration by other means.

93. d) Work in immunology and treatment of syphilis

The German medical scientist Paul Ehrlich was known for his pioneering work in haematology, immunology, and chemotherapy. He received jointly with Elie Metchnikoff the Nobel Prize for Physiology or Medicine in 1908. His preparation 606, later called Salvarsan, was extraordinarily effective and harmless despite a large arsenic content. The first tests, undertaken in the spring of 1910, proved to be surprisingly successful in the treatment of a whole spectrum of diseases; in the case of yaws, a tropical disease akin to syphilis, a single injection was sufficient.

94. a) Research on the theory of elementary particles

The Japanese physicist Hideki Yukawa proposed a new theory of nuclear forces in which he

---

The East German government erected the Berlin Wall that isolated East from West Berlin in 1961.

Siberia, in Russia and Northern Kazakstan, was considered a place of exile for criminals and political prisoners.

Did You Know?

predicted the existence of mesons, or particles that have masses between those of the electron and the proton. The discovery of one type of meson among cosmic rays by American physicists in 1937 suddenly established Yukawa's fame as the founder of meson theory, which later became an important part of nuclear and high-energy physics. After devoting himself to the development of meson theory, he started work in 1947 on a more comprehensive theory of elementary particles based on his idea of the so-called nonlocal field.

95. b) Russell Alan Hulse and Joseph Hooton Taylor, Jr.

The American physicists shared the Nobel Prize for Physics in 1993. Using the large radio telescope at Arecibo, Puerto Rico, they discovered dozens of pulsars, which are rapidly spinning neutron stars that emit rapid, regular bursts of radio waves. Irregularities in the radio emissions of the pulsar PSR 1913 + 16 led them to deduce that the pulsar had a companion neutron star with which it was locked in a tight orbit. Hulse and Taylor made this discovery in 1974.

96. c) Emil Theodor Kocher

The Swiss surgeon, in 1883, announced his discovery of a characteristic cretinoid pattern in patients after total excision of the thyroid gland; when a portion of the gland was left intact, however, there were only transitory signs of the pathological pattern. By 1912 he had performed 5,000 thyroid excisions and had reduced the mortality in such surgery from 18 percent to less than 0.5 percent. His other surgical contributions include a method for reducing dislocations of the shoulder and improvements in operations on the stomach, the lungs, the tongue, and the cranial nerves and for hernia.

The forceps and incision (in gallbladder surgery) that bear his name remain in general use.

97. c) Amnesty International

The international organization headquartered in London seeks to inform public opinion about violations of human rights, especially the abridgments of freedom of speech and of religion and the imprisonment and torture of political dissidents, and which actively seeks the release of political prisoners and the relief, when necessary, of their families. The organization was founded in London on May 28, 1961, through the principal efforts of Peter Benenson, who had been a defense lawyer for political prisoners in Hungary, South Africa, and Spain and who sought to establish a collective agency for the advancement of human rights.

98. a) Adolf Butenandt

The German biochemist, with Leopold Ruzicka, was awarded the 1939 Nobel Prize for Chemistry for his work on sex hormones. In 1929, almost simultaneously with Edward A. Doisy in the United States, Butenandt isolated estrone, one of the hormones responsible for sexual development and function in females. In 1931 he isolated and identified androsterone, a male sex hormone, and in 1934, the hormone progesterone. Butenandt's investigations made possible the eventual synthesis of cortisone and other steroids and led to the development of birth control pills.

99. c) Pearl Buck

The American author is noted for her novels of life in China. She received the Nobel Prize for Literature in 1938. Her novels include *East Wind, West Wind* (1930), *The Good Earth* (1931), *Sons* (1932), and *A House Divided* (1935).

100. b) Shmuel Yosef Agnon
The Israeli writer was one of the leading modern Hebrew novelists and short-story writers. Agnon's real literary debut was made with *Agunot* (1908; "Forsaken Wives"), his first "Palestinian" story. His first major work was the novel *Hakhnasat kalah*, 2 vol. (1919; *The Bridal Canopy*). His second novel, *Ore'ahNata' Lalun* (1938; *A Guest for the Night*), describes the material and moral decay of European Jewry after World War I. His third and perhaps greatest novel, *'Tmol shilshom* (1945; "The Day Before Yesterday"), examines the problems facing the westernized Jew who immigrates to Israel. All Agnon's works are the final result of innumerable Proust-like revisions, as is shown by the many manuscripts in existence and by the variety of the printed texts.

101. d) Anwar el-Sadat
The Egyptian army officer and politician was president of Egypt from 1970 until his death. He initiated serious peace negotiations with Israel, an achievement for which he shared the 1978 Nobel Prize for Peace with Israeli prime minister Menachem Begin. Under their leadership, Egypt and Israel made peace with each other in 1979.

102. c) Bertrand Russell
The English logician and philosopher who entered Trinity College, Cambridge, in 1890, was at once recognized as intellectually outstanding. He was winner of first-class honours in the Mathematical Tripos (honours examination) in 1893 and then turned to philosophy. His first published book—written from the orthodox liberal point of view—was *German Social Democracy* (1896). He remained a liberal until he joined the Labour Party in 1914.

103. a) Alexander Robertus Todd
The British biochemist began work on nucleosides, compounds that form the structural units of nucleic acids (DNA and RNA). In 1949 he synthesized a related substance, adenosine triphosphate (ATP), which is vital to energy utilization in living organisms. He synthesized two other important compounds, flavin adenine dinucleotide (FAD) in 1949 and uridine triphosphate in 1954. In 1955 he elucidated the structure of vitamin B_{12}.

104. a) International Physicians for the Prevention of Nuclear War
This international organization of doctors is opposed to the nuclear arms race and seeks to educate the public on the catastrophic medical consequences that would result from a nuclear war. International Physicians was founded (in 1980) and led by several American and Soviet physicians under the leadership of Bernard Lown and Yevgeny I. Chazov, respectively. The organization promotes research on the medical, psychological, and biospheric effects that a nuclear war would have.

105. b) Marshall Warren Nirenberg
The American biochemist demonstrated that, with the exception of "nonsense codons", each possible triplet (called a codon) of four different kinds of nitrogen-containing bases found in deoxyribonucleic acid (DNA) and, in some viruses, in ribonucleic acid (RNA) ultimately causes the incorporation of a specific amino acid into a cell protein. His work and that of Holley and Khorana helped to show how genetic instructions in the cell nucleus control the composition of proteins.

Between 1949 and 1961, about 2.5 million East Germans fled to the West.

The Marienkirsche in Berlin is Germany's oldest surviving church.

Hiram Bingham, a Yale University professor, discovered Machu Picchu in 1911.

Did You Know?

106. b) Lech Walesa

The labour activist helped form and lead (1980-90) communist Poland's first independent trade union, Solidarity. He went on to become the president of Poland (1990-95) and received the Nobel Prize for Peace in 1983. As president, Walesa helped guide Poland through its first free parliamentary elections (1991) and watched as successive ministries converted Poland's state-run economy into a free-market system. Walesa had displayed remarkable political skills as the leader of Solidarity, but his plain speech, his confrontational style, and his refusal to approve a relaxation of Poland's strict new prohibitions on abortion eroded his popularity late in his term as president. In 1995 he sought reelection but was narrowly defeated.

107. a) John Douglas Cockcroft

The British physicist, joint winner, with Ernest Thomas Stinton Walton of Ireland, of the 1951 Nobel Prize for Physics for pioneering the use of particle accelerators in studying the atomic nucleus. The British physicist was professor of natural philosophy at the University of Cambridge from 1939 to 1946. In 1932 he and Walton designed the Cockcroft-Walton generator and used it to disintegrate lithium atoms by bombarding them with protons. This type of accelerator proved to be one of the most useful in the world's laboratories.

108. c) Carbon-14 dating

The American chemist Williarm Frank Libby's technique of carbon-14 (or radiocarbon) dating provided an extremely valuable tool for archaeologists, anthropologists, and earth scientists. For this development he was honoured with the Nobel Prize for Chemistry in 1960. The carbon-14 dating technique is used to date material derived from former living organisms as old as 50,000 years. It measures small amounts of radioactivity from the carbon-14 in organic or carbon-containing materials and is able to identify older objects as those having less radioactivity.

109. d) Manfred Eigen

The German physicist was awarded the Nobel Prize for his work on extremely rapid chemical reactions. Eigen was able to study many extremely fast chemical reactions by a variety of methods that he introduced and which are called relaxation techniques. These involve the application of bursts of energy to a solution that briefly destroys its equilibrium before a new equilibrium is reached. Eigen studied what happened to the solution in the extremely brief interval between the two equilibria by means of absorption spectroscopy.

110. b) Elie Wiesel

The works of this Romanian-born American novelist provide a sober yet passionate testament of the destruction of European Jewry during World War II. All of Wiesel's works reflect, in some manner, his experiences as a survivor of the Holocaust and his attempt to resolve the ethical torment of why the Holocaust happened and what it revealed about human nature. He became a noted lecturer on the sufferings experienced by Jews and others during the Holocaust, and his ability to transform this personal concern into a universal condemnation of all violence, hatred, and oppression was largely responsible for his being awarded the Nobel Prize for Peace.

111. d) Georg Wittig

In investigating reactions involving carbanions, negatively charged organic species, the German chemist discovered a class of organic phosphorus compounds called ylides that mediate a particular type of reaction that became known as the Wittig reaction. This reaction proved of great value in the synthesis of complex organic compounds such as vitamins A and D_2, prostaglandins, and steroids.

112. c) Richard Robert Ernst

The Swiss researcher and teacher won the 1991 Nobel Prize. Ernst's refinements made NMR techniques a basic and indispensable tool in chemistry and also extended their usefulness to other sciences. Ernst discovered that the sensitivity of NMR techniques (hitherto limited to analysis of only a few nuclei) could be dramatically increased by replacing the slow, sweeping radio waves traditionally used in NMR spectroscopy with short, intense pulses.

113. a) Behaviour of subatomic particles

The German physicists Walther Bothe and Max Born won the Nobel Prize for Physics in 1954. Born's studies of the wave function led to the replacement of the original quantum theory, which regarded electrons as particles, with an essentially mathematical description representing their observed behaviour more accurately.

114. a) Walter Kohn

The Austrian-born American physicist was a corecipient of the Nobel Prize with John A. Pople. The award recognized their individual work on computations in quantum chemistry. Kohn's development of the density-functional theory made it possible to apply the complicated mathematics of quantum mechanics to the description and analysis of the chemical bonding between atoms.

Science

1. d) Stephen Hales
The English botanist, physiologist, and clergyman pioneered quantitative experimentation in plant and animal physiology. Hales measured blood pressure by inserting a tube into a blood vessel and allowing the blood to rise up the tube. In addition, he measured the capacity of the left ventricle of the heart, the output of the heart per minute, and the speed and resistance to flow of blood in the vessels.

2. a) Andreas Caesalpinus
An Italian physician, philosopher, and botanist, Caesalpinus sought a philosophical and theoretical approach to plant classification based on unified and coherent principles rather than on alphabetical sequence or medicinal properties. He helped establish botany as an independent science. His *De plantis libri XVI* (1583) is considered the first textbook of botany. The brief first book presents the principles of botany using the models of Aristotle and Theophrastus; the remaining 15 books describe and classify more than 1,500 plants.

3. c) Fields Medal
Officially known as International Medal for Outstanding Discoveries in Mathematics award, the Fields Medal is granted to between two and four mathematicians for outstanding or seminal research. It is granted only every four years and is given, by tradition, to mathematicians under the age of 40, rather than to more senior scholars. The first two Fields Medals were awarded in 1936.

4. d) Jan Ingenhousz
The Dutch-born British physician and scientist is best known for his discovery of the process of photosynthesis, by which green plants in sunlight absorb carbon dioxide and release oxygen. In 1779, he published the results of an ingenious study on the chemical effects of plant physiology, *Experiments Upon Vegetables, Discovering Their Great Power of Purifying the Common Air in Sunshine, and of Injuring It in the Shade and at Night.* Ingenhousz found that (1) light is necessary for this restoration (photosynthesis); (2) only the green parts of the plant actually perform photosynthesis; and (3) all living parts of the plant "damage" the air (respire), but the extent of air restoration by a green plant far exceeds its damaging effect.

5. a) John Wesley Hyatt
The U.S. inventor discovered the process in 1870, while searching for a substitute for ivory for making billiard balls. Hyatt combined nitrocellulose, camphor, and alcohol, heated the mixture under pressure to make it pliable for moulding, and allowed it to harden under normal atmospheric pressure. His discovery opened the way for the development of the modern plastics industry.

6. a) Barnes Neville Wallis
The British aeronautical designer and military engineer produced not only the dambuster bombs but also the 12,000-pound "Tallboy" and the 22,000-pound "Grand Slam" bombs. He was also responsible for the bombs that destroyed the German warship *Tirpitz*, the V-rocket sites, and much of Germany's railway system.

7. b) Johann Rudolf Glauber
The German-Dutch chemist made his living chiefly by the sale of secret chemicals and

medicinals. He prepared hydrochloric acid from common salt and sulphuric acid and pointed out the virtues of the residue, sodium sulphate—*sal mirabile*, or Glauber's salt; he also noted the formation of nitric acid from potassium nitrate and sulphuric acid. Glauber prepared many substances, made useful observations on dyeing, and described the preparation of tartar emetic. He urged that Germany's natural resources be developed and gave examples of such developments. His writings were reissued as *Glauberus Concentratus* (1715).

8. c) Harvey William Cushing
The American surgeon was a leading neurosurgeon of the early 20th century, Cushing developed many of the operating procedures and techniques that are still basic to the surgery of the brain, and his work greatly reduced the high mortality rates that had formerly been associated with brain surgery.

9. d) Anna Freud
The Austrian-born British founder of child psychoanalysis and one of its foremost prac-titioners also made fundamental contributions to understanding how the ego, or consciousness, functions in averting painful ideas, impulses, and feelings. She viewed play as the child's adaptation to reality but not necessarily as a revelation of unconscious conflicts. She worked closely with parents and believed that analysis should have an educational influence on the child.

10. b) Antonio Egas Moniz
A Portuguese neurologist and statesman, Moniz was awarded the 1949 Nobel Prize for Physiology or Medicine for the development of prefrontal leucotomy (lobotomy) as a radical therapy for certain psychoses, or mental disorders, along with Walter Hess.

11. c) G. Stanley Hall
The psychologist who gave an early impetus and direction to the development of psychology in the United States, Hall is frequently regarded as the founder of child psychology and educational psychology. A great teacher, he inspired research that reached into all areas of psychology. The first journal in the fields of child and educational psychology, the *Pedagogical Seminary*, later the *Journal of Genetic Psychology*, was founded by Hall in 1893. In 1887 Hall founded the *American Journal of Psychology*.

12. c) Z
An atom is first identified and labelled according to the number of protons in its nucleus. This atomic number is ordinarily given the symbol Z. The great importance of the atomic number derives from the observation that all atoms with the same atomic number have nearly, if not precisely, identical chemical properties.

13. d) Four
The human stomach is subdivided into four regions: the cardia (so named because it is nearest to the heart), an opening leading down from the esophagus; the fundus, an expanded area curving up above the cardiac opening; the body, or intermediate, region, the central and largest portion; and the pylorus, a narrowing where the stomach joins the small intestine. Each of the openings, the cardiac and the pyloric, has a sphincter muscle that keeps the neighbouring region closed, except when food is passing through. In this manner, food is enclosed by the stomach until ready for digestion.

14. d) Jean Piaget
The Swiss psychologist is thought by many to have been a major figure in 20th-century developmental psychology. In more than 50

Did You Know?

In Cuba, Carlos Finlay expressed the view, in 1881, that yellow fever is carried by the Stegomyia mosquito. Following his lead, the Americans Walter Reed, William Gorgas, and others were able to conquer the scourge of yellow fever in Panama and made possible the completion of the Panama Canal by reducing the death rate there from 176 per 1,000 to 6 per 1,000.

books and monographs over his long career, Piaget continued to develop the theme he first discovered in Paris, that the mind of the child evolves through a series of set stages to adulthood.

15. d) Mechanical
The windmills transformed the kinetic energy of wind into mechanical energy for pumping water and grinding grain.

16. c) Amedeo Avogadro
In 1808 the English physicist John Dalton suggested that each element consists of identical atoms, and in 1811 the Italian physicist Amedeo Avogadro hypothesized that the particles of elements may consist of two or more atoms stuck together. Avogadro called such conglomerations molecules, and based on experimental work he conjectured that the molecules in a gas of hydrogen or oxygen are formed from pairs of atoms.

17. c) Cell
It is the basic unit of which all living things are composed. All cells are similar in composition, form, and function. A single cell can be a complete organism in itself, as in bacteria and protozoans. Groups of specialized cells are organized into tissues and organs in multicellular organisms such as the higher plants and animals. Cells were first observed in the 17th century, shortly after the discovery of the microscope. Their significance, however, was not understood until the early 19th century, when improvements in microscopy permitted closer observation.

18. c) Blood platelets
They are the smallest cells of the blood, averaging about two to four micrometres in diameter. Although much more numerous

(150,000 to 400,000 per cubic millimetre) than the white cells, they occupy a much smaller fraction of the volume of the blood because of their relatively minute size. Like the red cells they lack a nucleus and are incapable of cell division, but they have a more complex metabolism and internal structure than have the red cells. When seen in fresh blood they appear spheroid, but they have a tendency to extrude hairlike filaments from their membranes. They adhere to each other but not to red cells and white cells. Tiny granules within platelets contain substances important for the clot-promoting activity of platelets.

19. c) Jean-Baptiste-Joseph Delambre
The French astronomer published in 1792 the *Tables du Soleil, de Jupiter, de Saturne, d'Uranus et des satellites de Jupiter* ("Tables of the Sun, Jupiter, Saturn, Uranus, and Jupiter's Satellites"). Delambre also wrote histories of ancient, mediaeval, and modern astronomy. His *Tables écliptiques des satellites de Jupiter* ("Ecliptic Tables of Jupiter's Satellites") was republished by the bureau of longitudes in 1817. A large crater on the Moon is named in his honour.

20. b) Red blood cells
The membrane of the red cell has on its surface a group of molecules that confer blood group specificity (that is, that differentiate blood cells into groups). Most blood group substances are composed of carbohydrate linked to protein, and it is usually the chemical structure of the carbohydrate portion that determines the specific blood type. Blood group substances are antigens capable of inducing the production of antibodies when injected into persons or animals lacking the antigen. Detection and recognition of the blood group antigens are accomplished by the use of serum containing these antibodies.

In 1948 the American aeronautical engineer Francis Rogallo patented a completely flexible kite with no rigid supporting spars, which was the forerunner of the delta kite and modern hang gliding.

The smallest living bird is generally acknowledged to be the bee hummingbird of Cuba, which is 6.3 cm (2.5 inches) long and weighs less than 3 gm (about 0.1 ounce).

Did You Know?

21. c) Rats and mice
Rodenticides kill by preventing normal blood clotting and causing internal haemorrhaging. Fumigants such as sulphur dioxide, carbon monoxide, hydrogen cyanide, and methyl bromide are also effective rodenticides. Phosphorus paste, barium carbonate salt, and powders such as zinc phosphide, white arsenic, thallium sulphate, strychnine, strychnine sulphate, and calcium cyanide are mixed with bait and placed where rodents will find and eat them.

22. d) Methyl isocynate
In December 1984 Bhopal was the site of one of the worst industrial accidents in history, when about 45 tons of the dangerous gas methyl isocyanate escaped from an insecticide plant in Bhopal that was owned by the Indian subsidiary of the U.S. firm Union Carbide Corporation.

23. d) Soranus
The Greek gynaecologist, obstetrician, and paediatrician was the chief representative of the methodist school of medicine. Soranus's writings set medical opinion concerning women's diseases, pregnancy, and infant care for nearly 1,500 years. Soranus wrote a life of Hippocrates, but the contents of this and later lives were largely traditional or imaginative.

24. b) Gregor Johann Mendel
The Austrian botanist and plant experimenter theorized that the occurrence of the visible alternative characters of the plants, in the constant varieties and in their descendants, is due to the occurrence of paired elementary units of heredity, now known as genes. The novel feature of Mendel's interpretation of his data, amply confirmed by subsequent observations on other organisms, including man, is that these units obey simple statistical laws.

25. c) 23
Among many organisms that have separate sexes, there are two basic types of chromosomes: sex chromosomes and autosomes. Autosomes control the inheritance of all the characteristics except the sex-linked ones, which are controlled by the sex chromosomes. Humans have 22 pairs of autosomes and one pair of sex chromosomes. All act in the same way during cell division.

26. d) Germany
Modern lethal chemical weapons employed the organophosphorus nerve agents first produced but not used by Germany during World War II. Related to certain insecticides but much more toxic to man, they would cause intense sweating, filling of the bronchial passages with mucus, dimming of vision, uncontrollable vomiting and defecation, convulsions, and finally paralysis and respiratory failure. Death would result from asphyxia, generally within a few minutes after respiratory exposure or within hours if exposure was through a liquid nerve agent on the skin.

27. c) Chlorine
Toxic smokes and other toxic substances were used occasionally in war from ancient times, but the earliest large-scale use of chemical warfare agents was in World War I. Preceded by both sides' sporadic use of various tear gases in artillery and other projectiles starting in 1914, It was the German attack with chlorine released from thousands of cylinders along a four-mile front at Ypres on April 22, 1915, that initiated the massive use of chemicals in that conflict.

28. b) Down Syndrome
It is caused by an extra chromosome on the chromosome 21 pair, thus giving the person a total of 47 chromosomes rather than the normal 46. Persons born with Down Syndrome are

characterized by several of the following: broad, flat face; short neck; up-slanted eyes, sometimes with an inner epicanthal fold; low-set ears; small nose and enlarged tongue and lips; sloping underchin; poor muscle tone; mental retardation; heart or kidney malformations or both; and abnormal dermal ridge patterns on fingers, palms, and soles.

29. c) Thales of Miletus
The philosopher is remembered for his cosmology based on water as the essence of all matter. Even though Thales as a philosopher renounced mythology, his choice of water as the fundamental building block of matter had its precedent in tradition. A likely consideration in this choice was the seeming motion that water exhibits, as seen in its ability to become vapour; for what changes or moves itself was thought by the Greeks to be close to life itself. To Thales the entire universe is a living organism, nourished by exhalations from water.

30. d) David Bushnell
The U.S. inventor, renowned as the father of the submarine, built a unique turtle-shaped vessel designed to be propelled under water by an operator who turned its propeller by hand. The craft was armed with a mine, or a torpedo, to be attached to the hull of an enemy ship. Several attempts were made with Bushnell's "Turtle" against British warships. Though the submarine gave proof of underwater capability, the attacks were failures.

31. c) A muscular digestive organ
Found in many birds, the gizzard is the hind part of the stomach especially modified for grinding food. Located between the saclike crop and the intestine, it has a thick muscular wall and may contain small stones, or gastroliths, that function in the mechanical breakdown of seeds and other foods.

32. c) Eric Berne
An influential therapy of the human potential movement was the technique known as transactional analysis. As practised by its founder, transactional analysis proved to be both a method of examining human interactions as well as a way of labelling and systematizing the information gained from observed transactions. The goal of this approach is to build a strong state of maturity by learning to recognize the "child" and "parent" aspects of personality in oneself and others.

33. c) Alfred Louis Kroeber
An influential American anthropologist of the first half of the 20th century, Kroeber's primary concern was to understand the nature of culture and its processes. His interest and competence ranged over the whole of anthropology, and he made valuable contributions to American Indian ethnology; to the archaeology of New Mexico, Mexico, and Peru; and to the study of linguistics, folklore, kinship, and social structure.

34. a) Hans Lippershey
He was a spectacle maker from the United Netherlands. Lippershey, on Oct. 2, 1608, formally offered his invention, which he called a *kijker* ("looker"), to the Estates of Holland for use in warfare. The Estates required its modification into a binocular device. His telescopes were made available to Henry IV of France and others before the end of 1608. The potential importance of the instrument in astronomy was recognized by, among others, Jacques Bovedere of Paris; he reported the invention to Galileo, who promptly built his own telescope.

DNA testing was first used in Britain in 1986 to prosecute serial rapist and murderer Colin Pitchfork. Today, DNA testing is regularly used to convict criminals, much as fingerprints have been for many years.

The kangaroo uses the tail to balance itself while jumping. Its tail is long and thick at the base.

Did You Know?

35. c) Tomography

Structures that are obscured by overlying organs and soft tissues that are insufficiently delineated on conventional X rays can be adequately visualized through tomography.

The simplest method is linear tomography. A more complicated technique is known as multidirectional tomography. A still more complex technique, variously called computerized tomography (CT), or computerized axial tomography (CAT), was also developed during the early 1970s.

36. c) Thomas Henry Huxley

The English biologist, educator, and advocate of agnosticism coined the word in 1869 at a meeting of the Metaphysical Society in London. He derived the word from the Greek *agnostos,* "unknowable", strictly speaking, the doctrine that humans cannot know of the existence of anything beyond the phenomena of their experience. The term has come to be equated in popular parlance with skepticism about religious questions in general and in particular with the rejection of traditional Christian beliefs under the impact of modern scientific thought.

37. b) Edward Acheson

The American inventor discovered the abrasive Carborundum and perfected a method for making graphite. He heated a mixture of clay and coke in an iron bowl with a carbon arc light and found some shiny, hexagonal crystals (silicon carbide) attached to the carbon electrode. Because he at first mistakenly thought the crystals were a compound of carbon and alumina from the clay, he devised the trademark Carborundum, after corundum, the mineral composed of fused alumina. Later, while studying the effects of high temperature on Carborundum, he found that silicon vaporizes at about 7,500° F (4,150° C), leaving behind graphitic carbon.

38. d) Ernest Orlando Lawerence

The American physicist won the 1939 Nobel Prize for Physics for his invention of the cyclotron. Lawrence first conceived the idea for the cyclotron in 1929. One of his students undertook the project and succeeded in building a device that accelerated hydrogen ions (protons) to an energy of 13,000 electron volts (eV). Lawrence then set out to build a second cyclotron; when completed, it accelerated protons to 1,200,000 eV, enough energy to cause nuclear disintegration. To continue the programme, Lawrence built the Radiation Laboratory at Berkeley in 1936.

39. c) Cheetah

The fastest land animal in the world over short distances, the cheetah, with its streamlined body and long legs, can run as fast as 100 km/h (60 miles per hour) and effectively outrun and capture its prey. Adult cheetahs can grow as large as 140 cm (55 inches long) and weigh up to 130 pounds (60 kg). Their fur is coarse sandy yellow with numerous black spots—the colouration and pattern of which differs slightly between the different subspecies. Unlike the other big cats, the cheetah does not roar—but it does purr and make a range of other sounds including high pitched yelps and barks.

40. c) Alfred Russel Wallace

A British humanist, naturalist, geographer, and social critic, Wallace became a public figure in England during the second half of the 19th century for his courageous views on scientific, social, and spiritualist subjects. His formulation of the theory of evolution by natural selection, which predated Charles Darwin's published contributions, is his most outstanding legacy, but it was just one of many controversial issues he studied and wrote about during his lifetime.

41. a) Paul Adrian Maurice Dirac

The English theoretical physicist is known for his work in quantum mechanics and for his theory of the spinning electron. In 1933 he shared the Nobel Prize for Physics with the Austrian physicist Erwin Schrodinger. In his book *The Principles of Quantum Mechanics* (1930), Dirac developed the so-called transformation theory of quantum mechanics that furnished a machinery for calculating the statistical distribution of certain variables when others are specified. He also stated his philosophical position with respect to theoretical physics.

42. b) Niels Bohr

The Danish physicist was the first to apply the quantum theory, which restricts the energy of a system to certain discrete values, to the problem of atomic and molecular structure. For this work he received the Nobel Prize for Physics in 1922. He developed the so-called Bohr theory of the atom and liquid model of the atomic nucleus. Einstein greatly admired Bohr's early work, but he never accepted Bohr's claim that quantum mechanics was the "rational generalization of classical physics" demanded for the understanding of atomic phenomena.

43. a) William Congreve

The English artillery officer and inventor's military rocket was a great advance in black-powder rockets. It provided the impetus for an early wave of enthusiastic utilization of rockets for military purposes in Europe. Congreve continued to improve his rockets' range and accuracy, leading many European countries to form rocket corps, usually attached to artillery units. The Congreve rockets were made obsolete by improved artillery and ordnance, but they continued to find uses for flares and ship rescue.

44. c) Isaac Newton

In his book, *Philosophiae Naturalis Principia Mathematica* (1687), he pointed out that a cannonball shot at a sufficient velocity from atop a mountain in a direction parallel to the horizon would go all the way around the Earth before falling. Although the object would tend to fall toward the Earth's surface because of gravitational force, its momentum would cause it to descend along a curved path. Greater velocity would put it into a stable orbit, like that of the Moon, or direct it away from the Earth altogether. On Oct. 4, 1957, nearly three centuries after Newton had proposed his theory, the Soviet Union launched the first Earth satellite, Sputnik I.

45. b) Rosalind Elsie Franklin

The British scientist contributed to the discovery of the molecular structure of deoxyribonucleic acid (DNA), a constituent of chromosomes that serves to encode genetic information. She collaborated on studies showing that the ribonucleic acid (RNA) in the tobacco mosaic virus was embedded in its protein and that this RNA was a single-strand helix, rather than the double helix found in the DNA of bacterial viruses and higher organisms.

46. b) Henri Dunant

The Red Cross arose out of the work of Henri Dunant, a Swiss humanitarian, who, at the Battle of Solferino, in June 1859, organized emergency aid services for Austrian and French wounded. It is a humanitarian agency with national affiliates in almost every country in the world. The International Movement of the Red Cross and Red Crescent began with the founding of the International Committee for the Relief of the Wounded (now the International Committee of the Red Cross) in 1863; it was established to care for victims of battle in time of war, but later national Red Cross societies were created to aid in the prevention and relief of human suffering generally. The Red Cross is the name used in countries under nominally Christian sponsorship; Red Crescent is the name used in Muslim countries.

47. b) South America
A nocturnal bird of South America, the oilbird lives in caves and feeds on fruit, mainly the nuts of oil palms. About 12 inches (30 cm) long, with fanlike tail and long broad wings, it is dark reddish brown, barred with black and spotted with white. It has a strong hook-tipped bill, long bristles around the wide gape, and large dark eyes.

48. d) Bird
Snail-kites are found only in the New World. They have sickle-shaped beaks adapted to feeding on snails, their only food. The best known is the Everglade kite (*Rostrhamus sociabilis*), now rare in Florida and Cuba but occurring in numbers in eastern Mexico, Central America, and most of eastern South America. It is a blackish or slate-coloured bird, about 50 cm long, with red eyes and white tail-base.

49. d) Bone to bone
A ligament is a tough, fibrous band of connective tissue that serves to support the internal organs and hold bones together in proper articulation at the joints. Ligaments may be of two major types: white ligament is rich in collagenous fibres, which are sturdy and inelastic; yellow ligament is rich in elastic fibres, which are quite tough even though they allow elastic movement. At joints, ligaments form a capsular sac that encloses the articulating bone ends and a lubricating membrane, the synovial membrane. Other ligaments fasten around or across bone ends in bands, permitting varying degrees of movement, or act as tie pieces between bones (such as the ribs or the bones of the forearm), restricting inappropriate movement.

50. a) A genetic disorder
It is a group of blood disorders characterized by a deficiency of haemoglobin, the blood protein that transports oxygen to the tissues. Thalassemia is caused by genetically determined abnormalities in the synthesis of one or more of the polypeptide chains that make up the globin part of haemoglobin.

51. c) Katherine Esau
The Russian-born American botanist did groundbreaking work in the structure and workings of plants. Her *Plant Anatomy* (1953) is a classic in the field. It became the foremost text in the United States on plant structure and was widely adopted abroad.

52. d) Mercury and Venus
A satellite is a natural or artificial object that revolves around a larger astronomical object, usually a planet. The Moon is the most obvious example. All the planets in the solar system except Mercury and Venus have natural satellites. More than 60 such objects have so far been discovered.

53. d) Jupiter
When ancient astronomers named the planet Jupiter, designated in astronomy for the ruler of the gods in the Greco-Roman pantheon, they had no idea of the planet's true dimensions, but

Did You Know?

The well-known work of William Hunter of London, *Treatise on the Theory and Practice of Midwifery,* published in three volumes in 1752-64, contained the first systematic discussion on the safe use of obstetrical forceps, which have since saved countless lives.

the name is appropriate, for Jupiter is larger than all the other planets combined. It has a narrow system of rings and 16 known satellites, one larger than the planet Mercury and three larger than the Earth's Moon. Jupiter also has an internal heat source, that is, it emits more energy than it receives from the Sun. This giant has the strongest magnetic field of any planet, with a magnetosphere so large that it would exceed the apparent diameter of the Moon if it could be seen from the Earth.

54. a) Flat-plate collectors
The sunlight that reaches the ground consists of nearly 50 percent visible light, 45 percent infrared radiation, and smaller amounts of ultraviolet light and other forms of electro-magnetic radiation. This radiation can be converted either into thermal energy (heat) or into electrical energy, though the former is easier to accomplish. Two main types of devices are used to capture solar energy and convert it to thermal energy: flat-plate collectors and concentrating collectors.

55. d) Aircraft and lighter-than-air ships
After a two-year tour (1913-14) of Europe to ascertain the state of development of aeronautics there, Hunsaker instituted the first American university course in aerodynamics and aircraft design in MIT and, with Donald W. Douglas, built the first wind tunnel. From 1916 to 1923 he was in charge of aircraft design for the U.S. Navy. In the spring of 1919, his NC4 seaplane made the first transatlantic flight, via the Azores. He also designed the *Shenandoah,* the first airship to use helium instead of hydrogen.

56. a) Enrico Fermi
In 1942 the Italian-born American physicist Enrico Fermi and his coworkers at the University of Chicago produced the first controlled self-sustaining fission reaction. They accomplished this feat with a simple nuclear reactor, the first such device ever constructed. Their so-called atomic pile consisted of large lumps of natural uranium embedded in hundreds of tons of specially purified graphite. The graphite was intended to slow down free neutrons to ensure their capture by the small number of uranium-235 nuclei in the natural uranium fuel.

57. a) Rubidium
A chemical element of Group Ia in the periodic table, the alkali metal group, rubidium (Rb) is the second most reactive metal. It is very soft with a silvery-white lustre. It was discovered (1861) spectroscopically by Robert Bunsen and Gustav Kirchhoff and named after the two prominent red lines of its spectrum. Rubidium occurs combined in such minerals as lepidolite, pollucite, and carnallite.

58. b) Sulphur
It was known from prehistoric times in native deposits and was also given off in metallurgic processes (the "roasting" of sulphide ores).

59. b) Ammonium chloride
The chloride of ammonia first became known to the West in the *Chou-i ts'an t'ung ch'i,* a Chinese treatise of the 2nd century AD. It was to be crucial to alchemy, for on sublimation it dissociates into antagonistic corrosive materials, ammonia and hydrochloric acid, which readily attack the metals. Until the 9th century it seems to have come from a single source, the Flame Mountain (Huo-yen Shan) near T'u-lu-p'an (Turfan), in Central Asia.

60. c) Richard Feynman
The American theoretical physicist was probably

the most brilliant, influential, and iconoclastic figure in his field in the post-World War II era. He was co-awarded the Nobel Prize for Physics in 1965 for his work which tied together in an experimentally perfect package all the varied phenomena at work in light, radio, electricity, and magnetism.

61. d) Albrecht von Haller

In 1747 in Berne, Switzerland, Albrecht von Haller, eminent as anatomist, physiologist, and botanist, published the first manual for physiology. Between 1757 and 1766 he published eight volumes entitled *Elementa Physiologiae Corporis Humani* (*Elements of Human Physiology*); all were in Latin and characterized his definition of physiology as anatomy in motion.

62. d) Box kite

The Australian aeronautical pioneer invented the box kite in the 1890s. The kite is named for its rectangular shape, the frame being twice as long as the width and the ends left uncovered, with one-third of the length covered around each end. The kite flies on one edge and needs no tail. The shape can be other than square in cross section: it may be oblong and fly on a wide side with a four-leg bridle; or it may be triangular, round (barrel kite), or even five- or six-sided. Hargrave also made important studies of wing surfaces and worked with rotary engines and gliders.

63. c) Claude Chappe

The French engineer and cleric converted an old idea into a reality by inventing the semaphore visual telegraph. In August 1794 the Chappe semaphore brought to Paris in less than an hour the news of the capture of Conde-sur-l'Escaut from the Austrians. Other lines were built, notably between Paris and Toulon, and the

system was soon widely copied elsewhere in Europe.

64. c) Bernard (-Ferdinand) Lyot

A French astronomer, Lyot's invention allowed the observation of the solar corona when the Sun is not in eclipse. Before Lyot's coronagraph, observing the corona had been possible only during a solar eclipse, but this was unsatisfactory because total eclipses occur only rarely and the duration of such eclipses is too short (no more than seven minutes) to allow prolonged scientific observation of the corona. In 1939, using his coronagraph and filters, Lyot shot the first motion pictures of the solar prominences.

65. d) Edwin Armstrong

The American inventor laid the foundation for much of modern radio and electronic circuitry, including the regenerative and superheterodyne circuits and the frequency modulation (FM) system.

66. b) Fungi

The term applies not only to mushrooms but to all of the large and diverse group of plantlike organisms to which the mushrooms belong. The fungi of most interest in microbiology are the yeasts and moulds. Many moulds are studied because of their economic importance.

67. d) Charles Bonnet

The Swiss naturalist and philosophical writer studied the habits of the aphid and found that the female insect was able to reproduce without fertilization by the male. Bonnet argued, in *Considerations sur les corps organisés* (1762; "Considerations on Organized Bodies"), that each female organism contains within its germ cells (eggs) an infinite series of preformed individuals, leading to an immortality and

The Kodiak bear, a variety of grizzly bear found on Kodiak Island, off the coast of Alaska, is the largest living flesh-eating land mammal.

The spectacled bear gets its name from the light-colored rings around its eyes.

immutability of species. He responded to fossil evidence of extinct species with *La Palingenesie philosophique* (1769; "The Philosophical Revival"), in which he theorized that the Earth periodically suffers universal catastrophes, destroying most life, and that the survivors move up a notch on the evolutionary scale. Bonnet was the first to use the term evolution in a biological context.

68. d) Plants dependent on other plants for support

Any plant that grows upon or is in some manner attached to another plant or object merely for physical support is an epiphyte. Epiphytes are primarily tropical in distribution and are often known as air plants because they have no attachment to the ground or other obvious nutrient source. They obtain water and minerals from rain and also from debris that collects on the supporting plants. Orchids, ferns, and members of the pineapple family are common tropical epiphytes. Lichens, mosses, liverworts, and algae are epiphytes of temperate regions. Mistletoes, which are partly parasitic on their host plants, are sometimes considered to be epiphytes.

69. b) Nitrogen

A carnivorous plant is especially adapted for capturing insects and other tiny animals by means of ingenious pitfalls and traps and then subjecting them to the decomposing action of digestive enzymes, bacteria, or both. They digest their prey through a process of chemical breakdown analogous to digestion in animals. The end products, particularly nitrogenous compounds and salts, are absorbed by the plants. Their adaptations for digesting nitrogen-rich animal proteins are thought to enable these plants to survive under otherwise marginal or hostile environmental conditions.

70. a) Venus's flytrap

A flowering perennial plant of the sundew family (Droseraceae), the *Dionaea* is notable for its unusual habit of catching and digesting insects and other small animals. The only member of its genus, the plant is native to a small region of North and South Carolina, U.S., where it is common in damp, mossy areas. The leaves of the plant are hinged along the midline so that the two nearly circular lobes, with spiny teeth along their margins, can fold together and enclose an insect alighting on them. This action is triggered by pressure on six sensitive hairs, three on each lobe. In normal daytime temperatures the lobes, when stimulated by prey, snap shut in about half a second. Glands on the leaf surface then secrete a red sap that digests the insect's body and gives the entire leaf a red, flowerlike appearance. About 10 days are required for digestion, after which the leaf reopens. The trap dies after capturing three or four insects.

71. a) Emu

The flightless bird of Australia is the second largest living bird. The emu is more than 1.5 m (5 feet) tall and may weigh more than 45 kgm (100 pounds). The emu is the sole living member of the family Dromaiidae (or Dromiceiidae) of the order Casuariiformes, which also includes the cassowaries.

72. c) Kookaburra

An eastern Australian bird of the kingfisher family (Alcedinidae), the kookaburra has a call that sounds like fiendish laughter. This gray-brown, woodland-dwelling bird reaches a length of 43 cm (17 inches), with a 8- to 10-cm (3.2- to 4-inch) beak. In its native habitat it eats invertebrates and small vertebrates, including venomous snakes.

The Malayan bear is the smallest of all bears at 27 to 36 kilograms (60 to 80 pounds).

The only mammals that fly are bats, and for this reason, they are often mistaken for birds.

Did You Know?

73. c) Joey
The young kangaroo, or Joey, is born alive at a very immature stage, when it is only about 2 cm (1 inch) long and weighs less than a gram (0.03 ounce). Immediately after birth it uses its precociously developed forelimbs (equipped with claws) to crawl up the mother's body and enter the pouch.

74. c) Protozoa
Protozoans are sometimes considered the most simple of all animals. First observed by Leeuwenhoek in the 17th century, protozoans are almost as ubiquitous as bacteria.

75. d) Free-tailed bat
These bats are found worldwide in warm regions. Their common name is descriptive of the way in which part of the tail extends beyond the membrane attached between the hind legs. Free-tailed bats are also known as mastiff, or bulldog, bats because of their supposed facial resemblance to these dogs.

76. c) Jamaican fruit bat
The tailless fruit-eating bat, belonging to the family Phyllostomatidae, inhabits the neotropical regions. The bat's body is characterized by the presence of a very small flight membrane between the hind legs. This species feeds mainly on fruit and will fly as much as 10 km (6 miles) to a feeding site. From there it carries fruit to a feeding roost in a nearby tree. The Jamaican fruit bat also eats insects, catching flies that approach the roost by hooking them in its wing tips. Its preferred roosts are caves or hollow trees; males may hang in the nearby foliage. The bat occasionally destroys fruit crops.

77. c) Lion
Lions are unique among cats in that they live in a group, or pride. A pride consists of several generations of lionesses, all of whom are related, their cubs, and one or two adult male lions who defend the pride's territory and mate with the females. The adult males are outsiders who may hold the pride for a few months to several years, depending on their ability to defend it against other outsider males. A pride may have as few as 4 or as many as 37 members, but about 15 is the average size. Each pride has a well-defined territory; where prey is abundant, its area may be as small as 8 sq miles (20 sq km), but if game is sparse, the territory may be up to 150 sq miles (400 sq km) in area. Male cubs are expelled from the pride at about 3 years of age and become nomads until they are old enough (at age 5) to try and take over another pride.

78. a) Goliath frog
The West African goliath frog, which is 300 mm (12 inches) from snout to vent and weighs 3.3 kg (7.28 pounds), is the largest anuran.

79. b) Andrew Meikle
Scottish millwright who constructed his first threshing machine in 1778, probably basing its design on a device patented in 1734 by Michael Menzies. The machine was a failure, as was a second, developed from a Northumberland model. Meikle analyzed these threshers and constructed a strong drum with fixed beaters that beat rather than rubbed the grain. The drum that made Meikle's machine a success may have been copied from the flax-scutching machine used to beat the fibres from flax plants.

80. b) Begins on a Monday and ends on a Sunday
The International Fixed Calendar is essentially a perpetual Gregorian calendar, in which the year is divided into 13 months, each of 28 days, with

The largest and tallest antelope is the African giant eland, about 69 inches (175 centimeters) tall at the shoulders and weighing about 1,764 pounds (800 kilograms).

The smallest antelope is the African royal, about 10 inches (25 centimeters) tall at the shoulders and weighing only about 6 pounds (2.7 kilograms).

an additional day at the end. Present month names are retained, but a new month named Sol is intercalated between June and July. The additional day follows December 28 and bears no designation of month, date, or weekday name, while the same would be true of the day intercalated in a leap year after June 28. In this calendar, every month begins on a Sunday and ends on a Saturday.

81. c) Thomas Savery
He was an English engineer and inventor. Savery's engine had many limitations, notably its weakness under high-pressure steam (above 8 to 10 atmospheres).

82. d) Avicenna
The Iranian physician is among the most famous and influential of the philosopher-scientists of Islam. He was particularly noted for his contributions in the fields of Aristotelian philosophy and medicine. He composed the *Kitab ash-shifa'* ("Book of Healing"), a vast philosophical and scientific encyclopaedia, and the *Canon of Medicine,* which is among the most famous books in the history of medicine.

83. c) Wilhelm Maybach
The German engineer and industrialist was associated with Gottlieb Daimler in developing efficient internal-combustion engines; their first important product, a relatively light four-stroke engine, was patented in 1885. In 1890 Daimler and Maybach formed the Daimler-Motoren-Gesellschaft, in Cannstatt, to manufacture automobiles; from 1895 Maybach was the firm's technical director. For the earliest Mercedes cars Maybach greatly improved an existing design for a 24-horsepower engine, providing mechanical inlet valves that could be throttled by the driver.

84. a) Hugo Junkers
A German aircraft designer and early proponent of the monoplane and all-metal construction of aircraft, Junkers' J-1 Blechesel ("Sheet Metal Donkey") monoplane was the first successful all-metal airplane (1915), and his F-13 was the first all-metal transport (1919). Many Junkers aircraft had a corrugated sheet-metal skin, which was copied by several American builders, including the Ford Motor Company.

85. a) Arm
Humerus is the long bone of the upper limb or forelimb of land vertebrates, which forms the shoulder joint above, where it articulates with a lateral depression of the shoulder blade and the elbow joint below, where it articulates with projections of the ulna and radius.

86. d) William H. Perkin
In 1856, the first commercially successful synthetic dye, mauve, was serendipitously discovered in England by William H. Perkin.

87. b) Fear of heights
Vertigo is a sensation that a person's surroundings are rotating or that he himself is revolving. Usually the state produces dizziness, mental bewilderment, and confusion. If the sensation is intense enough, the person may become nauseated and vomit. Aircraft pilots and underwater divers are subject to vertigo because the environments in which they work frequently have no reference points by which to orient their direction of movement.

88. c) Christiaan Barnard
Norman Schumway achieved the first successful heart transplant in a dog at Stanford University, California, U.S., in 1958. On December 3, 1967, Christiaan Barnard of South Africa

performed the first human heart transplant at the Groote Schuur Hospital, Cape Town.

89. d) Heinrich Rudolf Hertz
The German physicist produced electromagnetic waves in the laboratory and measured their length and velocity. He showed that the nature of their vibration and their susceptibility to reflection and refraction were the same as those of light and heat waves. As a result he established beyond any doubt that light and heat are electromagnetic radiations.

90. d) United States of America
The HST is a large reflecting telescope whose mirror optics gather light from celestial objects and direct it into two cameras and two spectrographs. The HST has a 94-inch (2.4-m) primary mirror, a smaller secondary mirror, and various recording instruments that can detect visible, ultraviolet, and infrared light. The most important of these instruments, the wide-field planetary camera, can take either wide-field or high-resolution images.

91. a) A steamboat
William Symington was a British engineer who developed (1801) a successful steam-driven paddle wheel and used it the following year to propel one of the first practical steamboats, the *Charlotte Dundas*. In 1801 he patented a new engine utilizing a connecting rod and crank, a system that proved superior for paddle-wheel operation. This engine was used in 1802 to propel the *Charlotte Dundas* on the Forth and Clyde Canal, thus launching the first steamboat fitted for practical operations.

92. a) Joseph Aspdin
Lime (calcium oxide), derived from limestone, chalk, or (where available) oyster shells, continued to be the primary pozzolanic, or cement-forming, agent until the early 1800s. In 1824 an English inventor, Joseph Aspdin, burned and ground together a mixture of limestone and clay. This mixture, called portland cement, has remained the dominant cementing agent used in concrete production.

93. a) Gravitational force
Being by far the weakest known force in nature, it plays no role in determining the internal properties of everyday matter. Due to its long reach and universality, however, gravity shapes the structure and evolution of stars, galaxies, and the entire universe. The trajectories of bodies in the solar system are determined by the laws of gravity, while on Earth all bodies have a weight, or downward force of gravity, proportional to their mass, which the Earth's mass exerts on them. Gravity is measured by the acceleration that it gives to freely falling objects.

94. b) Sodium bicarbonate
Layer cakes, cookies (sweet biscuits), biscuits, and many other bakery products are leavened by carbon dioxide from added sodium bicarbonate (baking soda). Added without offsetting amounts of an acidic substance, sodium bicarbonate tends to make dough alkaline, causing flavour deterioration and discoloration and slowing carbon dioxide release. Addition of an acid-reacting substance promotes vigorous gas evolution and maintains dough acidity within a favourable range.

95. b) To measure temperature
The device consists of two wires of different metals joined at each end. One junction is placed where the temperature is to be measured, and the other is kept at a constant lower temperature. A measuring instrument is

---

connected in the circuit. The temperature difference causes the development of an electromotive force that is approximately proportional to the difference between the temperatures of the two junctions. Temperature can be read from standard tables, or the measuring instrument can be calibrated to read temperature directly.

96. a) Phylogeny
Fundamental to phylogeny is the proposition, universally accepted in the scientific community, that plants or animals of different species descended from common ancestors. The evidence for such relationships, however, is nearly always incomplete, for the vast majority of species that have ever lived have become extinct, and relatively few of their remains have been preserved.

97. d) Ascanio Sobrero
Nitroglycerin is a powerful explosive and an important ingredient of most forms of dynamite. It is also used with nitrocellulose in some propel-lants, especially for rockets and missiles, and it is employed as a vasodilator in the easing of cardiac pain. Pure nitroglycerin is a colourless, oily, somewhat toxic liquid having a sweet, burning taste. It was first prepared in 1846 by the Italian chemist Ascanio Sobrero by adding glycerol to a mixture of concentrated nitric and sulphuric acids.

98. c) Magnification and diameter of lens
The first number indicates the magnification and the second the diameter of the objective lens in millimetres (one inch is about 25 mm). This latter figure is a measure of the light-gathering power of the instrument. In applications in which depth perception is not essential, a single telescope, called a monocular, may be employed. It is essentially one-half of a pair of binoculars.

99. b) Sun spots
These spots appear relatively dark against the bright yellow background of the general photosphere. Sunspots appear, migrate about the solar surface, and disappear as the plasma to which they are anchored moves under the influence of rotation and convection. The average number of sunspots increases and decreases more or less regularly in an 11-year cycle.

100. a) Clepsydra
One form, used by the North American Indians and some African peoples, consisted of a small boat or floating vessel that shipped water through a hole until it sank. In another form the vessel was filled with water that was allowed to escape through a hole, and the time was read from graduated lines on the interior measuring the level of the remaining water. It may have been an invention of the Chaldeans of ancient Babylonia; specimens from Egypt date from the 14th century BC. The Romans invented a clepsydra consisting of a cylinder into which water dripped from a reservoir; a float provided readings against a scale on the cylinder wall.

101. b) Antibodies
Antibodies are produced in response to substances called antigens, most of which are foreign proteins or polysaccharides. An antibody molecule can recognize a specific antigen, combine with it, and initiate its destruction.

102. c) Frequency
Sounds are higher or lower in pitch according to the frequency of vibration of the sound waves producing them. A high frequency (for example, 880 hertz [cycles per second]) is perceived as a high pitch; a low frequency (for example, 55 Hz) as a low pitch.

When the Empire State Building in New York City was completed in 1931, it was the tallest building in the world, at 381 m (1,250 ft). It was an engineering marvel because of the time it took to build (just over one year) and because its 102 floors far surpassed any other building at that time.

Did You Know?

Sports

1. b) Long-distance runner
The track athlete from Finland dominated long-distance running in the 1920s, capturing six gold medals in three Olympic Games (1920, 1924, 1928). For eight years (1923-31) he held the world record for the mile run: 4 min 10.4 sec.

2. a) London
Invented in England in the early days of the 20th century, table tennis was being played in many countries by the 1920s. The International Table Tennis Federation was founded in 1926 and the first world championships were held in London in 1927.

3. d) Guo Yuehua
The first World Cup was held in 1980. Guo Yuehua of China won the $12,500 first prize.

4. c) Scrabble
A board-and-tile game, Scrabble has two to four players competing in forming words with lettered tiles on a 225-square board; words spelled out by letters on the tiles interlock like words in a crossword puzzle. The game, based on the crossword puzzle and anagrams, was developed by Alfred M. Butts, an architect, in 1931. It was redesigned, renamed as Scrabble, and marketed by James Brunot in 1948. It was first sold in Great Britain in 1954.

5. d) Breaststroke
Much used in lifesaving and recreational swimming as well as in competitive swimming, the stroke is especially effective in rough water. As early as the end of the 17th century, the stroke was described as consisting of a wide pull of the arms combined with a symmetrical action of the legs and simulating the movement of a swimming frog, hence the usual term frog kick. The stroke is performed lying face down in the water, the arms always remaining underwater. The early breaststroke featured a momentary glide at the completion of the frog kick. Later the competitive breaststroke eliminated the glide. In the old breaststroke, breath was taken in at the beginning of the arm stroke, but in the later style, breath was taken in near the end of the arm pull.

6. a) Davis Cup
The trophy is awarded to the winner of an annual international lawn-tennis tournament originally for amateur men's teams. The official name is the International Lawn Tennis Challenge Trophy. The trophy was donated in 1900 by American Dwight F. Davis for a competition between teams from the United States and Great Britain. Davis himself played on winning U.S. teams in the first two meetings (1900 and 1902). Since 1912 the tournament has grown to truly international proportions, with the world divided into several zones and zone champions playing each other for the right to enter the finals.

7. c) Gaius Maecenas
Archaeologic al and other evidence shows swimming to have been practised as early as 2500 BC in Egypt and thereafter in Assyrian, Greek, and Roman civilizations. The Romans built swimming pools, distinct from their baths. In the 1st century BC the Roman Gaius Maecenas is said to have built the first heated swimming pool.

Whales move around in groups called schools, herds, pods, or gams.

The largest whale, the blue whale, may measure up to 110 feet (33.6 meters) and can weigh 150 tons (136,000 kilograms).

The mysticetous whales have whalebone, or baleens, instead of teeth.

Did You Know?

8. b) Polo
The game is played on horseback between two teams of four players each who use mallets with long, flexible handles to drive a wooden ball down a grass field and between two goal posts. A game of Central Asian origin, polo was first played in Persia (Iran) at dates given from the 6th century BC to the 1st century AD. Polo was at first a training game for cavalry units, usually the king's guard or other elite troops. To the warlike tribesmen, who played it with as many as 100 to a side, it was a miniature battle.

9. c) Polo
Polo is played on an outdoor grass field 274.3 m (300 yards) long by 146.3m (160 yards) wide. Centred at each end are lightweight goalposts 7.3m (8 yards) apart. A score is made by hitting the ball between the goalposts. A game consists of six periods of 7½ minutes each, called *chukkers*, *chukkars*, or *chukka*s. Eight chukkers are played in Argentina, and four is a common number in England and on the European continent.

10. a) Synchronized swimming
It is exhibition swimming in which the movements of one or more swimmers are synchronized with a musical accompaniment. Because of a similarity to dance, it is sometimes called water ballet, especially in theatrical situations. The sport developed in the United States in the 1930s. Synchronized swimming is an organized amateur sport in many areas of the world under the general supervision of the Federation Internationale de Natation Amateur (FINA; International Amateur Swimming Federation), which publishes a list of stunts (movements or figures) accepted in competition. The FINA recognized synchronized swimming in 1954. Synchronized swimming for women was admitted as Olympic competition in 1984. The competition originally consisted of solo and duet events, but both events were dropped at the 1996 Games in favour of a single team event.

11. c) Crawl
The almost unanimous choice of stroke for covering any considerable distance, the stroke was in use in the Pacific at the end of the 19th century and was taken up by the Australian swimmer Henry Wickham about 1893. The brothers Syd and Charles Cavill of Australia popularized the stroke in Europe in 1902 and in the United States in 1903. The crawl was like the old sidestroke in its arm action, but it had a fluttering up-and-down leg action performed twice for each arm stroke. In the crawl, the body lies prone, flat on the surface of the water, with the legs kept slightly under the water. The arms move alternately, timed so that one will start pulling just before the other has finished its pull, thus making propulsion continuous. Breathing is done by turning the head to either side during recovery of the arm from that side.

12. a) Butterfly stroke
The stroke differs from the breaststroke in arm action. In the butterfly the arms are brought forward above the water. The stroke was brought to the attention of U.S. officials in 1933 during a race involving Henry Myers, who used the stroke. He insisted that his stroke conformed to the rules of breaststroke as then defined. After a period of controversy, the butterfly was reco-gnized as a distinct competitive stroke in 1953.

Whales breathe through nostrils, or blowholes, located at the top of their heads.

The whale's spout is caused due to the condensation of moisture present in the breath of the whale.

The shape of the spout is an identifying characteristic of the various species of whales.

13. d) Squash
A singles or doubles game, squash is played in a four-walled court with a long-handled strung racket and a small rubber ball. Two different varieties of game are played: softball (the so-called "British", or "international", version) and hardball (the "American" version).

14. c) Gymnastics
Calisthenics are free body exercises performed with varying degrees of intensity and rhythm, which may or may not be done with light hand-held apparatuses, such as rings and wands. The exercises employ such motions as bending, stretching, twisting, swinging, kicking, and jumping as well as such specialized movements as push-ups, sit-ups, and chin-ups. Calisthenics promote strength, endurance, flexibility, and coordination and augment the body's general well-being by placing controllable, regular demands upon the cardiovascular system. The exercises can function as physique builders or serve as warm-ups for more strenuous sports or exertions.

15. c) Badminton
A court or lawn game, it is played with lightweight rackets and a shuttlecock, a small, cork hemisphere with 16 goose feathers attached and weighing about 80 grains (5 g [0.17 ounce]). A nylon shuttlecock with the apron furnished by feathers is also used. The game is named for Badminton, the country estate of the dukes of Beaufort in Gloucestershire, England, where it was first played in about 1873. It may have started much earlier in India. In the 1860s British army officers stationed there reportedly played the game out of doors and called it *poona*. The first unofficial All-England badminton championships for men were held in 1899, and the first badminton tournament for women was arranged the next year.

16. a) Gymnastics
A gymnastic apparatus, the pommel horse is a leather-covered form 1.6 m (63 inches) long, 34 to 36 cm (13.4 to 14.2 inches) wide, and (measured to its top) about 110 cm (43 inches) from the floor with a support in its centre. Curved wooden pommels (handholds), 12 cm (4.7 inches) (high, are inserted in the top of the horse 40 to 45 cm (15.75 to 17.72 inches) apart. The apparatus stems from a wooden horse introduced by the Romans and used to teach mounting and dismounting. They added it to the ancient Olympic Games. It is a gymnastics event for men only and is contested in the modern Olympic Games.

17. c) Maureen Connolly
An American tennis player, Connolly became, in 1953, the first woman to win the grand slam of tennis: the British (Wimbledon), U.S., Australian, and French singles championships. Dubbed "Little Mo" by an affectionate press, Connolly was deceptively slight and engaging off court, but in action she displayed awesome power in her drives and a distractingly expressionless face.

18. a) Drag racing
The first to the finish line is the winner. Both elapsed time and finishing speed are usually recorded. Competitions are run as a tournament, with losers eliminated and winners competing against others in their class until only one is left undefeated. Drag racing is practised with nearly every variety of motor vehicle, including boats, but most frequently

with automobiles; it originated in the southern California deserts in the 1920s. Its two major U.S. organizations, the National Hot Rod Association (nhra) and the American Hot Rod Association (ahra), were formed in the early 1950s.

19. c) Rally driving
The course is generally unknown to contestants until the start of the race. Such racing began in 1907 with a Peking-to-Paris race of about 12,000 km (7,500 miles). Rallies became very popular after World War II in Europe and elsewhere, and international competitions were instituted. Weekend rallies came to be common worldwide, ranging from those held by local clubs to events sponsored by larger organizations.

20. c) Golf
The Ryder Cup is a biennial professional team golf event first held in 1927. Until 1979 it was played between teams of golfers from the United States and Great Britain, but in 1979 and thereafter players opposing the United States were chosen from all of Europe. The trophy was donated by Samuel Ryder, a British seed merchant, for a biennial golf competition to alternate between British and U.S. venues.

21. b) Handicap
Handicapping takes many, often complicated, forms. In horse racing, a track official known as the handicapper may assign weights to horses according to their speed in previous performances; the presumed fastest horse must carry the most weight. In golf, two unequal players may have a close match by allowing the poorer player a handicap, a certain number of uncounted strokes based on earlier performances. The same is true in 10-pin bowling. In sailboat racing, the winner of a race may be not the first to finish but rather the boat that performs best in relation to its design.

22. d) Bowling
In the game a heavy ball is rolled down a long, narrow lane toward a group of objects known as pins, the aim being to knock down more pins than an opponent. The game is quite different from the sport of bowls, or lawn bowls, in which the aim is to bring the ball to rest near a stationary ball called a jack. There are many forms of bowling, but tenpins, the most widely played variation, is the principal form in the United States, Canada, western Europe, East Asia, Australia, New Zealand, and Latin America. Its many variations include duckpins, candlepins, fivepins, skittles, and ninepins, with differences within the framework of each of the games.

23. d) Michel-Gabriel Paccard
A young Genevese scientist, Horace-Benedict de Saussure, offered prize money for the first ascent of Mont Blanc, but it was not until 1786, more than 25 years later, that his money was claimed by a Chamonix doctor, Michel-Gabriel Paccard, and his porter, Jacques Balmat.

24. d) Harness racing
The sport consists of driving at speed a Standardbred horse pulling a light two-wheeled vehicle called a sulky. Harness racing horses are of two kinds, differentiated by gait: the pacing horse, or pacer, moves both legs on one side of its body at the same time; the trotting horse, or trotter, strides with its left front and right rear leg moving forward

Did You Know?

There were estimated to be more than a billion sheep in the world in the late 20th century.

The Rambouillet is the largest of fine wool sheep.

The Pamir argali, or Marco Polo sheep, standing up to 1.3 m (4 feet) high, is the largest living wild sheep.

simultaneously, then right front and left rear together. Harness racing is one of the two main kinds of horse racing; the other involves horse racing astride in a saddle. The sulky was originally a light, open, one-horse, four-wheeled vehicle with its single seat for only one person fixed on its shafts. Today, used primarily in harness racing, it consists of little more than a U-shaped shaft curving around the narrow seat where the driver perches.

25. d) Archery
Roving is a form of archery in which targets of different sizes or shapes are placed at varying distances in uneven, often wooded, terrain in an attempt to simulate hunting conditions.

26. c) American round
The target-shooting event is shot from distances of 55, 46, and 37 m (60, 50, and 40 yards). Two American rounds and two York rounds, consisting of 12 ends of 6 arrows each, constituted the U.S. men's championship until 1968, when other combinations of rounds were introduced. In the junior American round for boys and girls, 30 arrows each are shot from distances of 50, 40, and 30 yards.

27. b) Speed skating
The sport of racing on ice skates originated in The Netherlands, possibly as early as the 13th century. The blade of the modern speed skate is longer and thinner than that of the hockey or figure skate. When planted on the ice with weight upon it, the blade describes a nearly straight line. Only the last few feet of the stride curve slightly outward as the skate leaves the ice. The modern racing stride rarely exceeds 9 m (30 ft) and is usually about 5 or 6 m (16-20 ft).

28. b) 10,000 m run
The Finnish long-distance runner was the winner of three Olympic gold medals and two-time world-record holder for the 10,000-m run.

29. c) Kayak
One of the two common types of canoe used for recreation and sport, a kayak has a pointed bow and stern and no keel and is covered except for a cockpit in which the paddler or paddlers sit, facing forward and using a double-bladed paddle. The kayak was commonly built for one occupant but could be designed for two or three.

30. b) Surfing
The sport, which originated prehistorically in the South Seas, is now enjoyed throughout the world on open-ocean coastlines with surf. The best conditions for surfing occur when large, smooth ocean swells in deep water peak up into steep sets of waves, or breakers, as they encounter a shelflike reef or sandbar 90 to 900 m offshore. Surfers also look for another type of wave, more difficult to ride, the taller, plunging "dumper", which occurs with a steep rise of bottom to the beach. The lee side of a point of land or a jetty often has the proper contour for good rolling breaker waves. There is also the sport of bodysurfing where the surfer does not use a board.

31. c) Riding
One of the world's leading jockeys in thoroughbred flat racing, Piggott was the British riding champion 11 times (1960, 1964-71, and 1981-82).

32. b) Bobsledding
The sport originated as distinct from tobogganing in Switzerland about 1890. It

earned its name after competitors adopted the technique of bobbing back and forth to increase the speed of the sled. The four runners are generally mounted in pairs on two axles. Steering is accomplished by turning the front axle either with ropes or by a wheel linked to the axle by cables. The brake is a toothed bar that is pressed against the ice between the rear runners.

33. d) Slalom

The race was devised by British sportsman Arnold Lunn in the early 1920s. The course is carefully designed to test the skill, timing, and judgment of competitors. The gates are placed in varying combinations, and it demands great skill to achieve the best line of approach and exit with the different combinations. A skier who misses a gate (pairs of poles topped with flags) is disqualified. The gates are at least 30 inches (75 cm) wide and 13 ft (4 m) apart. When first developed, slalom gates were made from bamboo, which could snap back and hit competitors. To solve this problem, new plastic gates have been devised that have springs to regulate the motion of the gates, causing them to gently tilt.

34. c) Alice Marble

An American tennis player, Marble was known for her powerful serves and volleys and dominated the women's game during the late 1930s. In 1939 she became the first woman of the century to win the Triple Crown at Wimbledon—the mixed doubles with Bobby Riggs, the women's doubles with Sarah Palfrey, and the women's singles titles, all in the same tournament.

35. c) Curling

Two teams of four players (given the titles lead, second, third, and skip) participate in a curling match. Each player slides round stones, concave on the bottom and with a handle on the top, across the ice of a rink or a natural ice field toward the tee, a fixed mark in the centre of a circle (called the house) marked with concentric bands. The object of the game is for each side to get its stones closest to the centre. Each player delivers two stones alternately with his opponent, beginning with the lead of each team and ending with the skip, who is also the team captain. One point is awarded for each stone that comes to rest nearer the tee than does any rival stone. A team can score up to eight points with the 16 stones delivered in an end, or inning, unless no stone is in the house or the nearest opposing stones are equidistant, in which case there is no score.

36. a) Snowboarding

Three main styles of competition exist: Alpine, freestyle, and boardercross. Developed in the 1960s, snowboarding was believed to have originated in the United States, where several inventors explored the idea of surfing on the snow. The sport, however, quickly evolved, and the early, rudimentary boards gave way to designs that are specialized to meet the demands of different competitions. The basic design is a board (much like a wheelless skateboard) to which the rider's feet are attached with bindings. No poles are used; racers push off from stationary posts. The size and shape of a snowboard varies according to the intended use of the board and the size of the snowboarder.

37. b) Field archery

A form of archery it attempts to simulate hunting conditions. As an organized sport it dates from the formation in 1939 of the National Field Archery Association of the United States. A standard field contest, or round, includes 28 targets. The largest is 60 cm (24 inches) in diameter, and the longest shooting distance is 60 m (196.8 ft). The targets have a black aiming spot in the centre, a white inner ring, and a black outer ring. Field archery is practised with many variations, including use of life-size animal figures as targets.

38. c) Battery
As a fielder, the pitcher may function as an emergency first baseman, and he fields bunts or other infield grounders hit his way. The catcher, as a fielder, is mainly a catcher of high flies, usually fouls. On such flies, ability to perceive the angle at which the ball leaves the bat is necessary to get a quick start in the right direction from home plate.

39. d) Hazel Hotchkiss Wightman
The American tennis player dominated women's competition before World War I. She was instrumental in organizing the Wightman Cup match between British and American women's teams. The winner of 45 U.S. titles, Hazel Wightman overpowered her opponents in the U.S. championship from 1909 to 1911, winning every event she entered in each year: the women's singles, the women's doubles, and the mixed doubles. She went on to win another singles title in 1919 and also won six doubles titles (1909-11, 1915, 1924, and 1928), the last two with Helen Wills. In 1923 she donated a silver cup (the Wightman Cup) to the U.S. Lawn Tennis Association to be used as a prize for an annual match between British and American women's teams. Wightman led the United States to victory in

the first match, 7-0, and was captain of the team until 1948.

40. b) Fencing
The epee is a sword developed in the 19th century for use in fencing practice and contests. Although the use of swords dates to prehistoric times and swordplay to ancient civilizations, the organized sport of fencing began only at the end of the 19th century. Fencing for men had been part of the Olympic Games with their revival in 1896. Events for women fencers have been added to the Olympic contest over the years.

41. d) Kendo
The fencing style is derived from the fighting methods of the ancient samurai (warrior class). Kendo matches take place in an area 9 to 11 m (about 30 to 36 ft) square. Contestants wear the traditional *uwagi* (jacket), *hakama* (long divided skirt), *do* (chest protector), *tare* (waist protector), *men* (mask), and *kote* (padded gloves). The *shinai* varies from 110 to 118 cm (43 to 46 inches) in length and is made of four lengths of seasoned bamboo bound by waxed cord. All blows use the "cutting" edge of the *shinai*, though this is not sharp.

42. b) Bunt
Nearly every time a batter tries to hit a ball he takes a full swing, aiming to drive it as fast and as far as he can. There are times, however, when he tries to bunt the ball, to make it roll slowly along the ground in fair territory but off as much as possible to one side or the other of a straight line from catcher to pitcher. The bunt is usually intended to be a sacrifice; that is, the batter expects to be thrown out at first base, but one or more runners may be

able to proceed to their next base while the ball is being fielded and thrown to first base.

43. a) Balkline billiards
The three balls are red, white, and white with a spot and the table has lines are drawn parallel to all cushions and usually either 36 or 46 cm (14 or 18 inches) away from them. The object of the games is to score caroms by driving a cue ball against both object balls. The eight areas between the lines and cushions are called balks, and, when both object balls are within one of them, a player may score only once or twice (depending on the game played) before driving at least one of the balls out of the balk.

44. d) Rickey Henderson
Henderson's career in major league baseball began with the Oakland Athletics in June 1979. In 1980, his first full season, he became one of only three players ever to steal 100 bases, breaking Ty Cobb's American League record of 96 bases. In 1985 he scored a career-best 146 runs and hit 24 home runs, and in 1986 he scored 130 runs with 28 homers; for both seasons he led the league in steals.

45. c) Softball
The popular participant sport, it is generally agreed, developed from a game called indoor baseball, first played in Chicago in 1887. The fundamentals of softball are the same as those of baseball. Batting and fielding strategy are similar, but softball is played on a much smaller area, and a game is only seven innings long.

46. c) Fourteen
In the average good player's set there are usually either three or four wood clubs and nine or 10 irons. No two clubs in a set are the same. There are differences in length and suppleness of shaft, weight, size and shape of head, the angle at which the shaft ends and the head begins (the lie), and the angle of the face of the club from the vertical (the loft).

47. d) Biathlon
It probably developed from European military ski training and competitions. Either classical or freestyle (skating) techniques can be used in biathlon competition. Mass starts are used in relay events. Athletes in individual events start at one-minute intervals and race against the clock. A combined running and swimming event called the biathlon was instituted in 1968 in Great Britain, mainly to produce modern pentathlon performers.

48. a) Amphetamine
The prototype of a series of synthetic drugs that have pronounced stimulatory actions on the central nervous system. They allow athletes to draw upon their physical reserves and continue despite the extremes of exhaustion until they collapse and, occasionally, die. All amphetamines cause profound psychic effects, including wakefulness, mental alertness, increased initiative and confidence, euphoria, lessened sense of fatigue, talkativeness, and increased ability to concentrate.

49. a) Carl Hubbell
In this pitch, the ball, which is thrown with the same arm motion as a fastball, has reverse spin against the natural curve and, when thrown by a left-hander, breaks sharply away and down from right-handed batters.

Did You Know?

The lynx is a long-legged cat with hairy soles, a square head, and large paws adapted to moving through snow. Its sharp vision inspired people to believe that it could even see through stone.

The llama's hair is normally cut every two years for fibre.

50. d) Castling
A player castles by shifting the king two squares in the direction of a rook, which is then placed on the square the king has crossed. For example, White can castle kingside by moving the king from e1 to g1 and the rook from h1 to f1. Castling is permitted only once in a game and is prohibited if the king or rook has previously moved or if any of the squares between them is occupied. Also, castling is not legal if the square the king starts on, crosses, or finishes on is attacked by an enemy piece.

51. b) Howard Staunton
In 1841 Staunton founded the first English chess magazine, and in 1851 he took the lead in organizing the first modern international chess tournament in London, where, however, he came in only fourth. The standard tournament chess piece design was originated in about 1835, and patented in 1849, by Nathaniel Cook. Following Staunton's endorsement and extensive promotion, the design became known as the Staunton pattern.

52. a) Wilhelm Steinitz
He won the championship in 1866 from Adolph Anderssen and lost it in 1894 to Emanuel Lasker. Steinitz was the first to claim the authority to determine how a title match should be held. He set down a series of rules and financial conditions under which he would defend his status as the world's foremost player, and in 1886 he agreed to play Johann Zukertort of Austria in the first match specifically designated as being for the world championship. Steinitz reserved the right to determine whose challenge he would accept and when and how often he would defend his title.

53. c) Balk
It may occur when: (1) in pitching the ball to the batter, the pitcher does not have his pivoting foot in contact with the pitching plate; (2) the pitcher does not hold the ball in both hands in front of him at chest level before starting his delivery, or, once started, does not continue his motion; or (3) the pitcher starts to make a throw to first base when a runner is occupying that base but does not go through with the throw. When the umpire calls a balk, all runners on base advance one base each.

54. c) Football
A football game was played in China as early as 206 BC, and by AD 500 round footballs stuffed with hair were in use. In Ancient Greece a game with elements of football, *episkuros*, or *harpaston*, was played, and it had migrated to Rome as *harpastum* by the 2nd century BC. In 7th-century Japan there was a football game. In the 14th century *calico* ("kick") was played in Florence; it persists as a festival game. Also in mediaeval Europe there were mob games, called *melees*, or mellays, in which a ball was advanced by kicking, punching, and carrying.

55. c) Putout
To meet the offensive force of the team at bat, the rules provide the fielding team with ways of making putouts. A putout, commonly known as out, removes the player from offensive play until his next turn at bat. The batting team's inning continues until three putouts are made; then it goes into the field and the rival team comes to bat. Most putouts are made by (1) striking out the batter; (2) catching a fly; (3) throwing the batter out; or (4) tagging out a base runner. The batter is

struck out when the pitcher succeeds in preventing him from hitting the ball into fair territory within the limit of three strikes.

56. d) Bagatelle

The game, probably of English origin, was probably a modification of billiards. Bagatelle is played on an oblong board or table varying in size from 1.8 by 0.5 m (6 by 1.5 ft) to 3 by 0.9 m (10 by 3 ft), with nine numbered cups at its head, eight arranged in a circle and the ninth in its centre. Billiard cues and nine balls—one black, four red, and four white—are used.

57. b) Wood

Golf balls were originally made of wood, but in the early 17th century the feather ball was introduced. It was a slow and expensive process to manufacture these balls, which consisted of boiled feathers compressed into a hole left in a stitched leather cover. The invention of the cheaper gutta-percha ball about 1848 helped to make the game more popular. With the emergence of harder rubber balls at the turn of the 20th century came advances in club making, including laminated club heads and seamless steel shafts.

58. d) Carom

It is a game played with three balls (two white and one red) on a table without pockets, in which the object is to drive one of the white balls (cue ball) into both the other balls. Each carom thus completed counts one point.

59. c) Pocket billiards

The game is played with a white cue ball and 15 consecutively numbered coloured balls on a rectangular table with six pockets. To begin play, the 15 object balls are arranged in a pyramid formation with its apex on a spot near the foot of the table. The first player then stands at the head of the table and drives the cue ball into the formation to break it apart. To continue play, he is usually required either to pocket a ball or to drive two object balls in addition to the cue ball against the cushions. When a player fails to pocket a ball, his opponent begins play. The first player or side to pocket eight balls wins the round.

60. c) Lacrosse

The competitive sport has two teams of players who use long-handled, racketlike implements (crosses) to catch, carry, or throw a ball down the field or into the opponents' goal. The goal is defined by uprights and a crossbar framing a loose net. Lacrosse is a very fast game, the object of which is to send the ball through the opponents' goal as many times as possible and to prevent one's opponents from scoring. A goal counts one point.

61. c) Doggett's Coat and Badge

The race is a sculling contest between skiffs originally used to ferry passengers across the river. Watermen who have recently completed their apprenticeship man the boats. Thomas Doggett, an English comic actor, to commemorate the accession of George I in 1714, instituted the contest in 1715. Doggett provided for a cash prize and "an Orange coloured Livery with a Badge representing Liberty" to be awarded to the winner. Although the colour of the uniform has changed from orange to red and the cash prize is no longer awarded, Doggett's decree continues to be fulfilled

62. d) Pachisi

Sometimes called the national game of India, there are four players in the game in opposing partnerships of two attempting to move pieces around a cross-shaped track. Moves are determined by throws of cowrie shells or dice. Each player has four pieces, which begin at the centre space, move down the middle track nearest the player, and counterclockwise around the outer track of the board. The partnership whose pieces first complete the course by returning to the centre space is the winner.

63. a) Pass
The main types are: (1) the chest pass—ball is released from a position in front of the chest; (2) the bounce pass—the ball is bounced on the floor to get it past a defensive opponent; (3) the roll pass on the floor; (4) the hook pass (side or overhead); and (5) the baseball pass—the ball is thrown a longer distance with one hand in a manner similar to a baseball throw.

64. d) Richard Nicolls
He was the governor of the colony of New York. In 1665 he offered a silver cup to be run for at Hampstead Plain, Long Island. Thus began course racing in North America.

65. c) Rodeo
The sport involving a series of contests and exhibitions derived from riding, roping, and related skills was developed by cowboys during the era of the range cattle industry in northern Mexico and the western United States (1867-87). It was confined mainly to Mexico, the United States, and Canada. Rodeos had their origin in the United States when cowboys would gather together in the "cowtowns" at the end of cattle-driving trails and vie for the unofficial title of best bucking-horse rider, roper, and so on. As the cowboys' occupation

was curtailed in scope by the railroads and by fencing, the contests became regular, formal programmes of entertainment.

66. d) Hurdle race
The horse race is run over a course on which a number of obstacles, called hurdles, must be jumped. Hurdle racing, a kind of preparation for steeplechasing, originated in England and Ireland in the 18th century and by the second half of the 20th century had spread to the Commonwealth countries, Europe, and the eastern United States. Its hurdles are light and movable and are lower than steeplechase fences. There are usually at least six jumps in the first 1½ miles (2,400 m) of a hurdle race, then one in each succeeding 400 m (quarter-mile). The less challenging hazards allow racers to maintain a faster pace than in steeplechasing.

67. a) The Grand National
This steeplechase race is held annually in late March or early April at Aintree, near Liverpool, England, over a distance of 7,180 m (4 miles 855 yards) with 30 or so fences. It attracts more attention throughout the world than any other steeplechase. The race was instituted in 1839 by William Lynn, a Liverpool innkeeper, and its present name was adopted in 1847.

68. b) Golf
The trophy is awarded to the winner of a biennial international amateur competition open to teams of three or four players from all nations. The competition was first held, under sponsorship of the World Amateur Golf Council, in 1958, and the trophy was named for President Dwight D. Eisenhower, a golf enthusiast.

The star-nosed mole has 22 pink tentacle-like touch organs set radially on its nose.

The offspring of a lion and a tigress is called a liger; that of a tiger and a lioness, a tigon; that of a leopard and a lioness, a leopon.

Did You Know?

69. b) Giuseppe Farina
The Italian automobile racing driver was the Italian driving champion in 1937, 1938, and 1939. He won the world title in 1950 while driving for Alfa Romeo.

70. b) Grand Circuit
Begun in 1871 by Colonel Billy Edwards, a businessman from Cleveland, Ohio, the circuit, then known as the Quadrilateral Trotting Combination, held its first meetings in 1873 in Cleveland, in Utica and Buffalo, New York, and in Springfield, Massachusetts. In the second half of the 20th century, the Grand Circuit was the premier American harness attraction, visiting more than 20 tracks in the United States and Canada and awarding a total purse of more than $4,000,000 in events for two- and three-year-old trotters and pacers.

71. a) Jules Rimet Trophy
The trophy was named for the Frenchman who proposed the tournament. This cup was permanently awarded in 1970 to three-time winner Brazil (1958, 1962, and 1970), and a new trophy called the FIFA World Cup was put up for competition.

72. b) Belmont Stakes
Oldest of the three classic American horse races (with the Kentucky Derby and the Preakness) that constitute the Triple Crown of United States horse racing, it originated in 1867 and is named after the financier, diplomat, and sportsman August Belmont. The Belmont has been run at various distances and tracks in its history. Since 1905, however, it has been held at Belmont Park, near New York City; and the course has been about 2,400 m (1.5 miles) in length since 1926. The race is held early in June.

73. d) Boxing
The terms pugilism and prizefighting in 20th-century usage are practically synonymous with boxing, although the first term indicates the ancient origins of the sport in its derivation from the Latin *pugil*, "a fighter with the cestus (a hand covering)", related to the Latin *pugnus*, "fist", and derived in turn from the Greek *pyx*, "with clenched fist".

74. b) Middlesex
Cycling as a sport officially began with a 1,200-m (1,312-yard) race in Saint-Cloud Park near Paris on May 31, 1868. The first English race was held the next day at Hendon, Middlesex.

75. c) Cycle ball
The amateur cycling game is played primarily in Europe. In cycle ball, two opposing teams mounted on bicycles try to trap and drive a ball into their opponents' goal by manipulating the ball, which is 18-20 cm (7-8 inches) in diameter, with the wheels of their bicycles. Cycle ball is played indoors between teams of two riders, and as a field game between teams of six. The annual international competition, including an annual world championship, is governed by a subsidiary body of the International Federation of Amateur Cyclists.

76. d) Tour de France
Staged for three weeks each July—usually in some 20 day-long stages—the Tour typically includes 20 professional teams of 9 riders each and covers some 3,600 km (2,235 miles) of flat and mountainous country, mainly in France, with occasional and brief visits to Belgium, Italy, Germany, and Spain. Established in 1903 by Henri Desgrange

(1865-1940), a French cyclist and journalist, the race has been run every year except during the World Wars.

77. c) Motorcycle racing

Cyclists compete on a course marked out over open and often rough terrain. Courses vary widely but must be 1.5 to 5 km (1 to 3 miles) in length in international competition, with steep uphill and downhill grades, wet or muddy areas, and many left and right turns of varying difficulty. Supercross, which began in the United States in the early 1970s, is an indoor version of motocross. Supercross is run on artificial dirt tracks constructed in large arenas. While courses are typically shorter than those in motocross, they feature more frequent and longer jumps.

78. a) Motor-paced race

The bicycles used have small front wheels, enabling the rider to move close to a freely moving roller on a bar projecting from the rear of the pacing motorbike and thus to take full advantage of the air currents created by the motorbike's passage. The technique requires excellent teamwork by both the motorcyclist and the racer to keep from becoming separated and thereby losing ground.

79. b) Boxing

An amateur boxing competition, Golden Gloves was initiated by Arch Ward, sports editor of the *Chicago Tribune*. First sponsored by the *Tribune* in 1926, annual tournaments were held between Chicago and New York teams from 1927. In later years the idea was taken up by other cities, and national tournaments were held. In some years before and after World War II, U.S. Golden Gloves champions met a picked European team. Many Golden Gloves champions went on to become professional world champions.

80. a) John Lawrence Sullivan

The U.S. professional boxer was one of the most popular heavyweight champions and a symbol of the bare-knuckle era of boxing. Although Sullivan is generally considered to have been world heavyweight champion, some boxing historians regard him as a U.S. champion only.

81. c) George Foreman

The American boxer was twice the world heavyweight champion (1973-74, 1994-95). When Foreman regained the heavyweight title at the age of 45, he became the oldest world heavyweight champion ever. Foreman first captured the professional heavyweight belt by knocking out Joe Frazier in two rounds at Kingston, Jamaica, on Jan. 22, 1973. He had won all 40 of his professional bouts, including a sequence of 24 consecutive knockouts, until he fell to Muhammad Ali on Oct. 30, 1974. He retired from the ring in 1977. Foreman resumed professional boxing in 1987 at the age of 39 and found immediate success in a heavyweight division that was lacking quality fighters. Despite his age and more than 30 additional pounds, Foreman remained a devastating puncher and captured the world heavyweight title for the second time by knocking out Michael Moorer in 10 rounds at Las Vegas, Nevada, on Nov. 5, 1994. He resigned his title the following year, on June 28, 1995.

82. a) Daniel Mendoza

The bare-knuckle pugilist was sixth in the succession of English heavyweight champions and the first Jewish champion, whose style of boxing was a great change from the mauling style used until his time. He relied on his courage, strong arms, and excellent physical condition as well as on his revolutionary boxing skill.

83. c) Rocky Marciano
Born in Brockton, Massachusetts, U.S., Marciano became the world heavyweight boxing champion from Sept. 23, 1952, when he knocked out champion Jersey Joe Walcott in 13 rounds in Philadelphia, to April 27, 1956, when he retired from the ring. Marciano was undefeated in 49 professional fights, scoring 43 knockouts.

84. a) Spyridon Louis
The marathon commemorates the legendary feat of a Greek soldier who, in 490 BC, is supposed to have run from Marathon to Athens, a distance of about 25 miles (40 km), to bring news of the Athenian victory over the Persians. Appropriately, the first modern marathon winner in 1896 was a Greek, Spyridon Louis.

85. a) St. Petersburg
Shooting at a mark was recorded in 1737 when the empress Anna established a target-shooting range at her court. The marks shot at were live birds, and the most proficient marksmen were given gold- and diamond-studded cups. The royal shooting matches became a tradition. In 1806 the Society of Shooting Amateurs, formed in St. Petersburg, Russia, largely by military officers, had as its chief interest handgun shooting with flintlock pistols. The first shooting range or club was founded, also in St. Petersburg, in 1834 for rifles or handguns, where the public could shoot for a nominal fee.

86. c) 1930
FIFA organizes the World Cup Championship series, the first having been played at Montevideo in 1930 and won by Uruguay. The World Cup competition is scheduled every four years between the Olympic Games.

87. a) Match and stroke
There are two forms of play in golf: match and stroke (or medal) play. In match play two players generally compete against each other, and each hole is won by the player who holes the ball in the fewest strokes. In stroke play each player competes against every other player in the tournament, and the competitor who holes the round (or rounds) in the fewest strokes is the winner.

88. a) Don Budge
The grand slam consists of winning the four major singles championships of the time, Australia, France, Great Britain, and the United States—in one year. Don Budge won it in 1938.

89. a) Cycling
There are two major types of road races that are team events. The first, called a criterium, is run over a relatively short (4-5-km [2.5-3-mile]) closed course; racers ride a predetermined number of laps, the winner being the first to complete that number. The second type consists of races held on open roads and includes point-to-point, circuit, and stage events. Point-to-point and circuit races are generally one-day races, varying in distance from roughly 240 to 280 km (150 to 175 miles) for professionals and roughly 180 to 220 km (110 to 140 miles) for amateurs.

90. c) William G. Morgan
Designed as an indoor sport for businessmen who found the new game of basketball too vigorous, volleyball was invented in 1895 by William G. Morgan, physical director of the Young Men's Christian Association (YMCA) in Holyoke, Massachusetts, USA.

91. b) Three
The game, played by two teams consisting of usually six players to a side, in which the players use their hands to bat a light, inflated ball, back and forth over a high net, trying to make the ball touch the court within the opponents playing area before it can be returned. The opponents attempt to prevent this by one player batting the ball up and towards a team mate before it touches the court surface, the team mate then volleying it back across the net or batting it to a third team mate who volleys it across the net.

92. a) Ice hockey
Players are frequently substituted, rarely staying on the ice for more than two minutes. The goalies are the only exception, as it is their duty to protect the goal, from which they will only occasionally stray.

93. d) Tenley Albright
She won the championship in 1953 and an Olympic Games gold medal in figure skating in 1956. She was also the first to win the world, North American, and United States titles in a single year (1953).

94. c) Baseball
A left-handed hitter, Ruth broke the major-league home-run record in three consecutive years, 1919-21, and again with his 60 home runs in 1927—in a 154-game season. Ruth led the American League in home runs for 12 years; he hit at least 50 in 4 separate seasons and at least 40 in each of 11 seasons. Ruth played 22 major-league seasons and hit a lifetime total of 714 home runs, a major-league record that remained unbroken until Hank Aaron hit his 715th home run in 1974. Other major-league lifetime records established by Ruth include 2,056 bases on balls and 2,211 runs batted in. In 10 World Series (41 games) he batted .326 and hit 15 home runs. His lifetime batting average was .342.

95. a) Trot
Light and balanced, in the trot the fore and hind diagonal pairs of legs follow each other almost simultaneously—near fore, off hind, off fore, and near hind. Riders can either sit in the saddle and be bumped as the horse springs from one diagonal to the other, or they can rise to the trot, post, by rising out of the saddle slightly and allowing more of their weight to bear on the stirrups when one or the other of the diagonal pairs of legs leaves the ground. Posting reduces the impact of the trot on both horse and rider.

96. a) Formula One car racing
The Brazilian race-car driver was a fierce competitor who was renowned for his ruthless and risky manoeuvres on the Grand Prix circuit and dominated the sport with 41 Grand Prix titles and 3 circuit world championships (1988, 1990, and 1991).

97. d) Hang gliding
Deriving from the sailplane, or glider, the hang glider was developed in the 1960s from the design of Francis Rogallo of the U.S. National Aeronautics and Space

---

The Thomson's gazelle can run 50 miles (80 kilometers) per hour.

The impala can jump to a height of 10 feet (3 meters) and cover 30 feet (9 meters) in a bound.

Ants constitute the family Formicidae, which has at least 8,000 species.

Did You Know?

Administration for a flexible-wing parachute projected for use in steering space vehicles in re-entry. Many variations of his original design followed, both by Rogallo and others.

98. d) A metal ball
The implement used in the hammer throw is not a conventional hammer but a metal ball about 127 mm (5 inches) in diameter attached to a wire, the whole implement being about 1,200 m (48 inches) in length and weighing a minimum of 7.26 kg (16 pounds). The handle at the opposite end of the wire from the ball is gripped by the thrower and released after three or four body turns have developed maximum centrifugal force.

99. c) Korea
This is a Korean art of unarmed combat that is based on the earlier form of Korean self-defence known as tae kyon and on karate. The name tae kwon do was officially adopted for this martial art in 1955 after the South Korean general Choi Hong Hi, the principal founder of tae kwon do, had submitted that name.

100. a) Chess
This is a move used by the player using black pieces in chess. The Sicilian Defence is one of the best fighting defences for black. The Soviets devoted attention to this particular strategy.

101. a) *When We Were Kings*
Muhammad Ali met George Foreman on Oct. 30, 1974, in Kinshasa, Zaire (now Democratic Republic of the Congo). His eighth-round knockout of Foreman regained for Ali the undisputed world heavyweight title. An Academy Award-winning film, *When We Were Kings* (1996) documents this fight.

102. a) A card game
Whist belongs to a family that includes bridge whist, auction bridge, and contract bridge, each of which developed in succession from the original game of whist. The essential features of card games in the whist family are: four people usually play, two against two as partners; a full 52-card deck is dealt out so that each player holds 13 cards. The object of play is to win tricks, each trick consisting of one card played by each player.

103. b) Thirteen
Modern cards are divided into four suits—spades, hearts, diamonds, and clubs. There are 13 cards in each of the four suits. The set of 52 cards together is known variously as the pack or the deck. Two jokers, bearing the image of a mediaeval court jester, are usually included with the standard 52-card deck, although they are not always used in play.

104. c) Seven
A water-polo team consists of seven active players and up to six substitutes. Each team wears either blue or white caps (red for the goalkeepers, with a blue or white number one; other players are numbered from 2 through 13). No grease or oil is allowed on the body. The two referees have final authority in each game; other officials include one or two timekeepers; one or two secretaries, who keep records of the many kinds of fouls, such as holding or hitting an opponent; and two goal judges.

105. b) Croquet
This is a popular outdoor game, played on a lawn or court, with long-handled mallets with which the players hit balls through a series of

While in flight, cranes make a piercing, trumpet-like call that can be heard long after they have flown out of sight.

The cardinal is the state bird of Illinois, Indiana, Kentucky, North Carolina, Ohio, Virginia, and West Virginia.

wickets, or hoops. It involves running a mallet-driven ball through a hoop or hoops to touch a peg as a goal—into a somewhat more complicated sport involving a series of six or more hoops laid out in a pattern, which had to be run in a specified order.

106. a) Show jumping
It is a competitive equestrian event in which horse and rider are required to jump, usually within a time limit, a series of obstacles that have been designed for a particular show. The contest based on jumping ability alone, called Puissance, requires the horse to run over a set number of obstacles in progressively more difficult courses; there is a limit of four jump-offs for Puissance competitions.

107. c) Freestyle skiing
This is a winter sport that combines skiing and acrobatics. There are three freestyle events: acro, aerials, and moguls.

108. c) Madge Cave Syers
The British ice skater was the first woman to compete at the highest level of international figure skating. At the 1908 Olympic Games in London she won the first Olympic gold medal ever awarded in women's figure skating, as well as the bronze medal for pairs with her husband and coach, Edgar Syers.

109. d) Gene Sarazen
A prominent American professional golfer of the 1920s and '30s, Sarazen won the U.S. Open in 1922 and in 1932, also winning the British Open in 1932. He won the Professional Golfers' Association of America (PGA) championship three times (1922, 1923, 1933) and won the Masters Tournament in 1935. With that win at the

Masters he became the first player to achieve a career Grand Slam in golf (that is, winning the U.S. and British Open, the PGA championship, and the Masters Tournament during one's career).

110. b) Checkers
One of the world's oldest games, checkers is played by two persons who oppose each other across a board of 64 light and dark squares, the same as a chessboard. The 24 playing pieces are disk-shaped and of contrasting colours (whatever their colours, they are identified as black and white).

111. d) Australian Rules Football
It is played on an oval field that can vary in width between 110 and 155 m (120 and 170 yards) and in length between 135 and 185 m (145 and 200 yards). Two goal posts not less than 6 m (about 20 ft) in height are placed 6.4 m (about 21 ft) apart at each end of the ground. Two shorter posts, called behind posts, rise to a minimum height of 3 m (10 ft), with each one placed at the side of a goal post at a distance of 6.4 m (about 21 ft).

112. c) Thirteen
The football game is played with an oval ball, usually by teams with 13 (in professional matches) or 15 (amateur) members on each side. It is similar to association football (soccer) and U.S. football, but play is continuous and substitution is not allowed.

113. a) Franz Beckenbauer
The German association football (soccer) player is credited with inventing the modern attacking sweeper and hence "total football". Beckenbauer joined the Bayern Munich team in 1958 and made his first-team debut in

The famous chirping of male crickets is produced when a male cricket rubs a scraper located on one forewing along a row of about 50 to 250 teeth on the opposite forewing.

The thermometer cricket's chirps can be used to calculate temperature in Fahrenheit by counting the number of chirps in 15 seconds, and adding 40.

Did You Know?

1963. As captain from 1971 he helped the Bayern Munich team win three European Cup championships (1973-74, 1974-75, 1975-76) and four national titles.

114. d) Denis Compton
In a career that spanned almost three decades (1936-64), Compton scored 38,942 runs (average, 51.85) and 123 centuries. He scored 300 runs in 181 minutes, the fastest-ever triple-hundred in first-class cricket. An outstanding all-around athlete, he also played association football (soccer) for Arsenal from 1936 until 1950, when knee surgery ended his football career shortly after Arsenal won the FA Cup.

115. d) Archie Moore
The American boxer was the world light-heavyweight champion from December 1952 to 1962. He received critical praise for his portrayal of the slave Jim in *The Adventures of Huckleberry Finn* (1959).

116. c) Four
There are four basic punches: the jab, hook, uppercut, and cross. All other punches are modifications of these basic punches.

117. c) Six
In individual Olympic events, the award for first place is a gold (silver-gilt, with six grams of fine gold) medal, for second place a silver medal, and for third place a bronze medal.

118. c) Jackson Haines
The American skater was a ballet dancer who adapted ballet style and techniques to a sport that had previously comprised a limited number of figures executed in a tight, awkward manner. Having won the U.S. men's championship, he went to Europe in 1865. Although his style of skating was rejected in England, he became a great popular success in Sweden, Austria, and elsewhere on the Continent. In Vienna, the world "waltz capital" in the 19th century, he astutely offered instruction in waltzing on ice. Skating schools founded or inspired by Haines sprang up in numerous countries.

119. b) Oskana Baiul
The Ukrainian figure skater won, at the age of 16, the Olympic gold medal for women's figure skating at the 1994 Games in Lillehammer, Norway. She was the youngest woman to win the figure-skating title since Sonia Henie won at age 15 at the 1928 Games in St. Moritz, Switzerland. Known as the "Swan of Odessa", Baiul was one of the most graceful and artistically accomplished skaters in the history of the sport.